Kant's Aesthetic Theory

KANT'S
AESTHETIC
THEORY

Donald W. Crawford

The University of Wisconsin Press

Published 1974

The University of Wisconsin Press
Box 1379, Madison, Wisconsin 53701

The University of Wisconsin Press, Ltd.
70 Great Russell Street, London

First printing

Printed in the United States of America
For LC CIP information, see the colophon
ISBN 0-299-06510-3

Publication of this book was made possible
in part by a grant from the
Andrew W. Mellon Foundation

Contents

Preface   vii

References to Kant's Critiques   2

1   Introduction   3

   1.1 Problems in a Study of Kant's Aesthetic Theory   3
   1.2 The *Critique of Judgment* in Kant's Philosophical System   7
   1.3 The Faculty of Judgment   20
   1.4 The Judgment of Taste   23
   1.5 Argument of the "Critique of Aesthetic Judgment"   26

2   Kant's Analysis of the Judgment of Taste   29

   2.1 The Judgment of Taste Is Aesthetic   29
   2.2 The Judgment of Taste Is Disinterested   37
   2.3 Implications of the Analysis   54

3   Kant's Deduction of Judgments of Taste   58

   3.1 Empirical and Transcendental Deductions   58
   3.2 The Empirical Deduction: Disinterestedness   61
   3.3 The Antinomy of Taste   63
   3.4 Structure of the Transcendental Deduction   66
   3.5 The Transcendental Deduction—Stage I: Key to the
       Critique of Taste   69

4   Aesthetic Perception and the Cognitive Faculties   75

   4.1 The Transcendental Deduction—Stage II: The Harmony
       of the Cognitive Faculties in Free Play   75
   4.2 Aesthetic and Cognitive Perception   78

5   Kant's Aesthetic Formalism   92

   5.1 The Transcendental Deduction—Stage III: Formal
       Purposiveness   92
   5.2 Form, Content, and the Experience of the Beautiful   96
   5.3 The Epistemological Basis for Kant's Aesthetic
       Formalism   101
   5.4 Secondary Qualities in the Experience of the Beautiful   106
   5.5 Formal Purposiveness and Representation in Art   111
   5.6 Art as the Expression of Aesthetic Ideas   118

6   A Common Sense and the Supersensible   125
    6.1 The Transcendental Deduction—Stage IV: A Common
        Sense   125
    6.2 Aesthetics and the Supersensible   133

7   Aesthetics and Morality   142
    7.1 Interest in the Beautiful   142
    7.2 The Transcendental Deduction—Stage V: Aesthetics
        and Morality   145

8   Kant's Aesthetic Theory and Art Criticism   160
    8.1 Criticism and Appreciation   160
    8.2 Criticism and Creativity   162
    8.3 Reason-Giving in Kant's Aesthetic Theory   164
    8.4 Kant's Analysis of the Arts   171
    8.5 Conclusion   176

    Bibliography   181
    Index   185

Preface

MANY BOOKS could be written about Immanuel Kant's *Critique of Judgment*. The fact that so few have been written is one of the surprises in the history of philosophy. For although Kant's Third Critique, like his other works, is forbidding both in language and in philosophical detail, there is an obvious richness and depth to Kant's treatment of philosophical problems concerning our aesthetic experience. It cries out for attempts to make it more accessible, to show how it, like great art itself, repays careful attention and continued study.

No claim is made for the present book being a complete treatment of the topics that could be discussed legitimately and with profit under the same title. Interpretation of Kant's philosophy is necessarily selective, and selective treatment is implicitly critical. This study emphasizes Kant's theory on the beautiful and the sublime, with recourse to the larger issues involved in the relationship between the two parts of the *Critique of Judgment* only insofar as those issues bear on Kant's aesthetic theory. My major concern has been to demonstrate a significant and fully developed line of argument in the first part of the *Critique of Judgment*, the "Critique of Aesthetic Judgment," concerning the nature and importance of aesthetic experience. I hope that I have demonstrated a philosophical unity in the variety of topics therein considered by Kant. For Kant's aesthetic theory is the first full attempt to deal in a systematic way with the major problems of aesthetics: the nature of aesthetic attitude and experience, the work of art and the aesthetic object, natural beauty, the creative process, evaluation and criticism, the function of art in society, and the value of aesthetic experience generally. That his aesthetic theory is of more than mere historical importance should be evident.

I am inclined to generalize and say that every author, insofar as he attempts in his writing a mapping of the development of his thinking on a subject, hopes to find an audience that reads through his book as presented. In this case, it is more realistic to recognize that any extended discussion of Kant's philosophy is likely to be read selectively. If one of a book's potential virtues is its ability to develop a series of probes with sustained depth of inquiry, one of its potential vices is the inability of the independent probes to achieve comprehensibility. I have tried to come to terms with this realism, probably at the price of some repetition, by making many sections relatively self-contained, even though there is a single, ongoing theme to my interpretation of the various parts of Kant's aesthetic theory. But I should be satisfied if any of the parts contributed to further and better work on Kant's aesthetics.

My own study of Kant's aesthetic theory began in earnest in writing a Ph.D. dissertation for the University of Wisconsin—Madison in 1964–65. That experiment in philosophical research was completed in the spring of 1965, and as a new Ph.D. I promptly put that effort simultaneously in the library depository and in the back of my mind. I soon realized that in it I had raised many more questions than I had even attempted to answer, much less answered to my satisfaction, that my understanding of Kant's aesthetic theory was in many ways inadequate, and that the most important question of the interrelation of the parts of the first half of the Third Critique had been left largely untouched. However, the very limitations of that study eventually proved to be both a resource and a stimulus to further work. The present effort bears certain relations to its ancestor, though only occasional traces of the original remain.

That this work exists at all is due to the continued encouragement of a number of people, especially William H. Hay, first as thesis advisor and now as a valued colleague. Nor do I wish to forget the stimulation of a paragon of the philosophical scholar, inquirer, and teacher, the late Julius R. Weinberg. The Department of Philosophy and the Graduate School of the University of Wisconsin—Madison deserve my thanks for partial relief from teaching duties and for summer research grants at various times during the past few years. I would like to express my appreciation to Sherry Angell, Janet Holt, and Karen Krause for their cheerful assistance in preparing the manuscript. Professional gratitude of the highest order must go to Lewis White Beck for a number of valuable suggestions and helpful criticisms he made upon reading the penultimate version of the manuscript. I am also grateful to the editor of *The Journal of Aesthetics and Art Criticism* for permission to use my article, "Reason-Giving in Kant's Aesthetics," which appeared in volume 28, number 4 (summer 1970); part of it has been incorporated into chapter 8, section 3.

Finally, my deep thanks for indulgence and understanding beyond measure to my wife, Sharon, whose ear I bent whenever a new thought

on Kant's aesthetic theory occurred to me, and who assisted in the many
ways that either cannot or need not be conceptualized.

Donald W. Crawford

Madison, Wisconsin
May 1973

Kant's Aesthetic Theory

REFERENCES TO KANT'S CRITIQUES

First Critique: *Critique of Pure Reason* (*Kritik der reinen Vernunft*), 1781, 1787.

Second Critique: *Critique of Practical Reason* (*Kritik der practische Vernunft*), 1788.

Third Critique: *Critique of Judgment* (*Kritik der Urteilskraft*), 1790.

The standard edition of Kant's works is that of the Prussian Academy of Sciences: *Kant's gesammelte Schriften*, 22 vols. (Berlin, 1900–42). The First Critique is in volumes 4 (1781 first edition) and 3 (1787 second edition); the Second Critique is in volume 5; the Third Critique is in volume 5, and the First Introduction to the *Critique of Judgment* is in volume 20.

Critique of Judgment. References are threefold: (1) to the section (as numbered by Kant) and paragraph of the German text of the Academy edition—e.g., "Pref. 3" refers to the Preface, paragraph 3; "Intro. V.2" refers to the Introduction, section 5, paragraph 2; "§ 26.4" refers to section 26, paragraph 4; "§ 29. G.R. 3" refers to paragraph 3 of the "General Remark upon the Exposition of the Aesthetical Reflective Judgment," which follows § 29; (2) to the appropriate page of volume 5 of the Academy edition, abbreviated "Ak."; (3) to the appropriate page in the translation of J. H. Bernard, abbreviated "B.": *Immanuel Kant: Critique of Judgment*, trans. J. H. Bernard, Hafner Library of Classics (New York: Hafner, 1951). My translations follow those of Bernard except as noted.

First Introduction to the *Critique of Judgment* (=First Intro.). References are to section, paragraph, and page of the Academy edition, and to the appropriate page in the translation of James Haden, abbreviated "H.", which I follow: *Immanuel Kant: First Introduction to the Critique of Judgment*, trans. James Haden, Library of Liberal Arts (Indianapolis: Bobbs-Merrill, 1965).

Critique of Pure Reason. References are to the standard pagination of the 1781 first edition (=A) and the 1787 second edition (=B), which also appear in the margins of the translation of Norman Kemp Smith: *Immanuel Kant's Critique of Pure Reason*, trans. Norman Kemp Smith (London: Macmillan, 1929). My translation follows that of Kemp Smith.

CHAPTER 1

Introduction

1.1   Problems in a Study of Kant's Aesthetic Theory

A STAGGERING number of works in many languages have been devoted to Kant's epistemology, metaphysics, and ethics. By comparison there are relatively few works, especially in English, on his Third Critique, the *Critique of Judgment.*[1] The general barriers to the study of any part of Kant's philosophical corpus are considerable, but there is no prima facie reason they should be any greater to the study of the *Critique of Judgment.* If the First Critique, the *Critique of Pure Reason,* can be said to be a critical examination of the nature and status of claims to scientific knowledge, and the Second Critique, the *Critique of Practical Reason,* can be said to be a critical examination of the nature and status of our claims to moral knowledge, then it is not too misleading to say that the Third Critique is an examination of the nature and status of our claims to aesthetic knowledge—the beautiful and the sublime in nature and art— and our claims to teleological knowledge generally. This superficial unity of Kant's enterprise simply increases the mystery of the relative lack of intense and comprehensive treatment of the Third Critique.

Since each of Kant's major works reflects these difficulties, one must search elsewhere for an explanation of the peculiar lack of commentaries on and critical studies of the *Critique of Judgment.* All this would be a minor problem, of course, a mere curiosity in the history of ideas, if Kant's work in aesthetics were itself considered to be of only minor

1. *Kritik der Urteilskraft* should be translated literally as *Critique of the Power of Judgment* (or faculty of judgment), and not simply as *Critique of Judgment,* as is usually done.

3

importance. But such is far from being the case. Historians of philosophical aesthetics generally credit Kant with being the most important mem-
ber of any group that could reasonably be called the founders of modern
philosophical aesthetics. As Joseph Margolis has put it, "Aesthetics, as a
discipline, begins approximately with Kant's Critique of Judgment; . . .
it was Kant who gave a sense of philosophical importance to aesthetics
and who set certain of its central questions."[2]

Indeed, within the philosophical world, Kant is still considered the
major aesthetician, and there are few if any close competitors. Kant's
preeminence is partly explained by the fact that few other philosophers
of Kant's stature devoted as much attention to aesthetics. Also, Kant's
treatment of the problems of aesthetics is systematic—a thoroughgoing
attempt at a comprehensive aesthetic theory within a framework of
philosophical respectability. Kant usually seems quite aware of the
depths to which he must go to make his claims hold. Only Edmund Burke
before him, developing the epistemology of Locke, was ambitious
enough to attempt to integrate solutions to a wide variety of problems
into his aesthetic inquiry. Kant himself was impressed with Burke's
attempt,[3] saying that Burke "deserves to be regarded as the most important author who adopts this mode of treatment" (§ 29. G.R. 22, Ak.
277, B. 118). "This mode of treatment" is the empirical method of the
British aestheticians of the time, an attempt to enumerate and explain
the sources of our ideas of the beautiful and the sublime. The most
general question of those writers, men such as Addison, Hutcheson, and
Burke, whose opinions Kant incorporates into his own theory, was, What
qualities in objects occasion that particular pleasure or satisfaction we
refer to as Beauty?

Kant attempts to shift the main question of aesthetics away from this
straightforward empirical issue. Kant refers to the method of the empiricists as "physiological" and " psychological" (§ 29. G.R. 22, Ak. 277,
B. 118–19). The major philosophical question, as Kant sees it, concerns
our right to make judgments of the form "This is beautiful," which we
claim are valid, not simply egoistically (as reports of our liking the object
in question) but necessarily and universally, as judgments "which may
exact the adhesion of everyone" (§ 29. G.R. 24, Ak. 278, B. 119). For
Kant, this means that an a priori principle must lie at the basis of all

2. Joseph Margolis, ed., *Philosophy Looks at the Arts* (New York: Scribner,
1962), pp. 5–6.

3. Edmund Burke, *A Philosophical Inquiry into the Origin of Our Ideas of the
Sublime and Beautiful.* 1st ed., 1756; 2d ed., 1759; German trans. 1773.

such judgments. The problem then becomes one of discovering such a principle.

The structure of the *Critique of Judgment* is somewhat awesome, and itself presents a barrier to grasping its contents. In a short Preface, Kant declares that with the Third Critique he has completed his entire critical philosophy. There follows an Introduction, which was substituted prior to publication for a much lengthier introduction, retained in Kant's writings under the title "On Philosophy in General," but now known as the First Introduction to the *Critique of Judgment*. Each of these writings attempts to explain the central philosophical problem confronted by the work, outlines Kant's solution to that problem, and provides some indication of the divisions of the work to follow. Unfortunately, both introductions are highly opaque to anyone not familiar with the outlines of Kant's critical philosophy and his exceedingly technical terminology. Indeed, anyone who reads the Third Critique in the order of its presentation, by struggling first with the Preface and then with the Introduction, finds himself immediately immersed in the thicket of Kantian architectonic and jargon: judgments of the form "This is beautiful" are somehow supposed to "mediate" between the concept of universal causality (=determinism) in the natural ("phenomenal") world and the concept of freedom in some supersensible ("noumenal") world; this noumenal world, at least as an idea, is said to be a necessary condition for man's interpersonal actions and moral relationships; the faculty of judgment is said to bridge the gap between the mental faculties of pure knowledge and desire. This is a rather heavy beginning, indicating that an understanding of Kant's aesthetic theory may require some familiarity with the doctrines of both the *Critique of Pure Reason* and the *Critique of Practical Reason,* and perhaps more. That is no mean task for any philosopher, much less for someone primarily interested in the philosophy of art. Consequently, few have made the effort.

Secondly, in an attempt to fit the experience of the beautiful in art and in nature into his philosophical system, Kant finds it necessary to introduce the notion of teleology in the form of purposiveness. This makes Kant's way of looking at the problems of aesthetics, especially the question of the nature of our experience of art, appear quite different from our own. The *Critique of Judgment* is divided almost equally into two parts. The first part, the "Critique of Aesthetic Judgment," is concerned with out judgments on the beautiful and the sublime in nature and art. In Kant's terms, it is concerned with our judging the formal purposiveness of nature or art subjectively by means of the feeling of pleasure or pain (displeasure). The second part, the "Critique of Teleological

Judgment," deals with our judging purposive phenomena in nature objectively by means of our reason and understanding. It also has two subjects, our judging things as natural ends and our judging their relative purposiveness. The relationship between the two main parts of the Third Critique is puzzling, though it is clear that Kant's general approach to aesthetic theory assumes a framework of human faculties, knowledge, and judgment and the integration of the questions of aesthetics into a larger philosophical system.

Thus, some general features of Kant's aesthetic theory may partially explain the lack of concentrated study of his work by aestheticians. Although still much to be admired, Kant's goal of a complete and comprehensive system of philosophy may now seem to intrude upon an investigation of the relatively self-contained area of study we call "aesthetics." The very comprehensiveness of Kant's theory may partially explain why many philosophers have interpreted it mainly as an extension or completion of his work in the more central philosophical areas of epistemology and metaphysics,[4] while others, unwilling to treat the problems of aesthetics in that way, have accorded the *Critique of Judgment* only superficial treatment. The present work deals with the complex argument, wholly contained in the "Critique of Aesthetic Judgment," that unites many diverse elements in Kant's aesthetic theory.

Thirdly, Kant treats in detail two species of aesthetic judgments, judgments of beauty and judgments of the sublime, neither of which today seems a very natural way to characterize the results of our aesthetic experiences. Knowledge of previous treatments of the sublime, especially those by Longinus and by Burke, is helpful, but inadequate to explain the place of Kant's treatment of the sublime in his aesthetic theory. That the beautiful and the sublime are more than simply two independent divisions of aesthetic judgments for Kant is clear from the many similarities he finds between them, but the bases of these similarities remain obscure.

Fourthly, Kant found it necessary to couch many of his claims in a language of mental faculties. While some critics have held that his faculty language is harmless, others have maintained that the main issues of aesthetics are obscured and confused by it. Problems as to the nature of these faculties and their interrelationships keep emerging, but

---

4. Two examples of this rather unhelpful approach to the *Critique of Judgment* are the books by Macmillan (1912) and Cassirer (1938), the only comprehensive studies of the Third Critique in English. Two recent articles by Gotshalk (1967) and Elliott (1968) do attempt to explicate the unity of the doctrines of the first part of the Third Critique, while treating those doctrines critically and without heavy reliance on the Kantian philosophical system (see Bibliography for complete citations).

it is difficult to see how the data which an aesthetic theory is designed to unify and explain can be usefully dealt with in terms of mental faculties. Again, it would appear that one must become immersed in Kant's more general philosophical theories and vocabulary in order to understand, much less assess, his aesthetic theory.

Finally, Kant's own limited exposure to and rather provincial views on the various arts might be sufficient to drive anyone interested in the nature and ultimate value of art elsewhere for insights. How much can one expect from a man, great philosopher though he is, whose example of a great poem is an obscure verse by Frederick the Great (§ 49.8, Ak. 315–16, B. 159) and whose favorite music seems to have been Prussian marches?[5]

Part of the motivation for the present work is a belief in the insightfulness of Kant's aesthetic theory. In spite of the difficulties enumerated above, the study of Kant's aesthetic theory is valuable and enlightening, over and above its historical importance. Kant articulates relationships between various problems in aesthetics that had gone unnoticed before him and that are often overlooked or confused today. Kant's ability to incorporate the gains of previous writers on aesthetics and his acute critical powers enable him to penetrate to the heart of a number of the most important problems of aesthetics, to recognize their depth and interrelatedness, and to present forceful solutions to them. Kant's significance is greatly increased by his impressive attempt to resolve classicism and impressionism, objectivism and subjectivism in aesthetic theory. He fully understood the opposing ways of looking at our experience of and judgments upon the beautiful in art and nature. Some of the ideas contained in the *Critique of Judgment* are now of only historical interest, but many of them are of lasting importance. Nothing in the Third Critique is more modern than the way Kant begins his investigation, with a discussion of the "logic" of aesthetic judgments and an attempt to determine how the judgment that something is beautiful differs from the judgment that it is good, or pleasant, or useful.

1.2   The **Critique of Judgment** in Kant's Philosophical System

The Possibility of a Critique of Taste

UNTIL THE completion of the *Critique of Judgment* at the age of sixty-six in 1790, Kant's only published writing on aesthetics was his *Observa-*

---

5. See Rudolf H. Weingartner, "A Note on Kant's Artistic Interests," *Journal of Aesthetics and Art Criticism* 16 (1957–58):261–62.

tions on the Feeling of the Beautiful and Sublime (Beobachtungen über das Gefühl des Schönen und Erhabenen), written in 1763 and published in 1764 when Kant was forty.[6] It is illuminating to characterize that earlier work and place it in the context of similar writings of British aestheticians of the first part of the eighteenth century. Joseph Addison's "Essays on the Pleasures of the Imagination" originally appeared in numbers 411–421 of *The Spectator* in 1712, and in German translation in 1745. Francis Hutcheson's *An Enquiry into the Original of Our Ideas of Beauty and Virtue*, first published in 1725, appeared in German translation in 1762. The major direction and focus of Kant's *Observations*, as well as its style, give us some reason to believe that Kant was familiar with these early and very popular attempts to analyze the experience of the beautiful in terms of pleasure and to attempt to determine the specific qualities of objects that occasion such pleasure. Kant's attempts at these empirical determinations are more extensive than those of either Addison or Hutcheson. When Kant wrote his *Observations*, the more ambitious and philosophically sophisticated work of Edmund Burke, *A Philosophical Inquiry into the Origin of Our Ideas of the Sublime and Beautiful*, which treats explicitly of the sublime as distinct from the beautiful, was probably unknown to him. Burke's work was first published in 1756 when Burke was a relatively unknown man of twenty-eight. It was not translated into German until 1773.

In the *Observations*, and until the *Critique of Judgment* was actually conceived much later, Kant took a dim view of the possibility of a "critique of taste," any distinctly philosophical inquiry into the foundations of aesthetic experience and value. What we now call "aesthetics" he relegated to empirical studies, in the manner of the British authors mentioned above, or to traditional speculative philosophy, in the manner of G. W. Leibniz or A. G. Baumgarten.[7] The subject was deemed neither to require nor to be amenable to any special philosophical treatment. Kant's *Observations* is an easy-flowing, popular essay which attempts an empirical account of our experiences of the beautiful and the sublime as these experiences occur in different ages, sexes, nationalities, and temperaments. Indeed, Kant's essay is more about differences in human

6. Kant, *Observations on the Feeling of the Beautiful and Sublime*, trans. John T. Goldthwait (Berkeley and Los Angeles: Univ. Calif. Press, 1960).

7. G. W. Leibniz, "Principes de la Nature et de la Grace" (1714); translated as "Principles of Nature and Grace," in *The Philosophical Works of Leibniz*, trans. George Martin (New Haven: Yale Univ. Press, 1908). A. G. Baumgarten, *Meditationes philosophicae de nonnullis ad poema pertinentibus* (1735), translated by Karl Aschenbrenner as *Reflections on Poetry* (Berkeley: Univ. Calif. Press, 1954). Baumgarten, *Aesthetica*, 2 vols. (Frankfurt-an-der-Oder, 1750–58).

beings than it is about the concepts of the beautiful and the sublime. Judgments on the beautiful and the sublime were not thought to be susceptible to treatment in terms of rational principles. A writer on these topics could merely make observations on how different people respond, their different sensitivities and values. The essay is essentially social psychology of a primitive sort. As John T. Goldthwait puts it, "Although the *Observations* cannot be said to be based on an empirical philosophy, it does share with empiricism a concentration upon the particulars of experience and a use of the method of inductive generalization rather than deduction from first principles."[8] The poles of opposition Goldthwait presents are misleading, however, since Kant's later position in the *Critique of Judgment* is not accurately described as a method of deduction from first principles; but when he wrote the *Observations,* Kant seems to have viewed these two methods as the only alternatives for aesthetics, and his method in the *Observations* is more empirical than rationalistic. Kant's position in the *Observations* reminds one of David Hume's view of the status of principles of composition in art in his "A Standard of Taste" (1757): "Their foundation is the same with that of all the practical sciences, experience; nor are they any thing but general observations, concerning what has been universally found to please in all countries and in all ages."[9] In the *Observations,* Kant gives no indication of having read either this important essay by Hume nor the 1759 essay by Burke on the standard of taste;[10] Kant does not formulate the problem of a standard or principle of taste which would have universal validity. The subjective perspective of Kant in *Observations* is evident from the opening sentence: "The various feelings of enjoyment or of displeasure rest not so much upon the nature of the external things that arouse them as upon each person's own disposition to be moved by these to pleasure or pain."[11]

In a letter to Marcus Herz dated 7 June 1771, Kant indicates that he plans to connect his work then in progress titled "The Limits of Sensibility and Reason" (later to become the *Critique of Pure Reason*) with the nature of the theory of taste, metaphysics, and morals (Ak. *10*:183).[12]

---

8. Kant, *Observations,* trans. Goldthwait, p. 10.

9. David Hume, "A Standard of Taste" (originally in his *Four Dissertations,* 1757), par. 9.

10. Burke, "Introduction on Taste," *Philosophical Inquiry,* 2d ed., 1759.

11. Kant, *Observations,* trans. Goldthwait, p. 45.

12. I have not attempted to trace the development of Kant's thinking on the problems of aesthetics between the publication of *Observations* (1764) and the *Critique of Judgment* (1790). This history is carefully discussed by G. Tonelli in a number of publications, most especially in "Kant, dall'estetica metafisica all'esteti-

And in the first edition of the *Critique of Pure Reason* (1781), Kant is fully aware of the problem concerning the standards or principles of taste, although he is unwilling to commit himself to their being other than empirical generalizations. The relevant remarks occur as a footnote to the first section of the "Transcendental Aesthetic." Since some extremely important changes were made in this footnote in the second edition (1787), the footnote is quoted in its entirety, with the second-edition additions in square brackets:

> The Germans are the only people who currently make use of the word 'aesthetic' in order to signify what others call the critique of taste. This usage originated in the abortive attempt made by Baumgarten, that admirable analytical thinker, to bring the critical treatment of the beautiful under rational principles, and so to raise its rules to the rank of a science. But such endeavors are fruitless. The said rules or criteria are, as regards their [chief] sources, merely empirical, and consequently can never serve as [determinate] *a priori* laws by which our judgment of taste must be directed. On the contrary, our judgment is the proper test of the correctness of the rules. For this reason it is advisable [either] to give up using the name in this sense of critique of taste, and to reserve it for that doctrine of sensibility which is true science—thus approximating to the language and sense of the ancients, in their far-famed division of knowledge into αἰσθητὰ καὶ νοητά (sensible things and mind-like things) [—or else to share the name with speculative philosophy, employing it partly in the transcendental and partly in the psychological sense]. (A21n=B35n)

In the first edition, rejecting any attempt at a rationalistic critique of taste, Kant claims that there can be no a priori rules or principles determining the effect an object will have on the mind in terms of the feeling of pleasure or displeasure the perception of it will produce.

In 1781, then, Kant's views are in keeping with those of Hume and Burke; indeed, they reflect Hume's account, quoted above. Hume and Burke both confront the issue of whether there are standards of taste, argue affirmatively for such standards, but maintain that the standards are no more than empirical generalizations concerning how certain qualities and characteristics of objects, such as unity amid variety and eloquence of expression, affect normal observers. Two facts particularly impress Burke and Hume. Firstly, certain works of art endure, their values and reputations either do not change at all or, if they change, they increase through time; it is inconceivable to them that Milton or Homer

---

ca psicoempirica," *Memorie dell'Accademia delle Scienze di Torino,* ser. 3, vol. 3, pt. 2 (1955):77–345, and in "La Formazione del testo della *Kritik der Urteilskraft,*" *Revue internationale de Philosophie* 8 (1954):423–48.

should ever be judged second-rate poets. Secondly, certain men have recognizable abilities of discrimination and discernment (which Hume calls a "delicacy of taste") with respect to matters of beauty; in other words, there is such a thing as "good taste." Hence, for Hume and Burke there must be standards of taste, however difficult it may be for us to discover them. Kant challenges the adequacy of this argument because he is unable to see how such empirically derived standards will provide an objective basis for any individual claim that something is beautiful.[13]

The key question for Kant thus becomes, What right have I to suppose that my individual judgment that an object is beautiful commands the assent of others? Kant believes that it is part of the meaning of "This is beautiful" that the assent of others is demanded, even though it is frequently not forthcoming in fact. The implication is that others ought to find the object beautiful. What can possibly justify making such a demand or implication? How can one do any more than simply report how he is affected in a particular case? Until just prior to writing the *Critique of Judgment*, Kant did not believe that there were any principles underlying such judgments capable of supporting the meaning or implications we take them to have.

In the second edition of the *Critique of Pure Reason* in 1787, Kant's modifications in the above footnote indicate a change in his view that it is not possible to have a critique of taste, that is, to discover other-than-empirical (namely, a priori) principles underlying our judgments of taste. In the first edition Kant says that, because they are merely empirical, the rules or criteria of taste "can never serve as *a priori* laws by which our judgment of taste must be directed," but in the second edition he says they "can never serve as DETERMINATE *a priori* laws by which our judgment of taste must be directed" (capitalization added). This addition anticipates an important doctrine of the *Critique of Judgment*, that there is an a priori rule or principle of taste, but one that is indeterminate. Indeed, this is the doctrine that will constitute Kant's solution

---

13. Burke and Hume both seem to recognize this alleged inadequacy. Burke provides one true interpretation of the famous maxim *de gustibus non est disputandum*: "So that when it is said, Taste cannot be disputed, it can only mean, that no one can strictly answer what pleasure or pain some particular man may find from the Taste of some particular thing. This indeed cannot be disputed; but we may dispute, and with sufficient clearness too, concerning the things which are naturally pleasing or disagreeable to the sense" (Burke, "Introduction on Taste," par. 3). And in discussing individual artistic preferences, Hume remarks: "Such preferences are innocent and unavoidable, and can never reasonably be the object of dispute, because there is no standard, by which they can be decided" (Hume, "Standard of Taste," par. 30).

to his famous Antinomy of Taste. The Antinomy has a thesis and an antithesis. The antithesis is that judgments of taste must be based on some rule or principle, since if they were not there would be no point in claiming, as we do, that others ought to agree with us, that our judgment is valid for everyone; the thesis is that judgments of taste cannot be based on some rule or principle, since if they were we should be able to resolve quarrels about such judgments, to settle them by proofs, which we cannot do. Kant's solution to the Antinomy is to claim that the rule or principle on which judgments of taste are based must be an indeterminate one. Kant sees an indeterminate concept of the subjective purposiveness of nature as the resolution or synthetis of the subjective-objective dichotomy seemingly forced upon us by the logical features of judgments of taste. These logical features include significant similarities and differences between judgments of taste and both cognitive judgments (knowledge claims) and purely subjective judgments (liking-reports). Thus the direction, if not the structure, of the deduction of judgments of taste seems to have been in Kant's mind—at least it is hinted at—when he wrote the second edition of the *Critique of Pure Reason*. Another important change is the addition of "chief" to modify the empirical sources of the rules of taste. Where, before, Kant had claimed that the sources of the rules or criteria of taste are merely empirical, in the second edition he says that their *chief* sources are merely empirical.

A further significant addition to the a21=b35 footnote is Kant's suggestion of an alternative to giving up "aesthetic" in the sense of "critique of taste," the usage introduced by Baumgarten in his *Aesthetica* (1750–58). The alternative, Kant says, is "to share the name with speculative philosophy, employing it partly in the transcendental and partly in the psychological sense." A precise explanation of what Kant means by "aesthetic" will be provided in chapter 2, section 1, but here we can note that Kant anticipates the role of the a priori principle underlying judgments of taste as a "regulative employment of an idea of pure reason," to use the terminology of the latter part of the *Critique of Pure Reason* (a642–704=b670–732); that is, it is a principle of investigation which is psychologically grounded and which attempts to go beyond our actual and possible human knowledge (cf. Intro. IV–V, Ak. 179–86, B. 15–23). These changes indicate that Kant has come to believe in the possibility of a critique of taste within the framework of the transcendental method developed in the First Critique.

In the same year as publication of the second edition of the *Critique of Pure Reason* (1787), Kant wrote a letter to K. L. Reinhold revealing not only his new direction regarding a critique of taste but also the position of such a critique in the critical philosophy as a whole:

I am now at work on the critique of taste, and I have discovered a kind of a priori principle different from those heretofore observed. For there are three faculties of the mind: the faculty of cognition, the faculty of feeling pleasure and displeasure, and the faculty of desire. In the *Critique of Pure* (theoretical) *Reason,* I have found a priori principles for the first of these, and in the *Critique of Practical Reason,* a priori principles for the third. I tried to find them for the second as well, and though I thought it impossible to find such principles, the systematic nature of the analysis of the previously mentioned faculties of the human mind allowed me to discover them, giving me ample material for the rest of my life, material at which to marvel and possibly explore. So now I recognize three parts of philosophy, each of which has its a priori principles, which can be enumerated and for which one can delimit precisely the knowledge that may be based on them: theoretical philosophy, teleology, and practical philosophy, of which the second is, to be sure, the least rich in a priori grounds of determination. I hope to have a manuscript on this completed though not in print by Easter; it will be entitled "Critique of Taste."[14]

Kant's manuscript was not as quickly forthcoming as he had predicted, and when it finally appeared, three years later (1790), it had been expanded to cover not merely taste—judgments with respect to the beautiful and the sublime—but teleological judgment as well—judgments of natural phenomena in terms of ends or purposes.

The Three Critiques Juxtaposed

In the *Critique of Pure Reason,* Kant took his task, one of the central problems of traditional philosophy, to be to explain how it is possible to have synthetic a priori judgments of cognition—knowledge claims which are stronger than what is confirmed through experience but the denials of which are not self-contradictions. He interpreted this issue as the key to disputes between the rationalists and the empiricists. Kant questioned the basis of knowledge claims which, on the one hand, are both necessary and universally true (such as the causal maxim, the truths of mathematics and geometry), and hence not derivable from experience alone and which, on the other hand, extend our knowledge by being true not merely by virtue of the meanings of the constituent terms or concepts through which the truths are expressed. Kant's psychological assumptions were such that his inquiry took the form of a search for those prin-

---

14. Letter to K. L. Reinhold, 31 December 1787 (Ak. *10*:513–15); the translation is from *Kant: Philosophical Correspondence 1759–99,* ed. and trans. Arnulf Zweig (Chicago: Univ. Chicago Press, 1967), pp. 127–28.

ciples of the mind—or rather a part of the mind, the faculty of knowledge or cognition *(Erkenntnisvermögen)*—that can account for our ability to make such judgments. But Kant did not think of his inquiry as one belonging to empirical psychology or even to rational psychology. He conceived his method as purely philosophical, proceeding by reasoning about what must be the nature of the operations of the mind given the fact that we make synthetic a priori judgments. Kant's question concerns how our claim to synthetic a priori knowledge can be justified and whether certain operations of the mind can be deduced as being somehow necessary, given more general features of the nature of human consciousness and experience.

Similarly, in the Second Critique, the *Critique of Practical Reason* (1788), Kant attempted to show how synthetic a priori moral judgments are possible. Here too the search was for a priori principles of the mind— this time of the faculty of desire—which could provide a basis for moral judgments being universally valid and binding.

To complete this brief perspective of Kant's critical philosophy, Kant's objective in the *Critique of Judgment* may be said to be the uncovering of the a priori principles governing the faculty of judgment. A judgment, for Kant, is the bringing of a particular awareness under a universal or concept; it is thinking that a particular thing has a general characteristic or quality. For example, I judge that this thing in front of me is a piece of paper, that the painting hanging on my wall is beautiful. But my judgment about the painting is peculiar. In making it, according to Kant, I implicitly refer to a pleasure or satisfaction that I feel, but at the same time I implicitly claim others ought to find it beautiful and feel a pleasure as well. Thus, like synthetic a priori knowledge claims and like synthetic a priori moral judgments, the judgment that something is beautiful—the judgment of taste—implicitly claims a universality and necessity neither met with in experience nor derivable from an analysis of concepts or the meanings of terms.

In each of the three critiques, Kant begins with certain facts of human experience. These facts are, respectively, our beliefs that our judgments concerning (a) what we know, (b) what we ought to do, and (c) what is beautiful possess a necessity and universal validity. Kant then attempts to give such beliefs the critical justification they require. One can appeal neither to what simply is the case nor to the traditional use of pure reason, constructing arguments in the form of syllogisms, to justify the claims we would make in each of these cases. One cannot strictly prove that such judgments have necessary and universal validity. In a sense, then, our claims in each realm go beyond or are stronger than the empirical evidence at our disposal and the powers of traditional logic.

In other words, Kant attempts to show how our knowledge claims, moral judgments, and judgments of taste can have more than a private validity. For if that were all they had, they would be no more than disguised reports concerning our own inner states. The philosophical question concerns how these judgments can be objective, or what kind of objectivity they possess. In ethics and aesthetics, this becomes the familiar problem of the subjective-objective dichotomy. Kant's concern is to show on what basis it can be known that our moral and aesthetic judgments are not simply "true for me"—subjective reports. In his aesthetic theory, Kant tries to break down the subjective-objective dichotomy by explaining how a judgment based on feeling (of pleasure or displeasure) can at the same time legitimately lay claim to be universally true, true for all human beings. His method involves not only an inquiry into the principles necessary to ensure what he takes to be the facts of aesthetic experience and judgment, but also an extensive analysis of key aesthetic terms or concepts. In these various ways, then, the three critiques are united in methodology and content.

Kant's Architectonic and the Critique of Judgment

The overall structure of the *Critique of Judgment* bears a superficial resemblance to that of the *Critique of Pure Reason,* but there is little to be gained from any detailed comparison of the two. The most noticeable parallelism is one of division: both major parts of the *Critique of Judgment,* the "Critique of Aesthetic Judgment" and the "Critique of Teleological Judgment," are divided into an Analytic and a Dialectic, in the same manner as the "Transcendental Logic" of the *Critique of Pure Reason.* There is also one parallelism of content that is worth noticing:

Critique of Judgment	*Critique of Pure Reason*
First Part: Critique of Aesthetic Judgment	First Part (of Transcendental Doctrine of Elements): Transcendental Aesthetic
Second Part: Critique of Teleological Judgment	Second Part (of Transcendental Doctrine of Elements): Transcendental Logic

The parallelism is not immediately obvious. Both first parts deal with aspects of our experience that are independent of any appeal to definite concepts; while both second parts deal with rules of the understanding in general, which Kant calls "logic" (A52=B76).

Of more significance to the present study is the division of the "Analytic of the Beautiful" into four Moments. These four Moments correspond to the four basic heads of the Table of Judgments in the *Critique of Pure Reason* (A70=B95). Here is how Kant presents them in the *Critique of Pure Reason:*

If we abstract from all content of a judgment, and consider only the mere form of understanding, we find that the function of thought in judgment can be brought under four heads, each of which contains three moments. They may be conveniently represented in the following table:

I	II	III	IV
Quantity of	*Quality*	*Relation*	*Modality*
Judgments	Affirmative	Categorical	Problematic
Universal	Negative	Hypothetical	Assertoric
Particular	Infinite	Disjunctive	Apodeictic
Singular			(A70=B95)

The division of the "Analytic of the Beautiful" in the *Critique of Judgment* constitutes Kant's attempt to analyze the judgment of taste in terms of the above table of judgments, with a curious inversion in the order of Quantity and Quality. More significantly, the detailed correspondence to the table in the *Critique of Pure Reason* is inexact in each case.

In terms of the Quality of judgments of taste, Kant does not even mention the obvious point that the judgment that something is beautiful is an affirmative judgment; instead, he attempts to specify precisely what is affirmed. He argues that what is affirmed in the judgment of taste is not a concept, but a feeling of pleasure; a feeling of pleasure is affirmed of the person making the judgment and not of the object judged. In essence, Kant maintains that the grammatical form of the judgment of taste is not its logical form. The logical form, considered under the head of Quality, is affirmative. But it is not the affirmation of a concept to a particular; rather, it is analyzed by Kant as the affirmation of a feeling of pleasure to the person doing the judging of the object—the object found to be beautiful—which is the grammatical subject of the judgment.

There also seems to be a discrepancy between the table in the *Critique of Pure Reason* and the account in the *Critique of Judgment* with respect to the Quantity of the judgment of taste. In many places in the Third Critique, Kant notes that the judgment of taste is a singular judgment,[15] by which he means that it is the judgment that a particular thing is beautiful. Thus, one would expect Kant to say that, according to the Moment of Quantity, the judgment of taste is singular (and not universal

---

15. §§ 8.5, 23.1, 31.2, 31.3, 33.5, 37.1, 57.3; Ak. 215, 244, 280–81, 281, 285, 289, 339; B. 50, 82, 122, 123, 127, 131, 184.

or particular). Kant specifically claims that judgments such as "All roses are beautiful"—universal judgments—and "Some roses are beautiful"— particular judgments—are not, strictly speaking, judgments of taste (§ 8.5, Ak. 215, B. 50). But in the "Analytic of the Beautiful," Kant's claim is that, according to the Moment of Quantity, "the judgment of taste carries with it an *aesthetic quantity* of universality" (ibid.). Indeed, the Second Moment ends with: "*Explanation of the Beautiful Resulting from the Second Moment:* The *beautiful* is that which pleases universally without [requiring] a concept" (§ 9.10, Ak. 219, B. 54). Thus, although strictly speaking the judgment of taste does not take the universal form, Kant is claiming that it has the force of a universal judgment, namely: "Everyone ought to find this object beautiful."

The correspondence in the Moment of Relation is equally imprecise. The relation considered is that of purposes. In terms of the original table, one would expect Kant to claim that the judgment of taste under the head of Relation is categorical, but Kant never discusses it in these terms. Nor does a submodality of "purposes" occur in the original table, and Kant never discusses precisely how his analysis of the judgment of taste in terms of purposiveness is relational. Once again, Kant is anticipating one of the features of his analysis of judgments of taste; he is not describing anything which is obvious about the form of judgments of taste.

Under the head of Modality, Kant considers the judgment of taste to be a necessary judgment. "Necessary" seems to correspond in "apodeictic" in the Table of Judgments, but Kant does not use the term in this characterization in the *Critique of Judgment.*

Although these somewhat technical points shed light on Kant's analysis of judgments of taste, they have little bearing on the main line of argument developed in the *Critique of Judgment* itself. As in numerous other places, Kant is attempting to be thoroughly systematic; he wants his architectonic to work in all areas of philosophy, but he has to adapt it to meet his particular needs.

The Critique of Judgment *and the Critical Philosophy*

The place of the *Critique of Judgment* in Kant's philosophical system turns on his claim that the Third Critique shows how the faculty of judgment forms a mediating link between the cognitive faculty (understanding) and the faculty of desire (reason) (Pref. 3, Ak. 168, B. 4). Kant believed this was necessary for the completion of his philosophical system because the first two critiques had established two distinct realms —the phenomenal world of cause and effect, and the noumenal supersensible world of freedom. The problem concerns whether there can be a unity between these two realms. Kant intends his solution to the problem of the *Critique of Judgment* to show the possibility of such a unity, and he regards the critique of judgment "as a means of combining the two parts of philosophy into a whole" (title to Intro. III, Ak. 176, B. 12).

The same general point may be put in a different way. Kant believes he had shown in the *Critique of Pure Reason* that understanding contains constitutive principles of cognition a priori, and in the *Critique of Practical Reason* that reason contains constitutive principles a priori with respect to the faculty of desire. He thus takes the main systematic thrust of the *Critique of Judgment* to answer the question: "whether now the judgment, which in the order of our cognitive faculties forms a mediating link between understanding and reason, has also principles *a priori* for itself; whether these are constitutive or merely regulative (thus pointing out no special realm); and whether they give a rule *a priori* to the feeling of pleasure and pain, as the mediating link between the cognitive faculty and the faculty of desire" (Pref. 3, Ak. 168, 3 B. 4). These claims cannot be fully understood prior to working through the arguments of the *Critique of Judgment,* but something by way of general summary and comment is pertinent here.

Kant believes that the *Critique of Judgment* establishes that the aesthetic judgment "contains a principle which the judgment places quite *a priori* at the basis of its reflection upon nature, viz. the principle of a formal purposiveness of nature, according to its particular (empirical) laws, for our cognitive faculty" (Intro. VIII.3, Ak. 193, B. 30). This is not a principle of the objective purposiveness of nature, nor the claim that judgment is based on recognizing objective purposes in nature. Kant's claim is that the "transcendental principle [of judgment] already has prepared the understanding to apply to nature the concept of a purpose (at least as regards its form)" (ibid.). In other words, we make sense of nature as well as of art by attempting to determine its formal purposiveness, that is, the organic relatedness and significance of its form (formal characteristics, features, and relations). Precisely how Kant thought he had discovered this principle and its necessity, and how it applies specifically to our experience of the beautiful in nature and art, will be discussed in detail in succeeding chapters. The formal purposiveness of nature, it must be repeated, is not a commitment to there being an actual purpose in nature (either assumed or discovered).

This subjective purposiveness is, in Kant's language, "transcendental," however, because it is presupposed by our faculty of knowledge (cognition) in its attempt to understand natural phenomena in accordance with empirical laws. "The judgment has therefore also in itself a principle *a priori* of the possibility of nature, but only in a subjective aspect, by which it prescribes not to nature (autonomy), but to itself (heautonomy) a law for its reflection upon nature" (Intro. V.7, Ak. 185–86, B. 22).

How does this principle of the subjective formal purposiveness of nature relate to the feeling of pleasure? We endeavor to bring the dissimilar appearances or phenomena of nature under laws, and then to bring the dissimilar laws of nature under higher ones, to fit them ultimately into a unity. When we are successful, a pleasure or satisfaction results—a fact which seems fairly obvious. In Kant's analysis, this pleasure or satisfaction results from the perceived harmony of nature with the abilities and demands of our mental faculties. Thus, the pleasure we feel is caused by our apprehension of the form of the object (whether of nature or of art), when that form is such as to lead to a harmony in the operations of our cognitive faculties (imagination and understanding) in reflection upon it. In Kant's words:

He who feels pleasure in the mere reflection upon the form of an object without respect to any concept although this judgment be empirical and singular, justly claims the agreement of all men, because the ground of this pleasure is found in the universal, although subjective, condition of reflective judgments, viz. the purposive harmony of an object (whether a product of nature or of art) with the mutual relations of the cognitive faculties (the imagination and the understanding), a harmony which is requisite for every empirical cognition. . . . It [the pleasure] rests merely on reflection and on the universal, though only subjective, conditions of the harmony of that reflection with the cognition of objects in general, for which the form of the object is purposive. (Intro. VII.5, Ak. 191, B. 28)

How does the principle of judgment mediate between the understanding and the reason, and hence between cognition and morality? Here we must recall the conclusions of the first two critiques, that the realm of theoretical knowledge—the natural laws of the empirical world—is distinct from the realm of morality, since the freedom (of the will) necessary for the realm of morality is not a feature of the empirical or phenomenal world, which world is subject to causal determinism. What we find, however, is that the purposiveness of forms in nature leads us to believe that nature is adapted to our faculties, since the free play of our mental faculties in apprehending this purposiveness of form is pleasurable to us. Thus, the necessary assumption of morality, namely, the freedom of the will (in the noumenal world), is not simply an idle wish. The world of experience and the world of human freedom are not inextricably separated in principle.

Is Kant claiming that the supersensible concept or principle on which the rules of morality rest is identical with the a priori principle of judgment, namely, the formal purposiveness of nature? The function of judgment in its reflective capacity (that is, going from the particular to the universal, which is not given) "is to establish the possibility of their systematic subordination" (Intro. IV.2, Ak. 180, B. 16), which is to regard particular experiences and their unification in terms of natural laws as a system and not simply as an aggregate (First Intro. II.5, Ak. 203, H. 10). This means that "particular empirical laws . . . must be considered in accordance with such a unity as they would have if an understanding (although not our understanding) had furnished them to our cognitive faculties, so as to make possible a system of experience according to particular laws of nature" (Intro. IV.3, Ak. 180, B. 16). Thus, Kant claims, "the principle of judgment, in respect of the form of things of nature under empirical laws generally, is the *purposiveness of nature* in its variety. That is, nature is represented by means of this concept as if an understaning contained the ground of the unity of the variety of its empirical laws" (Intro. IV.4, Ak. 180–81, B. 17). "This transcendental concept of a purposiveness of nature . . . only represents the peculiar way in which we must proceed in reflection upon the objects of nature in reference to a thoroughly connected experience" (Intro. V.4, Ak. 184, B. 20). Thus, it is merely a subjective principle, not an objective principle of nature. But it is nonetheless a subjective principle of all our cognition. The problem Kant begins with in terms of his philosophical system as a whole is how the understanding makes "a connected experience out of given perceptions of nature containing at all events an infinite variety of empirical laws" (Intro. V.5, Ak. 184, B. 21). Determining the principle underlying the faculty of judgment is thus necessary to complete the Kantian philosophical system, the critical philosophy as a whole.

1.3   The Faculty of Judgment

Judgment and the Process of Cognition

In the *Critique of Pure Reason,* Kant identifies the ability to judge (=the faculty of judgment, *Urteilskraft*) with one of the three major faculties of the mind—the understanding *(Verstand)*. It is the mental capacity described positively as knowledge or cognition by means of concepts, and negatively as the "non-sensible faculty of knowledge" (a67=b92). A human being is exercising his faculty of judgment when he attempts to make or succeeds in making individual judgments. More generally, a judgment, as an act of the understanding, is the act of thinking a particular representation as being contained under a universal or concept.[16] What constitutes the particular representation in a given case

16. See   a68–69=b93–94,   a132–34=b171–73,   a320=b376–77,   a646=b764;

varies. It may be a sensation, or an intuition of an individual object, or a concept or universal. Kant is using "representation" *(Vorstellung)* here to mean whatever one is aware of. For example, the following sentences express judgments: "This [what I am presently seeing] is red," "This ball is red," "Red is a color." As a faculty, judgment is the power of subsuming under concepts that which is in some way given in experience, either through sense awareness itself or through the faculties of knowledge. The power of judgment is the "faculty of distinguishing whether something does or does not stand under a given rule" (A132=B171). According to Kant, rules are what enable us to unify or order the manifold of our experience—the great variety of stimulatory inputs we receive. The particular objects of our awareness at any given time are many and various; in Kant's language, there is a "manifold of intuition." Rules are necessary to conceptualize this manifold in such a way that we can communicate with other human beings. Bringing a particular awareness under a concept requires an act of synthesis—a unification of the variety of representations under one common representation—a universal or concept (A68=B93). For example, as I walk around my house I see, in turn, the various sides of the house, parts of the roof, a chimney, and so forth. This variety of representations (in Kant's language, this manifold of intuitions) I somehow, by means of rules, unify under one common representation—my house. I might have walked around the house in the opposite direction, or reversed my path several times, or had glimpses of clouds and trees interspersed with my views of the parts of the house. Still, I unify the manifold under one representation—my house. And in this case the rules are such that the order in which the various parts of the house appear to me does not matter—it is still the same house no matter how I go about seeing it. Concepts are thus the means one faculty of the mind—the understanding—has of gaining knowledge, through the making of judgments by means of concepts which it supplies. It supplies concepts by having at its disposal rules for the unification (synthesis) of the manifold of intuitions.

Of course, the understanding cannot by itself make judgments; it is not the only faculty of the mind necessary for making judgments. In the example given above, another mental faculty, the imagination *(Einbildungskraft)*, is required to reproduce continually the representations of the various parts of the house previously apprehended, to hold those representations before the mind, and to gather them together so that the understanding, which supplies the rules for conceptualization, can see

---

Intro. IV.1, Ak. 179, B. 15.

(=judge) that the rules for the application of the concept are fulfilled. Only then do we have knowledge (cognition) and succeed in making a judgment.[17]

Determinant and Reflective Judgment

In both versions of the Introduction to the *Critique of Judgment,* Kant distinguishes two types of judgment, determinant and reflective. The activity of the power of judgment in its *determinant* form occurs when the universal or concept is given (for example, my house), and I search for an object—a particular unification of representations, a synthesis of the objects of my awareness—to subsume under it. If successful, the judgment is made and knowledge is achieved. On the other hand, the activity of the power of judgment in its *reflective* form occurs when only the variety of particular representations is given and I search for a concept or universal under which the object of my awareness may be subsumed (Intro. IV.1, Ak. 179, B. 15; First Intro. V, Ak. 211–16, H. 16–21). For example, suppose I encounter a conglomerate assortment of building materials—bricks, boards, glass—and reflect on the assortment in an attempt to determine what it is that I have found. Is it just a pile of carelessly stored building materials, or the remains of an abandoned shed, or perhaps a contemporary sculpture? In my reflection on the objects of my apprehension, I shall try different unifications of the variety of things I see in an attempt to find a way in which they relate such that a definite concept is applicable to them. And this is to say that I come to recognize that, when the various objects of my awareness are perceived in a certain way, a set of rules for the application of a concept is fulfilled; I now see it as a dilapidated shed. No definite concept was initially given. Only the manifold of representations was given, and I exercised my power of judgment by reflecting on the manifold in an attempt to find a concept suitably exemplified, whereupon I could make a judgment and thus a claim to knowledge.

In the *Critique of Judgment,* Kant claims that in judging an object with respect to its beauty, whether in nature or art, the faculty of judgment is exercised in its reflective capacity. Particular representations (the various elements and their interrelations in the object) are perceived and reflected upon, with the mental powers attempting to discern whether the elements and relationships are organized in a purposive manner. Whether they can be said to be so organized is determined by

---

17. There are several accounts of the process of cognition in the *Critique of Judgment:* §§ 9.4, 21, 35.1; Ak. 217, 238, 287; B. 52, 75, 129. An extended account, of course, is to be found in the *Critique of Pure Reason.*

whether they can be seen as purposive. The question in matters of beauty is whether the elements and their relationships relate as if they can be subsumed under a definite concept, as if they were rule-governed, even though we have no definite concept at our disposal which fits their organization (except the indefinite concept of rule-governedness).

1.4 The Judgment of Taste

Necessity for a Critique of the Faculty of Judgment

A judgment of taste is simply a judgment that a particular thing is (or is not) beautiful. Kant means to include under the category of judgments of taste only *singular* judgments that a thing is beautiful, that is, only judgments of the form "This is beautiful" in which "this" refers to a single object of awareness and not to a class of objects. Thus, the judgment that all Michelangelo sculptures are beautiful is not, according to Kant's analysis and usage, a judgment of taste; it is a logical or cognitive judgment, an empirical generalization based on a number of judgments of taste.[18]

Kant begins the *Critique of Judgment*—the critical examination of the faculty or power of judgment—with an analysis of the judgment of taste. This analysis may be variously described as an inquiry into the meaning of such judgments, the logical implications of making them, and the basis or grounds underlying them. Kant sees the judgment of taste as a clear example of a *reflective* judgment; in it, the object is not judged with respect to any definite concept, but only with respect to whether the contemplation of its form produces in us a feeling of pleasure or displeasure. Although based on a feeling of pleasure or displeasure, the judgment of taste makes a claim to being universally valid; it thus goes beyond what is empirically given in experience. Consequently, Kant believes there must be a general a priori principle underlying the faculty of judgment as exercised in these cases:

. . . the possibility of a purely reflective judgment which is aesthetic and yet based on an a priori principle, i.e., a judgment of taste, if it can be shown actually to have a justifiable claim to universal validity, definitely requires a critique of the judgment as a faculty having distinctive transcendental principles (like the understanding and the reason), and only in that way qualifies for incorporation into the system of the pure faculties of cognition. (First Intro. XI.6, Ak. 244, H. 47–48)

An analysis of the judgment of taste will thus show the need for and provide the key to a critique of judgment.

18. See note 15.

In the footnote to the title of the First Moment of the "Analytic of the Beautiful," Kant remarks: "The definition of 'taste' which is laid down here is that it is the faculty of judging the beautiful. But the analysis of judgments of taste must show what is required in order to call an object beautiful" (Ak. 203n, B. 37n). In Kant's analysis, the judgment of taste is an aesthetic judgment. In judging that something is beautiful, one (implicitly) relates a representation (one's awareness) of an object to a feeling of pleasure in oneself, the judging subject. An aesthetic judgment is contrasted with a logical (conceptual, cognitive) judgment, in which a representation is related to a concept (for example, "This is a dog"). The judgment that something is pleasant and the judgment that something is sublime are also aesthetic judgments, in the sense defined. Each of these judgments is also singular in that the object of awareness or reflection is a single object. Judgments claiming that a particular thing is pleasant Kant calls "judgments of sense" (Sinnenurteile) or "material aesthetic judgments" (§ 14.1, Ak. 223, B. 59) or even "aesthetic judgments of sense" (First Intro. VII.4–5, Ak. 224, H. 28). Kant's analysis of judgments of taste consists in a delineation or subtractive definition of the concept of the beautiful and the faculty of judging it (=taste). The judgment of taste is analyzed on the basis of a disinterested pleasure, independent of charm, emotion, and the concept of perfection.

That the judgment of taste is disinterested and that it is aesthetic form the two cornerstones to Kant's analysis of our experience of and judgments upon the beautiful. Kant is not unlike many contemporary philosophers in insisting on beginning with what he takes to be common usage and what we take ourselves to mean when using certain expressions. In the case of judgments of taste, analysis shows that our ordinary conception of the force or meaning of calling something beautiful involves a positive felt pleasure or satisfaction on the part of the appreciator, and claims implicitly a universality in our judgment—that others also ought to find a satisfaction in their experience of the object. These are the cornerstones by which Kant critically assesses the domain and extent of the human power of judgment.

Pure and Impure Judgments of Taste

Some judgments of taste are pure (formal), others impure (material). In using the modifying terms "pure," "impure," "formal," "material," "free," and "dependent," Kant intends "judgment of taste" to mean the act of judging or asserting, or the proposition that a particular thing is beautiful. He cannot be using the expression "judgment of taste" in the strict sense he sometimes does to mean the activity of or the product of a disinterested act of judging an object noncognitively (§§ 41.1, 57.5; Ak. 296, 340; B. 138, 185) with respect to its form, for the expressions "pure judgment of taste" and "free judgment of taste" would then contain a redundancy, and "impure judgment of taste" would contain a contradiction.

What, then, is a "pure judgment of taste"? A pure judgment, representation, or mode of knowledge is characterized by Kant in the *Critique of Pure Reason* as one which is completely a priori. However, this characterization is ambiguous: it can mean (a) "necessary and in the strictest sense universal" (B4), or (b) having "no admixture of anything empirical" (B3), or (c) having in it "nothing that belongs to sensation" (A20=B34). Kant may have thought these characterizations equivalent, but it is by no means obvious that they are. Regardless of this, they raise difficulties in understanding Kant's views in the Third Critique, since none strictly applies to judgments of taste. Yet, at some time or other, each characteristic is applied by Kant to judgments of taste. (This is not uncharacteristic of Kant—modifying key terms to fit his purposes, interpreting them so as to make them applicable to each new area he investigates, urging his architectonic onward.) A judgment of taste is certainly not pure in terms of being completely a priori, at least not in the defining sense of being known "independent of experience and even of all impressions of the senses" (B2). For, as Kant realizes, "we cannot determine *a priori* what object is or is not according to taste; that we must find out by experiment" (Intro. VII.5, Ak. 191, B. 28). Nor is a judgment of taste pure in terms of being necessary and in the strictest sense universal, for if it were it would have to be either amenable to proof or demonstrable as a necessary condition of our experience. Kant categorically denies that judgments of taste are amenable to proof, and he speaks of their necessity and universality qualifiedly as being "exemplary" and merely "imputed." As for any demonstrable quality, it is inconceivable that any particular judgment of taste could ever be a necessary condition of experience.

What Kant really means is that it is possible for judgments of taste to have the characteristics we believe them to have only if they are made in accordance with an a priori principle and that when they are so made they are pure.[19] But if this is all Kant means, it is grossly misleading to say, as Kant does by implication, that a judgment of taste so made (or the class of judgments we call "judgments of taste") is itself a priori; and it is equally misleading, then, for Kant to speak of the deduction of judgments of taste as "transcendental," since a transcendental deduction,

19. See, e.g., Intro. VII.6, §§ 29.5, 37.1; Ak. 191, 266, 289; B. 28, 106, 131.

strictly speaking, is "the explanation of the manner in which concepts can . . . relate *a priori* to objects" (A85=B117).

In saying that a judgment of taste can be pure, and hence a priori, Kant means:

(a) A judgment of taste is pure insofar as it is made not on the basis of the pleasure taken in sensation alone (for example, the sense charm or emotional appeal of the object), but rather on the basis of a judging of (reflection upon, contemplation of) the form of the object (a specific painting, sculpture, musical composition).

(b) A pure judgment of taste is necessary—others ought to agree with it—but in the sense that this necessity is "exemplary" (§ 18), "conditional" (§ 19), and "subjective" (§ 20).

(c) A pure judgment of taste is universal insofar as it is based on what we can suppose in all men; but this universality is subjective, not dependent upon concepts, and is merely imputed to all other judges (§ 8).

Characterizations (b) and (c) concern the logical features or logical status of judgments of taste as a class of judgment. Together, they comprise one horn of the Antinomy of Taste (as presented in the "Dialectic of the Aesthetic Judgment") as well as one of the "peculiarities" of judgments of taste (§§ 32–33); they are thus part of what leads to the need for a "deduction" for judgments of taste. Characterization (a), on the other hand, is in essence the first part of the deduction itself.

1.5   Argument of the "Critique of Aesthetic Judgment"

Kant's claim to have developed the first truly philosophical theory of aesthetics rests on his attempt to explain the differences between judging something to be beautiful and simply judging it to be pleasant. Both kinds of judgment, Kant says, are "aesthetic," in that they are not conceptual judgments about things in the world but are reports on the relation between an object met with in experience and a feeling of pleasure in the judging subject. But the judgment that I find some particular thing beautiful, unlike the judgment that I find it pleasant, imputes this pleasure or satisfaction to others. I take this pleasure or satisfaction to be necessary in that I feel anyone else in the same situation should pass the same judgment on the object's beauty, and thereby the satisfaction I feel I allege to be a universal one: in making the judgment that the object is beautiful, I imply (assume, purport) that my pleasure or satisfaction should (the element of necessity) hold for all (the element of universality) men, that all others ought to find it the way I do.

However, as Kant notes, "to establish *a priori* the connection of a feeling of pleasure or pain as an effect with any representation (sensation or

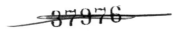

concept) as its cause is absolutely impossible" (§ 12.1, Ak. 221, B. 57). Hence, our use of the term "beautiful" requires justification. Kant calls the judgment that a particular thing is beautiful a "judgment of taste," simultaneously deferring to our ordinary beliefs and paving the way for claiming that a special faculty—not necessarily a skill, but at least an awareness—is involved. In Kantian terms, then, judgments of taste need to be "deduced": their validity as a class of judgment needs to be established because they claim a necessity and universality not met with in experience. In other words, how are such judgments possible? In the context of his critical philosophy, Kant's inquiry is obviously "transcendental."

It is pertinent to summarize Kant's deduction of judgment of taste. The claim to universal validity in judgments of taste is legitimate only on the assumption of similar subjective conditions for judgment in all men. A particular thing (a painting, building, musical composition, poem) can legitimately be claimed to be beautiful only if such a claim is made not on the basis of a feeling of pleasure accompanying the sensation, but rather on a feeling of pleasure accompanying the "judging of the object" *(Beurteilung des Gegenstandes)* (§ 9). This judging of the object is not to be identified with the judgment of taste *(Geschmacksurteil)*, which is simply the verdict or awareness that some specific thing is beautiful. The judging of the object, on the other hand, consists of those mental activities with respect to the object (actually, to the manifold of intuitions) which lead to the judgment of taste; it is an activity of reflection and contemplation on the form of the object. The (grammatical) subject of a particular act of judging the object need not be the object as a whole (the "this" of "This is beautiful"). For example, in the case of a painting, one aspect of judging the object could be to note that some of its spatial forms contrast with others, thereby creating a felt spatial tension. Such a notation is logically distinguishable, if not empirically distinct, from the verdict or awareness that the object is beautiful. For the judgment that something is beautiful to make a legitimate claim for objectivity (intersubjectivity) and hence universal validity, the feeling of pleasure to which it implicitly refers (and on which it is based), must be a consequent of the mental activities (contemplation, consideration, judging of the form of the object) such as exemplified above.

If the judgment of taste were made simply and directly on the basis of a pleasure in having a given sensation (simply sensing the object), it could make no claim to universal validity. The pleasures of mere sensation (that this smell, taste, texture, sound, or sight is pleasing to me) are completely subjective, in Kant's view; they may vary from individual to individual, and there is no basis on which mere pleasantness in sensation can be held to be the same for everyone. By relating the pleasure in the beautiful to the faculty of judgment, however, Kant claims to have shown how it is possible for judgments of taste to make this claim for universal validity. He maintains that the principle which underlies the faculty of judgment *(sensus communis)* is a condition for any experience whatsoever. In other words, the felt satisfaction which marks our awareness of the beauty of a thing is (must be) the result of the operation of the cognitive faculties—in free play, the imagination and understanding harmonize, as there is an awareness of purposiveness of form. Since this harmonious interplay of imagination and understanding is transcendentally necessary for any experience (or so Kant thought he had shown in the *Critique of Pure Reason*), it is a condition which can be supposed legitimately in all men. Hence our implicit claim that our judgments of taste hold for all men is (in principle) justified—the judgment of taste as a class of judgment has been legitimized. Furthermore, what we must contemplate or reflect upon in the experience of the beautiful is the form of that which we are considering. It is the form of our experience which we can communicate to one another; it is the form of intuitions which constitutes the basis for judgment.

This much of Kant's argument should be relatively uncontroversial, although the details may be obscure in this summary. However, the above argument does not complete the deduction of judgments of taste, for the specific reason that it neither explains nor legitimizes the fact that we impute our pleasure in the beautiful to others as necessary. The pleasure we feel underlying our judgments of taste "comes to be imputed to everyone, so to speak, as a duty *[Pflicht]*" (§ 40.7, Ak. 296, B. 138); we demand universal agreement (§ 8.2, Ak. 214, B. 49), and blame others if they judge otherwise and deny them taste (§ 7.2, Ak. 212–13, B. 47). The complete deduction of judgments of taste thus must show the basis on which we have an interest in the beautiful and in the judging of it. That basis must be found in nothing other than a link between beauty and morality. Given that the beautiful is the symbol of the basis of morality, there is a basis for demanding agreement on judgments of taste, because the requirement of moral sensitivity on the part of all human beings is justifiable.

CHAPTER 2

Kant's Analysis of the Judgment of Taste

2.1 The Judgment of Taste Is Aesthetic

An Arguable Thesis

KANT GAVE titles to almost every section of the *Critique of Judgment.* The title of § 1 is "The Judgment of Taste Is Aesthetic." It may be puzzling to see Kant putting this proposition forward as a claim and arguing for it. Today it seems obvious, perhaps even analytic, that the judgment that something is beautiful is an aesthetic judgment. Far from requiring argument, it seems to be true by virtue of the meanings of the terms involved. The judgment that something is beautiful is the classic and perhaps still the paradigmatic case of an aesthetic judgment, although we are now inclined to give greater attention and emphasis to aesthetic terms of praise other than "beautiful." The puzzle presented by Kant's argument cannot be removed simply by suggesting that Kant is using "aesthetic" as a technical term. As will be shown, Kant makes it clear elsewhere that he believes his use is etymologically sound, and in § 1 he does not proceed by giving or attempting to justify a definition but rather by giving reasons for his analysis of judgments of taste being aesthetic. In short, Kant feels that his claim uncovers one of the defining features of a class of judgments—judgments of taste. An explanation of the meaning and import of Kant's claim in § 1 thus requires a more detailed examination of the notion of "aesthetic."

"Aesthetic" in the Critique of Pure Reason

In the *Critique of Pure Reason,* Kant explicitly rejected Baumgarten's identification of "aesthetic" with a "critique of taste." Kant argued that

29

a critique of taste, by which he meant any attempt "to bring the critical treatment of the beautiful under rational principles, and so to raise its rules to the rank of a science," would be fruitless because "the said rules or criteria are, as regards their chief sources, merely empirical" (A21n= B35n; "chief" added in B). At the time of the writing of the first edition of the *Critique of Pure Reason,* Kant believed that there could be no a priori rules underlying taste and that hence our judgments of taste could not be derived transcendentally but only empirically (psychologically and anthropologically). On this basis in the first edition of the *Critique of Pure Reason,* Kant advised reserving the term "aesthetic" for "that doctrine of sensibility which is true science" (ibid.), that is, to use it as roughly synonymous with "sensible" or "perceptual," and thus approximate the Greek root. In the second edition, he added an alternative to this suggestion: "or else to share the name with speculative philosophy, employing it partly in the transcendental and partly in the psychological sense" (ibid.).

Kant consistently restricted his use of "aesthetic" to "sensible" in the First Critique. His "Transcendental Aesthetic" was an investigation of the a priori conditions for things being sensible to us. The two conditions he found—space and time—he maintained were necessary conditions for anything being an object of our awareness.

"Aesthetic" in the "Critique of Aesthetic Judgment"

As noted in chapter 1, Kant changed his opinion on the possibility of a critique of taste; indeed, he came to see it as the means of uniting the first two parts of the transcendental philosophy into a philosophical whole. Does Kant change his usage of "aesthetic" in the "Critique of Aesthetic Judgment," now that he has envisaged the possibility of a critique of taste? It is important to answer this question in order to determine precisely what is being claimed in § 1 in saying that the judgment of taste is aesthetic.

What does the adjective "aesthetic" modify in the passages in question? What we find is puzzling: Kant speaks both of *representations* and of *judgments* as being aesthetic. As applied to representations, Kant uses "aesthetic" in a sense of which "sensible" or "empirical" is one species, and the other species is a feeling-state. Kant holds that there are two kinds of sense perception: the first, *sensation (Empfindung),* gives us information about the world external to ourselves and our bodily states; the second, *feeling (Gefühl),* cannot give us any such information about an object of perception. "We understand by the word 'sensation' an objective representation of sense; and, in order to avoid misrepresentation, we shall call that which must always remain merely subjective and can constitute absolutely no representation of an object by the ordinary term 'feeling' " (§ 3.3, Ak. 206, B. 40). Both types of representations, sensations and feelings, are termed "aesthetic"; they are opposed, one may presume, to concepts and perhaps also to (pure) intuitions.

When "aesthetic" is applied to judgments, however, Kant does not mean what we might expect him to mean—that an aesthetic judgment is necessarily one in which the component representations are aesthetic. He says, for example, that the "given representation in a judgment can be empirical (consequently, aesthetical); but the judgment which is formed by means of them is logical, provided they are referred in the judgment to the object" (§ 1.2, Ak. 204, B. 38). He is saying that a judgment may be cognitive or logical (and hence not aesthetic) even if its constituent representations are aesthetic. Thus, an aesthetic judgment is not equivalent to a judgment with aesthetic constituent representations. An aesthetic judgment is one in which the representations, whatever their nature (that is, whether sensible, aesthetic, or rational), are referred or related in the judgment back to the subject rather than to an object. Aesthetic judgments are thus subjective judgments, according to Kant, in the literal sense of being "of the subject." The judgment of taste is aesthetic because it relates a representation (an object of art or nature) to the subject and his feeling of pleasure or displeasure. A judgment is aesthetic if and only if through the judgment the representation is related solely to the subject (his feeling) (ibid.). Another explicit formulation of this position occurs later in the deduction:

The concept of an object in general can immediately be combined with the perception of an object, containing its empirical predicates, so as to form a cognitive judgment; and it is thus that a judgment of experience is produced. . . .

But with a perception there can also be combined a feeling of pleasure (or pain) and satisfaction, that accompanies the representation of the object and serves instead of its predicate; thus there can result an aesthetical noncognitive judgment. (§ 36.1–2, Ak. 287–88, B. 130)

Kant's point here is one of semantics, not one of grammar or syntactics. It is, in more recent terms, a point about the depth grammar of judgments that a particular object is beautiful, and as such it requires argument. That argument Kant gives by presenting an analysis of the logic or meaning of statements of the form "This is beautiful"—judgments of taste; the "Analytic of the Beautiful" constitutes the major part of this analysis.

The Paradox of an Aesthetic Judgment

However, Kant's general account of the nature of judgment would seem to be inconsistent with the above interpretation of the meaning of an aesthetic judgment. As noted in chapter 1, section 3, a judgment is an act of the understanding; it is to think that a particular representation (whether a sensation, intuition, or concept) is contained under a universal or a concept. That this is Kant's view of the nature of judgment is quite clear. But according to this view an aesthetic judgment would be impossible because it would be self-contradictory. Kant has claimed explicitly that "This is beautiful" does not relate a particular thing to a concept of an object or a universal; hence, it does not strictly fulfill the criterion for its being a judgment. Rather, Kant has claimed that "This is beautiful" relates a particular thing to the subject and his feeling of pleasure or displeasure. Since, according to Kant, feelings of pleasure and displeasure are not universals or concepts, "This is beautiful" ought not to be called a judgment at all. Making it a special species of judgment ("aesthetic judgment") would not help to remove the inconsistency. That Kant should call "This is beautiful" an aesthetic judgment is thus paradoxical.

Kant himself recognized the paradoxical nature of the notion of an aesthetic judgment. In the First Introduction to the *Critique of Judgment,* Kant notes that "aesthetic representation" can be taken to mean a sensuous or empirical representation, relating to the manner in which the subject is affected (First Intro. VIII.1, Ak. 221, H. 25). *Sensibility* is the faculty being engaged here; it is defined by Kant as "the capacity (receptivity) for receiving representations through the mode in which we are affected by objects" (A19=B33). In the process of cognition, according to Kant, an aesthetic representation is transferred or applied to the object of which it is a representation. This is the first and basic sense of "aesthetic," the one Kant used in the *Critique of Pure Reason.*

The next step in Kant's attempt to resolve the paradox of an "aesthetic judgment" is found in his second use of "aesthetic": "It has long been customary, however, to call a representation aesthetic, i.e., sensuous, also to signify the intention of relating a representation not to the cognitive faculty but to the feeling of pleasure and displeasure" (First Intro. VIII.1, Ak. 222, H. 26). Kant remarks that it is also appropriate to call this feeling a sensation because it is a modification of our state, *sensation* being "the effect of an object upon the faculty of representation so far as we are affected by it" (A19–20=B34). But since it can never be used for knowledge of an object, it should be termed a subjective rather than an objective sensation. Nonetheless, it could be called "aesthetic," that is, sensible or sensuous, because it is a modification of the state of the subject just like other sensations, the objective ones on which knowledge of objects is based.

Kant then notes that the two senses of "aesthetic," as applied to representations, produce an ambiguity:

Hence an inevitable ambiguity is always present in the expression "an aesthetic mode of representation," if it is sometimes understood to mean that which arouses the feeling of pleasure and pain, and at other times that which concerns merely the cognitive faculty as regards knowledge of objects as appearances, through sensory intuition. (First Intro. VIII.1, Ak. 222, H. 26)

Kant believes that this ambiguity can best be removed by not applying the term "aesthetic" to intuitions, sensations, and representations, and restricting its use only to the operations of the faculty of judgment. But this removes the ambiguity of "aesthetic representation" at the cost of creating the contradictory notion of an *aesthetic judgment*. Kant clearly recognizes this contradiction:

For intuitions can indeed be sensuous, but judgments definitely belong purely to the understanding (taken in the broader sense), and *to judge* aesthetically or sensuously, supposing this to be *knowledge* of an object, is therefore a contradiction. . . . an *objective* judgment, in contrast, is always brought about through the understanding alone and thus cannot be called aesthetic. (First Intro. VIII.2, Ak. 222, H. 26)

Far from being disturbed by this contradiction, Kant believes it renders completely unambiguous the sense he wants to give to the term "aesthetic judgment":

The expression "an aesthetic judgment of an object" thus signifies that a given representation is indeed related to an object, but it is a judgment conveying the determination of the subject and its feeling rather than of the object. . . . A judgment is termed "aesthetic," i.e., sensuous, according to its subjective effect and not its ground of determination. (First Intro. VIII.2, Ak. 223, H. 27)

Although it is not the sensible representation of an object, the judgment of taste can thus be called aesthetic because it can be described as the sensible representation of the state of the subject—the way the subject is affected—in relation to the object. In these terms we can comprehend Kant's remark that by an aesthetic judgment we understand a judgment "whose determining ground can be no other than subjective" (§ 1.1, Ak. 203–4, B. 37), since it relates to a feeling of pleasure or displeasure. And, according to Kant, feelings of pleasure or displeasure can never be properties of an object but only of the subject—his mental state.[1]

In §§ 18–20 of the *Prolegomena to Any Future Metaphysics*,[2] Kant

1. First Intro. VIII.4, Ak. 224, H. 28; §§ 1.1, 3.3; Ak. 203–4, 206; B. 37–38, 40.
2. Kant, *Prolegomena to Any Future Metaphysics Which Will Be Able to Come*

distinguishes between judgments of experience, which are objectively valid, and judgments of perception, which are only subjectively valid: "All our judgments are at first merely judgments of perception; they hold good only for us (that is, for our subject), and we do not till afterward give them a new reference (to an object)."[3] Kant gives examples of those judgments of perception that can never become judgments of experience: "The room is warm," "Sugar is sweet," and "Wormwood is bitter." His reasoning is that "they refer merely to feeling, which everybody knows to be merely subjective and which of course can never be attributed to the object, and consequently never become objective."[4] In the terminology of the *Prolegomena,* such judgments can never become judgments of experience or judgments about objects; they must always remain subjective. In the terminology of the *Critique of Judgment,* they must be considered aesthetic judgments.

The *Prolegomena* passages are helpful in understanding how the root word "sensuous," or "perceptual," or "sensible" underlies each of Kant's uses of the term "aesthetic," and why Kant holds that there are two major species of aesthetic judgments: those for which we claim universal validity and those in which we merely claim that something is simply pleasurable or displeasurable. The former class consists in judgment on the beautiful (judgments of taste proper) and judgments on the sublime. The latter class Kant sometimes calls "judgments of sense" or "material aesthetic judgments" (e.g., § 14.1, Ak. 223, B. 59). They are concerned merely with the pleasurable to sense, e.g., "The rose is pleasurable (to smell)," "Canary wine is pleasant (to taste)," They make no claim to universal validity, and even though there may be considerable empirical agreement upon them, they remain wholly subjective. The pleasure to which they refer is produced directly by the sensing of the object. Judgments that a particular thing is beautiful or sublime, however, do make a claim to universal validity; they are offered as if they are valid for every human being. Even though there is no universal agreement on such judgments, everyone imputes or demands this agreement with respect to others. Aesthetic judgments of both species, however, are subjective in that their "ground of determination lies in a sensation

---

Forth as Science (*Prolegomena zu einer jeden künftigen Metaphysik, die als Wissenschaft wird auftreten können*) (1783), included in volume 4 of the Prussian Academy edition of Kant's works. I follow the translation by Lewis White Beck: *Kant: Prolegomena to Any Future Metaphysics,* Library of Liberal Arts (Indianapolis: Bobbs-Merrill, 1950).

3. *Prolegomena* § 18, Ak. 4:298, Beck 46.
4. *Prolegomena* § 19n, Ak. 4:299n, Beck 47n.

immediately connected with the feeling of pleasure and pain" (First Intro. VIII.4, Ak. 224, H. 28).

Kant's Support for His Claim

Kant is using "judgment" not in the strict sense in which he defined it but merely in the sense of any statement or proposition in which a representation is thought related to something else. But there is a problem in connection with Kant's criterion for distinguishing species of judgment. The statements "This is beautiful," "This is sweet," "This is triangular," and "This is mammalian" have the same grammatical form. Thus, the verbal or grammatical form of the judgment cannot be what determines whether, as in the last two examples, the predicate is related to an object, or whether, as in the first two examples, the predicate is related back merely to the subject—whether, that is, the judgments are logical (cognitive) or aesthetic.

Kant seems to be required to make a distinction between the grammatical form of judgments and their logical form. The problem is thus how the logical form of a judgment, in particular an aesthetic judgment, is determined. Suppose we grant that the distinction between aesthetic judgments and logical or cognitive judgments is clear. How is the distinction to be applied in any given case? How do we decide in a given case whether a judgment is logical or aesthetic?

Kant's support for the claim that judgments of taste are aesthetic is twofold, and contained in this support is the means for distinguishing aesthetic and cognitive judgments generally. In the first place Kant appeals to a logical point, in the second to a phenomenological observation.

The logical point in support of the claim that judgments of taste are aesthetic is the observation which constitutes the thesis of the antinomy of taste. It may be termed the absence-of-proof thesis. Judgments of taste do not relate a representation to a concept; if they did, they would be susceptible of proof, which they are not.

If one judges objects merely according to concepts, then all representation of beauty is lost. Thus there can be no rule according to which anyone is to be forced to recognize anything as beautiful. No one lets himself be talked into making a judgment, through reasons or principles, that a dress, a house, or a flower is beautiful. He wants to submit the object to his own eyes, just as if the satisfaction in it depended on sensation. (§ 8.6, Ak. 215–16; my translation, cf. B. 50)[5]

---

5. Cf. §§ 34, 35.1, 44.1, 56.2, 57.4; Ak. 186–87, 304–5, 338, 340; B. 127–28, 128–29, 147, 183, 185.

No amount of talking alone can get one to see that something is beautiful, and no reasons can be adduced from which a conclusion can be inferred that a particular thing is beautiful. General principles may guide our perception and our judgment, but they can never force them. The thesis that judgments of taste are not susceptible to syllogistic proof is tied to Kant's view that the beautiful pleases immediately, that the discovery of something's beauty requires a direct experience of the object. The last quotation brings these two views together and leads to the second consideration.

The phenomenological observation in support of Kant's claim is simply that there is a qualitive difference in the feeling or experience on which the judgment is based. In § 1 Kant says that to grasp *(befassen)* a building with our cognitive faculties is something entirely different from being aware *(sich . . . bewusst zu sein)* of this representation of a building with the feeling of pleasure. Here Kant seems to be appealing to what we are doing and feeling in the apprehension of something, such as looking at a building ordinarily contrasted with looking at it aesthetically. Kant's assumption is that a feeling of pleasure or displeasure cannot be affirmed of an object (such as a house or a painting); it can only be affirmed of a perceiving subject. Judgments of taste are thus a subspecies of aesthetic judgments; they are noted phenomenologically through our awareness of a feeling of pleasure or displeasure upon perceiving the object. That it is pleasure which is bound up in the experience is something that can only be felt. "That the representation of an object is immediately bound up with pleasure can only be internally perceived *[kann nur innerlich wahrgenommen werden]*, and if we did not wish to indicate more than this, it would give a merely empirical judgment" (§ 37.1, Ak. 289, B. 131). Kant appears to be adducing these facts of experience as evidence for his claim that judgments of taste are aesthetic and as a means of deciding, in a given case, whether a judgment is logical or aesthetic.

The conclusion we are led to is that the judgment of taste is aesthetic, that is, it is about that state of the subject in the perceptual or sensible apprehension of an object (for Kant, the representation of an object). This analysis of the judgment of taste as aesthetic forms the thesis of the antinomy of taste. Together with the analysis of judgments of taste as disinterested (and hence laying claim to universal validity), an opposition is produced which Kant interprets as necessitating a transcendental deduction of judgments of taste. Thus the claim that the judgment of taste is aesthetic is of central importance to the continuing argument of the *Critique of Judgment*.

2.2 The Judgment of Taste Is Disinterested

That the judgment of taste is aesthetic is the conclusion of an argument designed to show that the grammatical form of the judgment of taste belies its logical form. The judgment of taste is basically a disguised liking-report, although Kant will argue that it is a liking-report of a very special kind. The judgment that something is beautiful is unlike the judgment that it is square, or that it is a feline or that it is a book, in which a particular awareness (representation, in this case an intuition) is related to a concept or universal; rather, the judgment of taste indicates a relation between the particular awareness (to which the "this" refers) and a feeling of pleasure on the part of the judging subject. Such is the import of § 1. In §§ 2–5, Kant begins to analyze this view by examining the nature of the pleasure felt to be the basis of the judgment that something is beautiful. The first and key step is the claim that the pleasure is a disinterested pleasure.

Kant vacillates between using the expression "judgment of taste" in a weak sense and using it in a strong sense. On the one hand, he says that if a judgment that something is beautiful is based on an interested (as opposed to disinterested) pleasure, it is not a judgment of taste (see, for example, the title to § 2). On the other hand, he says that such a judgment is a judgment of taste by virtue of its form ("This is beautiful"), even though it may not be a pure judgment of taste (for example, § 2.1, Ak. 205, B. 39). Kant's ambivalence is due to the theoretical conflict between treating judgments as verbal actions or products of verbal actions and treating them as the exercise of a particular human faculty. Probably the least ambiguous language is to retain "judgment of taste" for the claim that something is beautiful and allow "pure judgment of taste" to function normatively, applying only when the necessary conditions for universal communication are met. By retaining "judgment of taste" in the descriptive sense, Kant's position is that only if the pleasure is disinterested can the judgment be a pure judgment of taste.

Disinterestedness

The notion of disinterestedness in aesthetics did not originate with Kant. Like many other central concepts in the Third Critique, such as genius, form, and the sublime, it is to be found in the writings of earlier eighteenth-century British aestheticians such as Shaftesbury, Hutcheson, Gerard, and Burke, with some of whose works Kant is known to have been familiar.[6] The centrality of the concept of disinterestedness in mod-

6. See Milton C. Nahm, *The Artist as Creator* (Baltimore: Johns Hopkins Univ.

ern aesthetics predates Kant, and Kant characteristically fails to indicate his indebtedness. The lack of specific investigation of the concept and its continued assumption perhaps are partly due to "disinterested" having come to mean "unbiased" or "impartial" (see, for example, the *Oxford English Dictionary's* listing of historical usages). If we suppose, as a point of necessity, that judgments of taste are to claim universal validity, to use Kant's terminology, it is reasonable to suppose that they ought to be "disinterested" in this sense. In an essay tracing the origin and development of the notion of disinterestedness in eighteenth-century British aesthetic theory, Jerome Stolnitz has expressed what has been a central question in much modern and even very recent aesthetic inquiry: "Given the meaning of 'disinterestedness,' which faculty or which contents of awareness or which objects can alone satisfy the conditions which it specifies?"[7] The notion of disinterestedness plays a central role in the development of Kant's aesthetic theory. The following section thus consists of (a) an analysis of the relevance of the concept of disinterestedness in Kant's aesthetic theory, and (b) a discussion of whether a purely aesthetic interest in an object can be defended. The latter question is essential in any attempt to assess Kant's view that our judgments of taste must be disinterested if they are to satisfy the logical requirements of their use.

Interest and Pleasure

Kant characterizes disinterestedness in terms of the absence of interest, and he defines "interest" as "the satisfaction which we combine with the representation of the existence of an object" *(Das Wohlgefallen das wir mit der Vorstellung der Existenz eines Gegenstandes verbinden)* (§ 2.1, Ak. 204, B. 38). Kant considers interest as a particular kind of state of mind, a feeling of pleasure. The ground of this feeling of pleasure is "the representation of the existence of an object." This interested state of mind contrasts with the experience of the beautiful, which, although also characterized as a feeling of pleasure, is disinterestedly based on the formal subjective purposiveness in the object. (In Kantian terminology, this becomes: the formal subjective purposiveness in the representation through which an object is given and in the contemplation of which our cognitive powers, the imagination and the understand-

---

Press, 1956); republished as *Genius and Creativity* (New York: Harper and Row, 1965).

7. Jerome Stolnitz, "On the Origins of 'Aesthetic Disinterestedness,'" *Journal of Aesthetics and Art Criticism* 20 (1961–62):141.

ing, are in harmony and free play.) But the support Kant can muster at this point for the thesis that the "satisfaction which determines the judgment of taste is disinterested" (the title of § 2) is limited at this stage of his argument; he cannot appeal to his later conclusions concerning the objectivity of formal purposiveness to deny that the feeling of pleasure characterized by interest is identical with or a component of the feeling of pleasure in the beautiful. To do so would be question-begging at this point. Also, such a procedure would remove some of his support for his later claims, since it is partly on the basis of the exclusion of interest that Kant is able to arrive at the conclusion of formal subjective purposiveness. In other words, the disinterestedness thesis plays a basic role in the development of Kant's argument as a whole, leading to the deduction of judgments of taste. The problem is to exhibit the centrality, but simultaneously to show the limitations of that role.

The German phrasing of Kant's definition of "interest" is ambiguous, given Kant's own use of the term *"Vorstellung." Vorstellung* is often simply a surrogate term for Kant, given his peculiar epistemological view that what we are aware of is always a representation, be it a particular sensation, empirical object, or a universal. A representation *(Vorstellung)* is simply any object of awareness, anything of which we are immediately aware. Thus, it can be argued that the inclusion of "representation" or "idea" *(Vorstellung)* in this definition of "interest" has no special force, that its occurrence is explicable through Kant's epistemological view that whatever is present to the mind is a representation, be it a datum of sense, a concept or universal, or the consciousness of an inner state. Understood in this way, one can say that Kant's use of *Vorstellung* is either redundant or readily replaceable by a more precise term. Which term replaces it depends upon the context. If the occurrence of *Vorstellung* is redundant in the definition of "interest" being considered, Kant is maintaining that to be interested in something is to feel pleasure in that thing's existence.

Other passages dealing with the notion of interest tend to support the contention that *Vorstellung* has no special force in the original definition of "interest" and is therefore redundant. In § 4, Kant equates interest with "a satisfaction in the *presence [Dasein]* of an object or action" (§ 4.1, Ak. 207, B. 41). In making pure judgments on the sublime, Kant claims that "we have no interest whatever in an object—i.e., its existence is indifferent to us" (§ 25.4, Ak. 249, B. 87). In § 41, where Kant is inquiring whether any interest can be combined with the judgment of taste after the judgment of taste has been given as a pure aesthetic judgment, he refers to *"pleasure in the existence [Existenz] of an object"* as "that wherein all interest consists" (§ 41.1, Ak. 296, B. 139). In the same paragraph he remarks that both empirical and intellectual interest "involve a satisfaction in the presence *[Dasein]* of an object." These passages tend to support the view that, in his definition of "interest" as "the satisfaction which we combine with the representation of the existence of an object," Kant is using *"Vorstellung"* ("representation" or "idea") in the fairly neutral sense of the particular awareness or experience of the object, as an object present to us.

In spite of these passages, there is a difficulty in interpreting Kant's definition of interest as the pleasure in the existence of an object. The difficulty is simply that one can be interested in or have an interest in something without that thing actually existing—indeed, without its even being possible to exist. One can be interested in dog racing, for example, although it is prohibited by law; in the Fountain of Youth, although it does not exist; and in squaring the circle, although it is impossible. "To be interested in," like "to endeavor to" but unlike "to see," does not have the existence of that denoted by its grammatical object as a condition of the truth of simple statements in which it is the main verb. A second interpretation of Kant's definition of "interest" thus presents itself, construing *Vorstellung* as having special force in the original definition of "interest" in § 2: the satisfaction which we combine with the idea of the existence of an object. In this second interpretation, Kant is being given credit for recognizing that interest cannot be analyzed as a feeling (of pleasure or of any other sort) that will necessarily occur upon experiencing some existent object. Interest, if taken to be a mental state at all, must be conceived as a present state of mind directed toward or related to an object, which object need not actually exist. Of course it is true that an interest can and usually does lead to action directed toward bringing about the existence and direct experience of the object and that some sort of pleasure or satisfaction usually accompanies the achievement of such efforts. But that feeling cannot be a necessary and sufficient condition for the application of the term "interest." With regard to this second interpretation, then, Kant is saying that if one is interested in something, one is pleased with the idea of that thing existing and continuing to exist.

A brief look at a competing, rather behavioristic characterization of interest may help put Kant's view in perspective. In this view, to be interested in an object is to be inclined to give one's attention to that object, the object of interest. Such a dispositional analysis in terms of behavior cannot completely avoid reference to feelings or states of mind. "To feel interest in anything is to feel attracted to it; to *feel inclined* to give attention to it. . . . To feel interest is also to *want* to pay attention to the object of one's interest."[8] If one accepts the view that one wants to pay attention to the object of one's interest, then it would seem, following Kant, that one also either desires the existence of the object of one's interest in order to be able to pay attention to it, or feels pleasure in the idea of the existence of the object of one's interest. In that case, Kant's analysis is not so far removed from the dispositional account as it might seem. To take an interest in something is certainly to direct one's attention to it, but directing one's attention to something is itself an intentional act. Thus, the behavioral criterion of interest leads one back to the mental state of the subject (a felt pleasure in something), which is where Kant began.

The ultimate plausibility of either account of interest need not concern us here. Certainly it can be questioned whether an interest in any way entails a feeling of pleasure or satisfaction. The important point for the development of Kant's aesthetic theory is that in either interpretation discussed above, as well as in the dispositional account, interest involves desire or will and, according to Kant, therefore a need or a want (see § 5.2, Ak. 210, B. 44). Pleasures based on a need or a want and not determined by concepts are individually determined so that no two people finding satisfaction in a work of art would have any basis for presuming they were or could be sharing an experience, and the feeling that others ought to agree with our judgments of taste could have no objective basis. In order to lay claim to holding for all men, the judging of a work of art as beautiful must be free, not determined by needs or wants; hence, disinterested.

Kant's Support for His Claim

Kant recognized that "disinterested" refers to a concept the content of which is given by its negation, "interested." Kant's basis for his claim that the judgment of taste is disinterested is thus not simply a matter of definition of "judgment of taste." The major support is an appeal to what we inquire into or about when we want to know if a given object is beautiful. Kant appeals to what, he says, everyone admits: that a judgment of taste in which the slightest interest mingles is highly partisan and is not a pure judgment of taste (§ 2.1, Ak. 205, B. 39).

Kant's underlying argument seems to be a type of verification argument. If a given property or characteristic is the determining ground of the judgment "This is beautiful," then when we ask "Is this beautiful?"

---

8. Alan R. White, "The Notion of Interest," *Philosophical Quarterly* 14 (1964): 320.

we must be asking whether the object has the given property or characteristic. With respect to judgments of taste, however, we do not inquire into either our own or others' desire for something to exist (or pleasure in the idea of the object existing) in order to find out whether we find the object beautiful. This sort of inquiry, Kant argues, is completely beside the point. (Kant's argument looks like the first step toward showing that Beauty is not a natural property; and indeed this is Kant's position.) Although Kant does believe that the experience of the beautiful is marked by the feeling of pleasure, "beautiful" does not mean "pleasurable." Only a pleasure of a certain kind, one with a certain type of ground, marks the experience of the beautiful. And this ground, the formal subjective purposiveness of a representation, is not a concept for which empirical or natural determinations can be given.

But this looks like a poor argument. Given that x is based on or grounded in y, it does not follow that any inquiry into x is to be recognized as an inquiry into y. Kant is relying on more than a verification argument here. He is appealing to each individual's awareness of the grounds of his judgment of taste.

This line of reasoning seems inconsistent with Kant's further goals since he wants to argue that if we are to legitimately claim what we purport to claim when we make a judgment of taste, we must base our judgment on the formal subjective purposiveness of the object; in no other way can the judgment have a claim for universal validity, and that it have such a claim is part of the meaning of saying that something is beautiful. Given these goals, how can Kant at this point claim that the judgment of taste in which any interest mingles is highly partisan and not a pure judgment of taste, which is to say it cannot claim universal validity? To do so at this point is to beg the question. This first argument, then, designed to show that the judgment of taste is disinterested, cannot be sufficient to prove that the judgment of taste is universally valid. That the judgment of taste is disinterested may be a reason to suppose that it has universal validity, but it cannot be a reason to conclude that it is universally valid.

There is a second argument in these sections, however; it may be termed the elimination argument. It consists in characterizing disinterested pleasure as the absence of the occurrence of all members of an enumerated set of interested pleasures. Kant continually speaks of the pleasure in sensation, the pleasure in contemplation or reflection, the pleasure in the good, and so forth. Pleasures are distinguished in terms of their grounds. Kant's argument depends, as he himself all but admits in § 2, upon there being no other kinds of interest than those he goes on to specify: interest in an object because it is good (either for something or in itself), or interest in an object because it is pleasant (pleasurable to sense). Disinterested pleasure, then, is pleasure not based on interested grounds.

Kant's belief that there are only two kinds of interest, that in the good and that in the pleasurable, makes plausible the examples he uses to support the argument that interest makes the judgment of taste impure. In § 2, Kant claims that the following replies to the question "Do you find this (palace) beautiful?" are obviously and completely irrelevant:

(1) I do not like things which are made only to be stared at.
(2) I only like buildings in Paris that are restaurants.
(3) It is wrong to waste the sweat of the people on such superfluous things.

These are examples of a lack of interest in the existence of the object (the palace), respectively due to:

(1) The lack of instrumental good—the palace is considered "good for nothing" in the first example.
(2) The lack of sense pleasure or delight—the palace is not a Parisian restaurant and hence does not give pleasure to the Iroquois chief who can only think of a building's contents.
(3) The lack of intrinsic good—in the third example it is considered morally wrong to bring such a thing into existence through human labor.

These replies are irrelevant, Kant correctly observes, because in asking whether something is beautiful we are not asking whether it is pleasant, good for something, or good in itself (at least not in any moral sense). We need not accept Kant's own analysis of judgments of taste in order to agree with his critical remarks here. Kant's observations merely serve to eliminate irrelevant bases for the judgment of taste; we can agree that these bases are irrelevant without concurring with Kant's positive view of the basis of the judgment of taste. That Kant thought this basis necessary is irrelevant at this point in his argument. Kant's remarks can best be viewed as preparing the way for the actual "deduction" of judgments of taste. In other words, these examples, although they may lend prima facie support to Kant's conclusion, in the absence of examples of any other kind of interest, do not entail, as Kant seems to think they do, that when we inquire into the beautiful "we do not want to know whether anything depends on or can depend on the existence of the thing, either for myself or for anyone else" (§ 2.1, Ak. 204, B. 38). Such a conclusion depends upon there being no other kinds of interest than those exemplified, but Kant provides no argument to support the exhaustiveness of his enumeration.

Kant does go on to give a fourth and rather peculiar example:

Finally, suppose that I found myself on an uninhabited island without hope of ever again coming among men and that I could by my mere wish conjure up such a palace. I can quite easily convince myself that I would not exert even this little effort if I already had a hut that was comfortable enough for me. (§ 2.1, Ak. 204–5; my translation, cf. B. 39)

Kant seems to be saying that outside of society, even supposing that all the necessary means are at one's disposal and no practical problems exist to interfere with the creation of such a palace, one can conceive of not wanting to create an object for which there was no use. This anticipates Kant's view (in § 41) that interest in the beautiful arises only in society. The striking feature of this fourth example is the implication resulting from the several conditions Kant attaches to it. It is suggested that one can convince himself that he should not want to create such a palace, but only outside of society, on an uninhabited island with no hope of ever again coming into contact with other human beings.[9] Kant believes these conditions to be necessary because he is willing to allow that within society one could not convince oneself of this. Kant appears to be hedging a little here; he seems to allow that there is an interest in the beautiful not based on sense pleasure, instrumental or moral good, but then explains it by saying that it is not essentially bound up with the beautiful alone, as this example shows, but is grounded in society, that is, in our social nature. "Judgments of taste, however, do not in themselves establish any interest. Only in society is it *interesting* to have taste" (§ 2.2n, Ak. 205n, B. 39n; cf. § 41.2, Ak. 296–97, B. 139).

The fourth example thus carries weight in supporting the claim that the judgment of taste is disinterested only on the assumption that interest in the existence of a beautiful object that is not based on moral, prudential, or sensual considerations can be explained on purely social grounds. Kant is in a difficult position here, however, since the conditions he puts on this example indicate that in society it is perfectly appropriate and relevant, in asking whether something is beautiful, to inquire into an interest we or others might have in its existence—provided that interest is not merely sensual, moral, or prudential. It is not obvious that the interest we have in society in the existence of beautiful objects is itself always one of these kinds. In society, Kant would seem

9. Cf. Kant's *Anthropology from a Pragmatic Viewpoint*, § 67: "Any *presentation* [*Darstellung*] of one's own person or art with taste presupposes a societal state (a state of communicating oneself to others). . . . Nobody living in complete solitude will adorn or trim himself or his house; nor will he do so for those who belong to him (wife and children), but only for strangers to show himself to advantage" (Ak. 7:240). In Kant, *Analytic of the Beautiful*, trans. Walter Cerf (Indianapolis: Bobbs-Merrill, 1963), p. 64.

to hold, our social natures are both constant and universal (that is, characteristic of all men) and thus would not be a variable factor in interfering with the truth of a judgment of taste. In other words, if the beautiful is interesting in society, then in society it would seem relevant to inquire into whether we are interested in the object under consideration, provided we can find a means of distinguishing this social interest from sensual, moral, and prudential interests. Kant's fourth example may have proved too much.

Perhaps making this distinction is no different from distinguishing pure from impure judgments of taste generally. If the beautiful interests us in society, then how is it that within society no talk of interest is at all relevant? This objection does not refute Kant's conclusion that the satisfaction which determines the judgment of taste is without any interest, because this social interest is determined or produced by, and does not itself determine, the judgment of taste. But it does show that Kant's claim regarding what we want to know or what we inquire into when we are interested in whether something is beautiful is not sufficient to establish this conclusion. The elimination argument is thus not strong enough.

Kant concludes his support of the claim of § 2 with the following remark:

Everyone must admit that a judgment about beauty, in which the slightest interest mingles, is very partial and is not a pure judgment of taste. We must not be in the least prejudiced in favor of the existence of the things, but be quite indifferent in this respect, in order to play the judge in things of taste. (§ 2.1, Ak. 205, B. 39)

Although this appears to be merely a restatement of the argument already considered (the verification argument), there is an additional appeal to what we all admit. But in what sense do we admit this? It is true that we admit it with regard to the interests specified in the first three examples (sense pleasure and the good), and it is also true that we admit it in the sense in which "interest" means "self-interest"—in the sense, that is, in which a judgment that is not disinterested is considered biased or partisan. But the first sense is the elimination argument, already shown to be insufficient; and the second sense is also unsatisfactory, not merely because it begs the larger question of the validity of judgments of taste, but also because Kant himself does not want to say that all interests are biased or partisan. Certain judgments, such as those moral judgments made in accordance with the Categorical Imperative, are both interested and impartial. Thus, the more restricted uses of "interested" and "disinterested" cannot be the ones operative here.

Is Kant aware of the weakness of his argument? Perhaps. For he suggests that we must elucidate the proposition that the satisfaction which determines the judgment of taste is disinterested by taking a more detailed look at "the pure disinterested satisfaction in judgments of taste" (§ 2.2, Ak. 205, B. 39). In other words, the grounds of the pleasure in the beautiful have not been positively characterized, although Kant has argued that certain grounds are irrelevant.

Kant's arguments to show that the pleasure in the beautiful (on which the judgment of taste is based) is not itself based on any interest are insufficient if they are viewed as attempts to deduce an objective basis for judgments of taste capable of ensuring their claim to universal validity. However, if Kant is interpreted merely as narrowing the field of inquiry, his effort makes more sense. It may be seen as part of his continuing attempt to delineate the ground for the judgment of taste consistent with the meaning of such judgments and sufficient to justify the claim to universal validity (in principle).

In an aesthetic judgment a representation (a mental awareness) is related back to the state of the experiencing subject, and in particular to his feeling of pleasure or displeasure. The aesthetic judgment is thus contrasted with a cognitive (logical, conceptual) judgment, in which there is a relating of a representation to an object by means of concepts. The only modifications of one's mental state ("sensations," in the broadest sense) which are always subjective and which, therefore, can never be a ground for knowledge of objects in the world are the feelings of pleasure and displeasure (Intro. VII, § 1.1; Ak. 188–92, 203–4; B. 25–29, 37–38). It is to these feelings, then, that representations must relate in aesthetic judgments—judgments of taste and judgments of sense alike. When the question is whether something is beautiful, "we wish only to know if this mere representation of the object is accompanied in me with satisfaction" (§ 2.1, Ak. 205, B. 39). Kant thus distinguishes the feeling of pleasure in the experience of the beautiful from the feeling of pleasure in all other experiences by distinguishing different grounds (bases, causes) of the pleasure. The "Analytic of the Beautiful" may be understood as a subtractive exposition of the basis for making judgments of taste. More specifically, the inquiry is an attempt to determine a basis for the felt pleasure in the beautiful. Kant's first technique for distinguishing these different grounds of pleasure is the concept of *interest*. As we have seen, interest is itself defined in terms of pleasure; it is a pleasure having a certain basis or ground, namely, pleasure taken in the "representation of the existence of an object." Kant's most general claim here is that the pleasure in the beautiful is not determined by any interest on our part, and is thus not connected to desire or the will.

Pleasure, Desire, and the Experience of the Beautiful

Pleasure, for Kant, is an irreducible feeling. As Walter Cerf points out, the feelings of pleasure (*Lust*) and displeasure (*Unlust*) are, for Kant, psychic ultimates unanalyzable into, and irreducible to, components.[10] Cerf's interpretation is supported by many of Kant's remarks, the most explicit of which occurs in the First Introduction:

> It can readily be seen that pleasure and displeasure, not being modes of cognition, cannot be defined in themselves; they can be felt, but not understood. One can see, therefore, that they can only receive an explanation, a very inadequate one at best, through the influence which a representation exerts by means of this feeling on the activity of the mental powers. (First Intro. VIII.note 8, Ak. 232, H. 36)

In other words, we cannot explain or define (*erklären*) the feelings of pleasure and displeasure; we can only point to or feel their occurrence and describe their effects upon us. We can say how the mind's activities are influenced by such feelings, and we can talk about the causes of (what occasions) a given feeling of pleasure or displeasure.

In spite of his clear pronouncement that pleasure and displeasure cannot be defined, Kant gives several general characterizations of the concepts in terms of their effects. For example:

> The consciousness of the causality of a representation, for *maintaining* the subject in the same state, may here generally denote what we call pleasure; while on the other hand pain is that representation which contains the ground of the determination of the state of representations into their opposite [of restraining or removing them]. (bracketed words added in 2d ed. [1793], § 10.1, Ak. 220, B. 55)

A similar characterization in terms of cause and effect appears in the second book of Kant's *Anthropology from a Pragmatic Viewpoint:* "That which directly (through the sense) incites me to *leave* the state in which I am (to get out of it) is the *displeasurable;* it causes me pain. That which directly incites me to *maintain* my state (to remain in it) is *pleasurable;* it causes me pleasure."[11]

Given certain desires, needs, or interests, the feeling of pleasure or displeasure may produce the desire to acquire or produce an object. For example, the discomfort of hunger, one type of displeasure, generally

---

10. Kant, *Analytic of the Beautiful,* trans. Cerf, p. x. J. H. Bernard translates *Unlust* as "pain," which is much too narrow; "displeasure" would be a slightly better translation.

11. Kant, *Anthropology from a Pragmatic Viewpoint* (1798), book 2 (Ak. 7: 231), in *Analytic of the Beautiful,* trans. Cerf, p. 60.

produces the desire to acquire food, and the pleasant taste of one potato chip generally produces the desire to acquire and eat another. These may be called "practical pleasures." But not every pleasure is practical; specifically, contemplative or disinterested pleasure is the exception:

The pleasure which is necessarily connected with desire (for an object whose representation affects feeling in this way) may be called practical pleasure, whether it is the cause or the effect of the desire. On the other hand, the pleasure which is not necessarily connected with a desire for an object and which, therefore, is really not a pleasure taken in the existence of the object of the representation, can be called mere contemplative pleasure, or passive delight. The feeling of the latter kind of pleasure is called taste.[12]

This merely contemplative pleasure "is in no way practical . . . but yet it involves causality, viz. of *maintaining* without further design the state of the representation itself and the occupation of the cognitive powers" (§ 12.2, Ak. 222, B. 58). Apparently, in contemplative pleasure, the representation (of the object judged to be beautiful) affects the judging subject in such a way that he is incited to remain in that state (contemplating the beautiful object.) Quite obviously, the state of the judging subject need not actually continue to be maintained for the experience to have been one of pleasure. What tends to be maintained is the state of mind of the subject, which we shall see below is the pleasure grounded on the harmony of the mental faculties. Kant calls this an "inner causality" and claims that it "determines the subject's activity in respect to the animation of its cognitive powers" (ibid).

Kant's thesis here is extremely difficult to interpret in a way that is consistent with his doctrine that the pleasure in the beautiful is disinterested, when that view is taken to mean "independent of any desire or interest." The natural way to interpret the claim about an "inner causality" is to say that the representation (the object judged to be beautiful) affects the judging subject so that he desires to remain in that state—experiencing the beautiful object, which is pleasurable. Such a desire can, of course, at times conflict with other desires (for example, practical desires, moral desires), and then there is what we with no hesitation call a "conflict of interests." Thus one may suspect that the notion of interest has slipped back into Kant's analysis of the pleasure in the beautiful through Kant's own analysis of pleasure. If I am incited to maintain my state, then am I not interested in remaining in it? But, if

12. Kant, *The Metaphysics of Morals (Metaphysik der Sitten)* (1797), Introduction to pt. 1 (Ak. 6:212), in *The Metaphysical Principles of Virtue*, trans. James Ellington (Indianapolis: Bobbs-Merrill, 1964), p. 10.

so, Kant's analysis of pleasure would seem to be incompatible with his analysis of judgments of taste.

However puzzling these details may be, Kant's larger aim is clear. He wants to be able to contrast the pleasure in the beautiful with other experiences of pleasure. The difficulty the above observations present for Kant's analysis of the judgment of taste is due to the necessary link Kant himself sees between the faculty of desire and interest. Pleasure arising from sensation alone—sense pleasure—excites a desire for repetition and possession, thereby resulting in an interest in the object; pleasure arising from objects of utility—that which is good for something—or objects of intrinsic value—that which is good in itself—excites a desire for their insured existence, and thereby an interest in their existence. But Kant does not want to say that pleasure in the beautiful is positively related to the faculty of desire in any way, because desire is tied to interest and hence to the existence of objects, whereas in the experience of beauty we are concerned only with how things appear to us. "To wish for something and to have a satisfaction in its existence, i.e. to take an interest in it, are identical." (§ 4.5, Ak. 209, B. 43) Kant wants to maintain a clear separation between the pleasure in the beautiful and the appetitive faculties (desire and the will) because he believes that an important aspect of our experience of the beautiful is that the mental powers are free. They must be free to reflect on the qualities of the object in any way whatsoever; reflection and contemplation must not be determined by a previous interest:

An object of inclination and one imposed on our desire by law of reason leave us no freedom by ourselves to turn anything into an object of pleasure. Any interest presupposes a need, or brings one forth, and if interest is the determining ground of the approbation, the judgment on the object is no longer allowed to be free. (§ 5.2, Ak. 210, my translation, cf. B. 44)

In other words, pleasure in what is merely pleasurable to sense is determined for an individual; it is simply the way he responds—a passive response. Pleasure in the good is also determined, since the concept of the good is imposed by a law of reason. Kant does not want to fit pleasure in the beautiful into a causal chain, so he must deny any connection between such pleasure and the faculty of desire. But, as we have seen, Kant does fit pleasure in the beautiful into a causal chain of a special sort—what he calls "inner causality" (§ 12.2, Ak. 222, B. 58). One is tempted to coin another paradoxical phrase to add to the many already contained in the text of the *Critique of Judgment* (for example, "purposiveness without a purpose," "conformity to law without a law"); disinterested interest. In Kant's own analysis, there seems to be an interest, in accordance with a desire, bound up with the experience of the beautiful, but it is not directed toward the existence of an empirical object but only toward maintaining the state of the judging subject.

The foregoing conclusion must be tempered somewhat in the light of certain other remarks Kant makes. Kant repeatedly denies any direct connection between the experience of the beautiful and the faculty of desire or interest. He defines "pleasure" as "the consciousness of the causality of a representation, for maintaining the subject in the same state" (§ 10.1, Ak. 220, B. 55), and he later says that in the case of the pleasure in the beautiful it is the consciousness of an "inner causality (which is purposive) in respect to cognition in general"—a consciousness of a "determining ground of the activity of the subject in respect of the excitement of its cognitive powers" (§ 12.2, Ak. 222, B. 58). There is no reference whatsoever in the above to the faculty of desire, the will, or interest. To summarize Kant's position: In the experience of the beautiful, the cognitive powers are in free, harmonious play and are caused to continue in that state, not through any act of will or desire on the part of the experiencing subject, but solely through the formal purposiveness of the representations themselves—the lawlike manner in which the formal qualities of the object appear to us when we freely reflect upon them. The cognitive powers are determined to be active, but they are not determined in their specific activity.

Kant's insight is basically sound, even if obscure. He wants to maintain that the pleasure in the experience of the beautiful is based upon (or determined by) the free experience of the object and not by any interest on our part. But the insight is clouded in several ways. Firstly, Kant does characterize that experience as one of a feeling of pleasure, yet it ends in being a pleasure of a very peculiar kind—it does not have any direct relation to desire or interest. The issue is clouded because the most natural way to explicate Kant's analysis of pleasure is by reference to desire and then to interest. Secondly, Kant's analysis precludes us from doing what seems most natural: attempting to find a desire or interest that is produced by or connected with the experience of beautiful things as a means of identifying that experience. Thirdly, Kant does appear to admit that in society the judgment of taste and the beautiful objects they are judgments of can produce an interest. It remains somewhat problematic why Kant thinks this interest arises only in society and why he should think it is totally irrelevant to inquire about that interest when inquiring about an object's beauty.

Interest and Aesthetic Objects

We have noted Kant's categorical denial that the judgment of taste itself entails an interest in, or desire for, the existence of any object. That is, he denies that any interest forms the basis of a pure judgment of taste, and he also denies that a judgment of taste by itself (for example, apart from society) produces any interest in the existence of an object.

Kant may have been misled by his theory here. Consider a view which seems plausible but appears incompatible with Kant's position. It is the view that there can be, and often is, a purely aesthetic interest in the existence of the object one judges to be beautiful and that this aesthetic interest does not render the judgment of taste "highly partisan and not a pure judgment of taste" (§ 2.1, Ak. 205, B. 39). A convenient initial argument is to make use of Kant's own elimination argument and maintain that the aesthetic interest about to be described does not cause a biased or partisan judgment of the beautiful because it does not involve moral, prudential, sensuous, or social interests. Rather, it is a purely aesthetic interest—an interest in the object as an object of aesthetic contemplation and experience.

Beautiful objects tend to maintain and hold our interest, and they do so in two main ways. Firstly, they maintain our interest by holding our attention when we are experiencing or contemplating them, to the extent that we tend to ignore, disregard, or even forget about other things. Our perceptual field is narrowed or, as in the case of the laughter of an audience at a play or film, incorporated into our experience to modify the object of our attention. The happenings of the everyday world, our practical concerns, are for the moment pushed aside. We become absorbed in attending to the beautiful object and may even lose sense of the passing of time. Artificial devices are often used to facilitate this narrowing of attention and break from our practical lives: picture frames, stages, lighting alterations, even physical comforts such as plush seats, all aid the creation of an object of attention which completely absorbs us. They create an aesthetic context. Secondly, beautiful objects hold our attention by keeping us interested in them, even after the experience of them has ended. We tend to return to those works of art, and even to natural objects of beauty, that we have found beautiful. We desire to experience them again and again, not simply because a pleasant experience generally creates a desire for its repetition, but because beautiful objects, like certain people, promise greater rewards in future encounters, even though great effort may be necessary. We return not merely for a repetition of the previous experience but with hopes of an even more rewarding experience. Beautiful objects, good works of art, tend to maintain appreciation. They become like friends: the renewal of acquaintance (their reexperience) is a sought-after delight, and the development of a true friendship produces experiences that far surpass in value the pleasure of an initial acquaintanceship.

Artists do create physical objects or the blueprints for the production of objects of experience, what we ordinarily call works of art (paintings, sculptures, musical compositions, and the like). People buy these objects to keep in their possession and support ventures for their public acquisition and display. It is an open question whether these activities on the part of individuals can be completely accounted for simply on economic, moral, sensual, and social grounds. Suppose we provide an artist or an appreciator of art with all his needs and remove him from society (if this were possible). Would he still desire objects of no apparent usefulness merely to look at, listen to, contemplate? Kant did not think so (§§ 2.1, 41.3; Ak. 204–5, 297; B. 39, 139–40). He thought the actual existence of beautiful artifacts explicable on social grounds. In society men wish to share their experiences, display their taste, draw attention to their persons and possessions. But one need not deny these facts in order to challenge Kant's view. One can challenge Kant's belief simply by maintaining what seems quite obvious, that an interest in the existence of objects of art can, and often does, arise on purely epistemological grounds and from perceptual, purely aesthetic considerations. Without reference to motives of moral or instrumental good, sense pleasure, economics, one's social nature, and the like, one can be interested in the existence of an object simply because one knows that it will, or is likely to, provide aesthetic satisfaction, either because one wants to reexperience it or because one has other knowledge that the experience of it will likely be aesthetically satisfying.

Objects of aesthetic value lend themselves to the desire for objectification. Indeed, it is only through objectification that anyone, appreciator or artist, can verify what he has created or experienced. It is only through objectification that the experience of the beautiful can be controlled in such a way as to insure the possibility of its being shared or being experienced again by the same appreciator. With respect to artistic and natural beauty alike, beautiful objects tend to be marked off from their surrounding environment, protected and maintained in order to insure the possibility of their reexperience and the sharing of the satisfaction they provide. Only through such objectification can the permanence and stability necessary for their reexperience and the sharing of the experience of them be assured. Although each of us may have a personal reason for being interested in the existence of a particular object we judge to be beautiful, we need not conclude, as Kant seems to, that this interest is thereby a self-interest, a private interest which precludes the objectivity of the judgment of the object.

Imagine that people are standing before a statue in a museum. One of them looks furtively about, and when the museum guard is out of sight pulls out a hammer from under his coat and begins to attack the statue, apparently with the intent of turning it to dust. Suppose a second person forcefully restrains the would-be destroyer of the statue. There are any number of reasons this second person might have for restraining the first: fear of himself being implicated in the destruction of the statue, an interest in the insurance company which would take a loss were it destroyed, a moral conviction that one ought to prevent the destruction of public property. Independently, however, he might have taken the action merely because he did not want that which he had previously found to be beautiful no longer to be available for his contemplation and experience. A desire that originated with or immediately resulted from his experience of the object was about to be permanently frustrated. Cannot his interest in the object's continued existence best be described as a purely aesthetic interest? Kant's doctrine does not seem to allow for this possibility.

Kant denies the relevance of any interest in the existence of an object either as a ground or as an immediate consequent of the judgment of taste (finding the object to be beautiful). I have attempted to provide grounds for doubting the second part of this claim, and I conclude that although our interest in beautiful objects is, or can be, different from our interest in objects generally (and even works of art under some circumstances), it is misleading to say that there is no interest in them directly due to their beauty.

In Kant's first claim, no interest in the existence of an object can be the ground of a pure judgment of taste. Kant's insight here still stands in the face of the above comments. But Kant expresses his point rather poorly. Kant wants to say, correctly, that the pure judgment of taste must be based on the immediate experience of the object—on the judgment, reflection, and contemplation of it alone. Kant believes he has independent grounds for this claim, namely, that this is a necessary condition for the universal validity we claim for our judgments of taste. But if my above argument is sound, if an interest in the existence of an object of beauty can be determined to be purely aesthetic, then it would be relevant to inquire into such an interest if one were inquiring into an object's beauty. How could such a purely aesthetic interest be ascertained? Kant's account of interest recognizes that there are not different kinds of interest in a given object in any sense other than that they have different grounds. It is only by ascertaining that the interest in the beautiful (or the judgment of taste) is itself based upon, or is a direct result of, the experience or contemplation of the object that one could claim that it is a purely aesthetic interest. In other words, Kant's insight is correct, even if his architectonic and systematic definitions of key terms obscure that insight.

These considerations show Kant's premature dismissal of interest in or desire for the existence of something as having any relevance to the experience of the beautiful or to the judgment of taste. The first reason is that Kant's own characterization of the experience of the beautiful in terms of pleasure and his account of interest are not logically distinct in the way that his argument requires. The second reason is that there are independent, epistemological considerations of our experience of the beautiful which relate it to interest in the existence of objects in the world. In short, although the experience of the beautiful, the good, and the merely pleasurable to sense may be distingishable in terms of kinds of interest, they do not seem to be distinguishable in terms of the presence or absence of some interest or other. The question remaining for aesthetic inquiry is whether there is reason to suppose a basis for an aesthetic interest in an object (of reflection, contemplation, or perception generally).

Kant's question and the one I have posed are not, however, different in principle. Kant is attempting to link the ground of the pleasure in the beautiful to features in the object of beauty sufficient to justify (in principle) a judgment claiming universal validity. I have argued that there is a legitimate question as to a purely aesthetic interest in an object. The further question involves the features and characteristics in objects producing or satisfying such an interest. In attempting to answer this further question, Kant tries to bridge the subjective-objective dichotomy in aesthetics.

2.3   Implications of the Analysis

Two theses emerge to form the cornerstone of Kant's aesthetic theory: the judgment of taste is aesthetic and the judgment of taste is disinterested. These two theses are combined in the concept of a disinterested pleasure, upon which Kant claims judgments of taste are based. The pivotal status of these theses for Kant's aesthetic theory can be shown through a discussion of the conclusions that can be derived from them as Kant continues his exposition of judgments of taste in the "Analytic of the Beautiful."

The Beautiful, the Pleasant, and the Good

§§ 3–5 contain a variety of observations on the nature and interrelationships of the judgments on the beautiful, the pleasant, and the good.

Insofar as these observations contribute to the inquiry into the basis of our judgments of taste, they are conclusions drawn from the basic claims that the judgment of taste is aesthetic and disinterested, together with observations about the satisfaction in the good or the pleasant.

In § 3, for example, Kant argues that satisfaction in that which pleases in sensation alone, the merely pleasurable to sense, is bound up with an interest, since "by sensation it excites a desire for objects of that kind" (§ 3.4, Ak. 207, B. 41). Consequently, although the judgment that something is pleasant is an aesthetic judgment, in the sense defined in § 1, it differs from the judgment of taste in that it is not a disinterested judgment. In other words, the pleasure on which it is based is not a distinterested pleasure, but one which gratifies by satisfying an interest, need, or want. It is not the product of reflective judgment.

Similarly, in § 4 Kant argues that in the pleasure in the good, both the good-in-itself and the good-for-something, "there is always involved . . . a satisfaction in the *presence* of an object or an action, i.e., some kind of interest" (§ 4.1, Ak. 207, B. 41). Satisfaction in the good, like that in the pleasurable to sense, is always tied to an interest in an object (cf. § 4.5, Ak. 209, B. 43). Thus, the pleasure in the beautiful is not to be identified with the pleasure in the good, and the judgment of taste and the judgment of the good are distinct kinds of judgment. Kant's conclusion is unequivocal: "We may say that, of all these three kinds of satisfaction, that of taste in the beautiful is alone a disinterested and *free* satisfaction; for no interest, either of sense or of reason, here forces our assent" (§ 5.2, Ak. 210, B. 44).

Beauty, Charm, and Emotion

In § 13 Kant argues that the pure judgment of taste is independent of charm and emotion and that the experience of the beautiful is quite distinct from the appeal of sensual charms and emotional qualities. This conclusion is clearly drawn from the thesis of the disinterestedness of judgments of taste. "That taste is always barbaric which needs a mixture of *charms* and *emotions* in order that there may be satisfaction, and still more so [i.e., more barbaric] if it makes these the measure of its assent" (§ 13.1, Ak. 223, B. 58). The disinterestedness of the satisfaction in beautiful, or more precisely our consciousness of its disinterestedness, leads us to claim universal validity for our judgments of taste. But judgments based on, or even mixed with, what is charming or emotionally appealing to us can make no claim to impartiality. These appeals are peculiar to each individual, tied to his own wants and desires, and thus cannot but detract from a pure judgment of taste.

Kant's elucidation of this conclusion by means of examples (§ 14) is quite confusing, not only because Kant is unable to deside whether colors are just qualities that charm us or whether we can reflect on their formal components, but also because he gives no clear examples of what sort of qualities would merely charm us or appeal to the emotions. He is inclined to say that the colors in painting and drawing, and the pleasant tones of an instrument in a musical composition are merely charming, that they do not contribute to the beauty of the object, but he is hesitant to exclude them categorically as completely irrelevant. The reasons for his hesitation are examined in chapter 5, dealing with Kant's formalism. Indeed, §§ 13–14 shed more light on Kant's positive view, that the pure judgment of taste is based on the pleasure in the formal purposiveness of an object, than on what is being excluded when one excludes charm and emotion. Clearly, however, that the judgment of taste is disinterested is the basis for such an exclusion.

Beauty and the Concept of Perfection

In § 15, Kant is arguing against Baumgarten, who held the view that beauty is perfection apprehended, however confusedly, through the senses. Kant's argument is straightforward, and there is no need to go into the details of it here. Briefly, Kant argues that since the judgment of taste is aesthetic, it is therefore (by definition) not a conceptual judgment; and since the judgment that a thing is perfect requires a concept of a definite (Kant says "objective") purpose, which the object is then judged to have perfectly fulfilled, the judgment of taste is quite distinct from the judgment of perfection. Again, Kant is simply drawing out the implications from one of his two initial theses.

Free and Dependent Beauty

In § 16, Kant draws the distinction between judging that something is beautiful *simpliciter* and judging that something is a beautiful thing of some kind (for example, a beautiful horse, knife, church). He claims that these are basically different kinds of judgment, that the judgment that something is beautiful *simpliciter* is not the same as the judgment that it is a beautiful something. His reason is simply that the latter type of judgment "presupposes a concept of the purpose which determines what the thing is to be, and consequently a concept of its perfection" (§ 16.4, Ak. 230, B. 66). Kant recognizes that we commonly use the term "beautiful" in this way as well, and he calls this kind of beauty "dependent" or "adherent" as opposed to "free." Strictly speaking, however, a judgment of beauty dependent upon a concept (such as perfection of a kind) is not an aesthetic judgment and hence not a judgment of taste. A judgment of taste is a free judgment, in no way dependent upon considerations of what sort of thing the object ought to be. The details of this view are discussed in chapter 4, section 5; here we simply note that the opinion is a consequence of the thesis that the judgment of taste is aesthetic.

CHAPTER 3

Kant's Deduction of Judgments of Taste

3.1 Empirical and Transcendental Deductions

IN THE *Critique of Pure Reason,* Kant discusses two ways of justifying the use of concepts: empirically and transcendentally. Ordinally, he remarks, the use of concepts requires no justification, "since experience is always available for the proof of their objective reality" (A84=B116). In other words, if someone demands to know what right we have to employ the concept "tree," it is only necessary to show him a tree. To put the matter linguistically rather than conceptually, Kant is suggesting that ordinarily a question as to the right to use a referring term is often quickly settled by producing or designating an object denoted by such a term or by describing the conditions under which such an object could be recognized. The use of some concepts cannot be justified in the above manner, however, and among these concepts "are some which are marked out for pure *a priori* employment, in complete independence of all experience" (A85=B117). The concepts Kant is referring to include those of space, time, and the categories of understanding. Kant claims that the use of such concepts can never be justified empirically, and yet their use always demands justification. "The explanation of the manner in which concepts can thus relate *a priori* to objects I entitle their transcendental deduction" (ibid.). An empirical deduction, on the other hand, is one which "shows the manner in which a concept is acquired through experience and through reflection upon experience, and which therefore concerns, not its legitimacy, but only its *de facto* mode of origination" (ibid.).

The application of Kant's distinction to judgments of taste is not immediately apparent. Far from being an a priori concept of an object, beauty, according to Kant, is not a concept at all (§ 38 Remark 1, Ak. 290, B. 133). The judgment of taste is aesthetic (§ 1), which entails that it is not a conceptual judgment. Hence, in the judgment of taste there can be no question of a concept relating a priori to an object, since there is no concept involved. And judgments of taste are certainly not a priori in the sense that it is possible to make them independently of experience. Judgments of taste are based on an immediate feeling of pleasure; they are aesthetic in the defined sense of relating the object of experience to the feeling of pleasure or displeasure in the experiencing subject. Kant explicitly denies that judgments concerning the experience of pleasure or displeasure can ever be made a priori: "To establish *a priori* the connection of the feeling of pleasure or pain as an effect with any representation (sensation or concept) as its cause, is absolutely impossible (§ 12.1, Ak. 221, B. 57). And even in those passages where Kant insists that when we call something beautiful we think of it as having a necessary reference to satisfaction, it cannot be "cognized *a priori* that everyone *will feel* this satisfaction in the object called beautiful by me" (§ 18.1, Ak. 236–37, B. 73). The sense in which the judgment of taste is a priori is elusive. Hence it is important to determine precisely Kant's reason for thinking that the class of judgments he terms judgments of taste requires a transcendental deduction.

Kant believes our use of "is beautiful" requires justification since the pleasure in the beautiful (to which the judgment of taste implicitly refers and which is found in experiencing the object) is imputed to everyone. It is the claim to universal validity, which Kant claims is part of the meaning of a judgment of taste, that makes it necessary to justify its use not merely empirically, but transcendentally:

[T]his claim to universal validity so essentially belongs to a judgment by which we describe anything as *beautiful* that, if this were not thought in it, it would never come into our thoughts to use the expression at all, but everything which pleases without a concept would be counted as pleasant. (§ 8.2, Ak. 214, B. 48)

The judgment of taste is thus said to be a priori in the sense that it claims to be universally valid and necessarily demands assent, independent of any actual empirical agreement; no empirical explanation would justify its use.[1] Such judgments must be based, according to Kant, on a priori principles if they are to be legitimate. Hence a transcendental justifica-

---

1. See §§ 9.7, 18, 36.3–4, 38; Ak. 218, 236–37, 288–89, 289–90; B. 53, 73–74, 130–31, 132.

tion is necessary (§ 36, Ak. 287–89, B. 130–31). Kant also states this position quite unambiguously in the "First Introduction":

[I]f a judgment is represented as universally valid, and thus lays claim to the *necessity* of its assertion, this professed necessity may rest either on a priori concepts of the object or on a priori subjective conditions underlying the concepts: thus, if one grants the claim of such a judgment, it would be preposterous to justify it by accounting psychologically for the origin of the judgment. For this would be self-defeating; if the desired explanation were completely achieved, it would prove that the judgment has no claim to necessity whatsoever precisely because its empirical origin is demonstrable.

Now, aesthetic reflective judgments, which we will analyze hereafter under the name of judgments of taste, are of the type mentioned above. They claim to be necessary, and assert, not that everyone does judge thus—in that event they would be a subject for explanation by empirical psychology—but that one *should* so judge, which is to say that they have a principle a priori. (First Intro. X.4, Ak. 238–39, H. 42–43)

Thus, no merely empirical account of the beautiful will be sufficient to justify what we claim when we make a judgment of taste. Kant sharply contrasts his "transcendental exposition of aesthetic judgments" with the merely empirical exposition of them given by Burke, whose efforts Kant describes both as "psychological" and as "physiological" (§ 29. G.R. 22, Ak. 277, B. 118–19). As observed in chapter 1, Kant's own previous work in aesthetics, his *Observations on the Feeling of the Beautiful and Sublime* (1764), would also be judged incomplete according to the account in the *Critique of Judgment* of what kind of treatment the notion of beauty requires:

Thus, the empirical exposition of aesthetic judgments may be a beginning of a collection of materials for a higher investigation; but a transcendental discussion of this faculty is also possible, and is an essential part of the "Critique of Taste." For if it had not *a priori* principles, it could not possibly pass sentence on the judgments of others, and it could not approve or blame them with any appearance of right. (§ 29. G.R. 24, Ak. 278, B. 120)

Kant is claiming that neither a strict empiricism, such as that of Hume, not a strict rationalism, such as that of Leibniz or Christian Wolff (1679–1754), can justify our right to make judgments of taste, with their implicit claim to universal and necessary validity. Essentially the same question of the justification for making judgments is the concern of each of the three critiques—knowledge claims in the First, moral claims in the Second, and aesthetic claims in the Third. One way of characterizing Kant's procedure is as an attempt to find the necessary conditions for making such claims, thereby showing how they are possible, and thus attempting to refute the skeptic's claim that they are not possible. By further showing that these conditions for the possibility of the judgments in question are at the same time conditions for experience in general, a complete justification for the right to make such judgments is provided. This is the famed *transcendental* method of justification, the *transcendental deduction*. Justification for judgments of taste is based on a principle which transcends particular experiences and which thus relates to the conditions for experience in general. The transcendental method is clearly as much a part of the *Critique of Judgment* as it is a part of Kant's other major works.

Prior to the transcendental deduction itself, Kant does two things: (a) he provides an empirical deduction of judgments of taste—an explanation of how we come to believe that judgments of taste have universal validity or what the empirical basis is for the claim to universal validity, namely, a consciousness of the disinterestedness of our judgment; (b) he provides a statement of what he insightfully labels the "Antinomy of Taste" (§ 56–57), which involves two seemingly incompatible propositions concerning the "logic" of judgments of taste, each of them seeming to be unimpeachable taken alone. The empirical deduction is, of course, insufficient to legitimize our right to make judgments of taste; it simply shows the source of our belief in their universal validity in certain cases. The antinomy of taste is a concise way of presenting what Kant takes to be *the* problem for philosophical aesthetics: How can a nonconceptual judgment, admittedly based on individually felt pleasure, implicitly claim to hold for all men and to demand their agreement? The answer to this question is the "deduction" of judgments of taste—their legitimation as a class of judgment.

3.2   The Empirical Deduction: Disinterestedness

The title of sentence of § 6 declares that the beautiful is that which is represented, without reference to concepts, as the object of a universal pleasure. Kant claims that when we judge something to be beautiful we believe that we are entitled to expect and hence demand a similar pleasure in everyone, that anyone else who contemplates the object aesthetically should also declare it to be beautiful. Kant says that our belief in judgments of taste being universally valid is a consequent of the consciousness that the pleasure in the object is entirely disinterested. Since we can find no private conditions as exclusively personal reasons for our pleasure, we must therefore regard the pleasure as grounded in what we may also presuppose in everyone else. Consequently, Kant concludes that "a claim [*Anspruch*] to subjective universality is necessarily connected with [the judgment of taste]" (§ 6.1, Ak. 212, B. 46).

The words "belief" and "claim," above, should be emphasized; it is the claim to or belief in the universality of our judgment to which the consciousness of the distinterestedness of the judgment gives rise. According to Kant's distinction between empirical and transcendental deductions discussed above, this explanation of the claim to universal validity on the part of judgments of taste constitutes an *empirical* deduction, for it "shows the manner in which a concept is acquired through experience and through reflection upon experience" (A85=B117). Kant purports to have explained why one believes that he is entitled to expect agreement from everyone else. But since this is merely an empirical statement of the origin of belief, this explanation cannot also constitute a justification of our right to make such a claim. It is not, in other words, a *transcendental* deduction. Textual analysis bears out this observation; in § 6 Kant speaks only of the belief in or the claim to universality, not the actual fact of universality of the judgment of taste.

An interest defeats impartiality. "Every interest spoils the judgment of taste and takes from its impartiality. . . . Hence judgments so affected can lay no claim at all to a universally valid satisfaction . . ." (§ 13.1, Ak. 223, B. 58). However, disinterestedness by itself does not guarantee the legitimacy of judgments of taste generally. To discover whether the proclaimed universal validity is possible in principle, a person must investigate its necessary condition, namely, that which "he may also presuppose in everyone else" (§ 6.1, Ak. 211, B. 46). Legitimation of the claim to universal validity on the part of the judgment of taste thus requires showing that such a presupposition both is possible and can be given content.

The idea of a universally valid judgment of taste may arise as the result of our being unable to find any purely private grounds for our judgment, simply in the belief that our pleasure is a disinterested one. And if the pleasure is not disinterested, if there are purely private grounds, the judgment is not a pure judgment and we have no right to use the term "beautiful." But, since judgments of taste are aesthetic, it remains to be shown whether, and if so, how, an actual common ground is possible. In short, the claim to universal validity cannot be justified unless it can be shown how, in an aesthetic judgment, something can be universally or intersubjectively communicated. Since Kant firmly believes that "nothing can be universally communicated and shared except cognition and representation, so far as it belongs to cognition" (§ 9.3, Ak. 217, B. 51), the noncognitive judgment of taste must somehow be linked to the cognitive faculties. In this way we are led to the transcendental deduction proper. Clearly, new elements are being introduced into the argument. Disinterestedness is part of the logic of judgments of taste, but it does not by itself constitute their deduction.

3.3 The Antinomy of Taste

In §§ 7–8, Kant makes and reviews observations in support of the view that judgments of taste require transcendental justification because their implicit claim to universal validity can be justified neither by experience nor by reason. These observations parallel the ones which constitute the so-called Antinomy of Taste (§ 56), in which the conflicting principles underlying every judgment of taste are expressed in explicitly contradictory forms. In § 57, Kant remarks that these principles "are nothing else than the two peculiarities of the judgment of taste exhibited above in the Analytic [of the Beautiful]" (§ 57.1, Ak. 339, B. 184). His mention of the "two peculiarities" refers to §§ 32–33. Thus the problem that sets the stage for the actual transcendental deduction is explicitly presented in at least three separate places. And we shall find, not surprisingly, that successive versions of the deduction follow these separate presentations of the Antinomy of Taste.

A true "antinomy" in Kantian philosophy is constituted by a double-pronged argument, each part of which begins with the same basic premise but ends with a conclusion contradicting the other part. In the Antinomy of Taste, the basic premise is that we dispute matters of taste without logical resolution. This is the same as the thesis that Kant refers to in § 56.3 as "the third proposition between these two commonplaces" —the two commonplaces being that everyone has his own taste and that there is no disputing about taste. The third proposition is that *there may be a quarrel about taste* (although there can be no controversy)" [über den Geschmack lässt sich streiten *(obgleich nicht disputieren)*] (§ 56.3, Ak. 338, B. 183). The thesis and antithesis of the Antinomy draw out the seemingly contradictory aspects of this fact; the solution to the Antinomy shows how the apparent contradiction is not a real contradiction.

The explicit *thesis* of the Antinomy of Taste is that the judgment of taste is *not* based upon concepts. The reasoning given in § 57.4 (Ak. 339–40, B. 185) is that a judgment determinable by concepts could be proved. The implication is obvious: since the judgment of taste cannot be proved, it is not based upon concepts, which is to say that it is not a conceptual (cognitive, logical) judgment and that Beauty is not a concept. The exact statement of the thesis of the Antinomy reads: "The judgment of taste is not based upon concepts, for otherwise it would admit of controversy *[liesse sich darüber disputieren]* (would be determinable by proofs)" (§ 56.4, Ak. 338, B. 183–84). The statement of the "second peculiarity of the judgment of taste" reads: "The judgment of taste is not determinable by grounds of proof, just as if it were merely *subjective*" (§ 33.1, Ak. 284, B. 125).[2]

Kant's underlying view here is that a concept has determinations, which are criteria or rules for its application, such that in principle one can get to the point in a dispute where it must be admitted that the determinations are exemplified, that the criteria for the application of the concept are fulfilled, and that the concept applies in a given case. But with the judgment of taste, no such point in a dispute can be reached; that is, we do not know what such a point is like in disputes about taste. Agreement cannot be forced in this way; it can only occur when the other person *feels* the pleasure in the beautiful object himself and on that basis alone makes a concurring judgment. The pleasure in the beautiful is an immediate satisfaction, marked by the judgment of taste, just as if it were merely subjective—a simple liking-report. The key point in support of the thesis of the Antinomy of Taste in its various formulations is absence of proof for our judgments of taste. This is the same point used in support of the claim of § 1—that the judgment of taste is aesthetic and not conceptual. No new material is presented in the thesis of the Antinomy of Taste; there is only a slightly different formulation of the thesis that the judgment of taste is aesthetic, with the basis for that thesis and its consequences expressed succinctly.

The explicit *antithesis* of the Antinomy of Taste is that the judgment of taste *is* based upon concepts. The reasoning given in § 57.4 (Ak. 339–40, B. 185) is that a judgment not determinable by concepts would not be the subject of controversy. The line of reasoning is that since we do quarrel over and engage in controversy about our judgments of taste, thinking that others ought to agree with us, the judgment of taste is based upon concepts and can make a legitimate claim to being universally valid. The exact statement of the antithesis of the Antinomy reads: "The judgment of taste is based on concepts, for otherwise, despite its diversity, we could not quarrel about it [*liesse sich . . . darüber auch nicht einmal streiten*] (we could not claim for our judgment the necessary assent of others)" (§ 56.4, Ak. 338–39, B. 184). The statement of the "first peculiarity of the judgment of taste" reads: "The judgment of taste determines its object in respect of satisfaction (in its beauty) with an accompanying claim for the assent of *everyone*, just as if it were objective" (§ 32.1, Ak. 281, B. 123).

This puzzling argument seems to rely upon the Aristotelian assump-

2. Other explicit formulations of this observation occur at §§ 8.6, 20.1, 34.1, 44.1, 56.2, 57.4; Ak. 215, 237–38, 285–86, 304–5, 338, 340; B. 50, 74–75, 127–28, 147, 183, 185.

tion that no natural human activity is in principle pointless, that the possibility of a resolution of disagreements of taste is a necessary condition for the activity of engaging in controversy over such judgments. But this argument is no better than arguing that God must exist because people pray to Him. Kant's point in the antithesis is better expressed: The distinction we all recognize between judgments of sense (which claim only private validity) and judgments of taste (which claim universal validity) is legitimate only on the assumption that the judgment of taste is based on some concept or principle. For if judgments on the beautiful were no different in principle than judgments on the merely pleasant to sense, controversy over the former would be pointless and impracticable, and we would not regard them with any notion of necessity (§ 20.1, Ak. 237–38, B. 75).

Preparation for the transcendental deduction of judgments of taste results in the following paradox: (1) since judgments of taste cannot be proved, they must be based not on principles or concepts but on what can never yield knowledge of an object, namely, pleasure and displeasure; (2) since judgments of taste make a claim for universal validity and thus engage us in controversy over them, they must be based on principles or concepts and not simply pleasure and displeasure. When put in this way, it is possible to see that Kant is posing a general question for critical philosophy: How is a synthetic a priori judgment possible? The specific form this question takes in philosophical aesthetics (what Kant calls a "critique of taste") is: How is it possible for a judgment based on pleasure or displeasure to make a legitimate claim of universal validity, that is, to hold necessarily for all men? The problem arises because the judgment that the experience of an object produces a feeling of pleasure is always a synthetic judgment, while the universality and necessity claimed by the judgment but not met within experience must be a priori, namely, based on a priori principles.

Kant's solution to the problem, as explicitly expressed in the Antinomy of Taste, is to argue in his characteristic way that there is an equivocation on a key term common to both thesis and antithesis, that when the term "concept" is properly interpreted, both the thesis and antithesis are true, without contradiction. The judgment of taste is not based on a determinate concept, but rather on an indeterminate one. This indeterminate concept, we are told, is "the concept of the general ground of the subjective purposiveness of nature for the faculty of the judgment" as well as, "the concept of that which may be regarded as the supersensible substrate of humanity" (§ 57.5, Ak. 340, B. 185). This particular formulation of Kant's solution to the Antinomy of taste is discussed further in chapter 4, section 1.

3.4 · Structure of the Transcendental Deduction

The structure of Kant's major connected argument in the *Critique of Judgment* does not correspond to the architectonic structure he himself imposes on his work. In the Third Critique, Kant follows the architectonic scheme established in his previous work: approaching the subject first in an analytical and then in a dialectical fashion, and labeling the particular section in which the deduction occurs. But this arrangement is inaccurate and misleading, artificial and repetitious; it tends to mask the actual development and the logically distinct stages of Kant's argument, and obscures the unity of his aesthetic theory. Kant himself observes that "the analysis of judgments of taste must show what is required in order to call an object beautiful" (note to title of First Moment, Ak. 203, B. 37). Although never succinctly presented in a complete form, significant parts of the central argument justifying the universal validity of judgments of taste are found in many different sections of the *Critique of Judgment*.[3]

The complete deduction of judgments of taste, the justification of our right to make judgments of the form "This is beautiful" that demand the assent of others, is an extended and complicated argument occupying the entire first part of the *Critique of Judgment,* the "Critique of Aesthetic Judgment." I shall present, analyze, and discuss the argument analytically rather than seriatim. The question whether Kant himself ever conceived his argument in this way cannot be answered by a consideration of the text of the *Critique of Judgment* alone, but he gives little indication of thinking through his entire argument at any one time.

The Five Stages

The logical development of Kant's major argument of the *Critique of Judgment* may be divided into five stages. Each of these stages constitutes an important aspect of his aesthetic theory. They follow the order of the development of the extended argument of the Third Critique in the sense that each stage is a further specification of what the judgment of taste must be based upon if it is to make a legitimate claim to hold for all men, to demand their agreement, and not simply to be a report of one's personal satisfaction in an object. Since the judgment of taste has been analyzed as an aesthetic judgment and not merely a report of sense pleasure, the argument is essentially a continued specification of that on which the pleasure in the beautiful is grounded. The first stage of the

---

3. The major locations are Intro. VII.5, § 9, §§ 10–17, §§ 35–40, § 57; Ak. 191, 216–19, 219–36, 286–96, 339–41; B. 28, 51–54, 54–73, 128–38, 184–87.

deduction shows that this is the direction the inquiry must take if it is to have any hope of success. The transcendental deduction is thus the positive counterpart to those sections in the "Analytic of the Beautiful" earlier described as a subtractive exposition of the judgment of taste. There it was explained that the pleasure in the beautiful could *not* be based upon the interested, the good, the merely pleasurable to sense, charm, emotion, and perfection. The deduction, on the other hand, explains what the pleasure in the beautiful must be based upon to legitimize the class of judgments Kant calls judgments of taste.

Presented below are summary statements of the five stages of the transcendental deduction of judgments of taste, each of which is discussed in detail in succeeding sections and chapters.

STAGE I. The key to the critique of taste. The conclusion of Stage I is that pleasure in the beautiful—that pleasure which is related in the judgment or taste—must be based upon a universally communicable mental state. Kant argues that otherwise the judgment of taste could not legitimately be distinguished from the judgment of sensuous pleasure, for which we claim no universal validity. At this stage Kant has given no content to such a universally communicable mental state on which the pleasure is based, nor has he argued that there is such a state. He has merely argued that the possibility of the legitimacy of judgments of taste as a class of judgment depends upon the possibility of there being a universally communicable mental state on which the pleasure in the beautiful is based. Such a mental state is a necessary supposition for the possibility of judgments of taste. Whether it is a reasonable or legitimate supposition is not yet in question. Stage I is discussed in detail in the following section.

STAGE II. The conclusion of Stage II is that such a universally communicable mental state must be based on the cognitive faculties (the imagination and the understanding) being harmoniously related in their free play, satisfying the general conditions for cognition. Since, in Kant's view, nothing can be universally communicated except cognition or mental states insofar as they relate to cognition, the subjective state of the mind on which the universally communicable pleasure is based must be the same as that generally obtaining for cognition, namely, the harmony of the cogntive powers of the mind—the imagination and the understanding. But since the judgment of taste is aesthetic and not conceptual, the state of mind on which the pleasure in the beautiful is based cannot be that of a definite act of cognition (judging a particular to be subsumable under a concept). The only remaining possibility, if judgments of taste are to be legitimate, is that the pleasure, which is the consciousness of the harmony of the cognitive faculties, is based upon "the state of mind, which is to be met with in the relation of our representative powers to each other, so far as they refer a given representation to *cognition in general*" (§ 9.3, Ak. 217, B. 52). In other words, the cognitive powers must be harmonious and in free play, not determined by concepts. Stage II is discussed in detail in chapter 4, section 1. Since this stage of Kant's argument relates to his general theory of cognition, a comprehensive summary of that theory is presented in chapter 4, section 2.

STAGE III. Formal purposiveness. The conclusion of Stage III is that harmony of the cognitive powers must be based upon the mere formal purposiveness of the object, which is distinct from the object being judged to have a definite purpose (that being a conceptual judgment). In the experience of the beautiful, we reflect on the purposiveness (designedness, rule-governedness) of the formal internal features and relations of the object as experienced. Stage III is discussed in detail in chapter 5, section 1.

STAGE IV. A common sense. The procedure of the power of reflective judgment in the reflection upon the beautiful—the harmonious interplay of the powers of cognition in general reflection upon the formal purposiveness of the object as experienced—is a procedure that must be exercised in the commonest experience, that is, in any experience whatsoever. The pleasure in the beautiful is thus based on that subjective element which we can presuppose in all men, since it is necessary for all possible cognition. This subjective element or principle is a common sense *(sensus communis)*. The conclusion of Stage IV, then, is that the subjective principle underlying judgments of taste is the same as the subjective principle underlying all judgments, and since it is a necessary supposition for all experience, it is justifiable to assume its existence. Stage IV is discussed in detail in chapter 6, section 1.

STAGE V. Aesthetics and morality. Stages I–IV have shown how a pleasure can be based on that which is universally communicable and so itself be universally communicable. But they do not show that the mere universal communicability of a feeling of pleasure can be imputed to everyone, so to speak, as a duty. In other words, the deduction through Stage IV has not shown that we are justified in making judgments of taste that imply that others ought to agree with us. Thus the transcendental deduction of judgments of taste is still incomplete.

Completion of the deduction requires making a transition from the aesthetic realm to the realm of morality. This transition and conclusion of the deduction is Stage V of the deduction. A hint of the transition is given in Kant's claim that to take an immediate interest in the beauty of nature is always the mark of a morally good human being (§ 42.2, Ak.

298–99, B. 141). But this is only a hint. It does not complete the deduction, (1) because it is only a mark or indication of a good man, and (2) because the same does not hold true for an immediate interest in the beautiful in art. Kant's argument is rather that the beautiful is a symbol of the morally good, and consequently it gives pleasure with a justifiable claim for the agreement of everyone.

The argument of Stage V is an extension of the continuing argument of Stages I–IV in the following way. Kant earlier argued that the subjective formal purposiveness on which the judgment of taste is based (Stage III) is an indeterminate concept of the subjective conditions of the possibility of cognition in general—a common sense (Stage IV). In Stage V it is argued that this indeterminate concept of formal purposiveness (which is the same as the subjective principle underlying all cognition—the common sense) is based on an indeterminate concept of "the general ground of the subjective purposiveness of nature for the [faculty of] judgment" (§ 57.5, Ak. 340, B. 185), which may be regarded as the supersensible substrate of phenomena. It is the idea that nature was designed for our cognition. Beauty is the symbol of this idea in art because it presents the idea to sense in a microcosm. Since this idea is the same as the principle of the purposes of freedom and of the agreement of freedom with its purposes in the moral sphere (§ 57 Remark II.4, Ak. 346, B. 191), beauty is the symbol of morality. On this basis, then, we impute to others, as a duty, the agreement with our judgments of taste in each and every case, whether our judgment is in fact correct or not, because we have a right to expect moral sensitivity in other human beings. This concluding stage of the deduction is discussed in detail in chapter 7, section 2.

3.5 The Transcendental Deduction—Stage I: Key to the Critique of Taste

In the title of § 9 (Ak. 216, B. 51), Kant raises the question whether in the judgment of taste the feeling of pleasure precedes the judging of the object or the judging of the object precedes the feeling of pleasure. He immediately remarks that the solution to the problem raised by this question "is the key to the critique of taste, and so is worthy of all attention" (§ 9.1, Ak. 216, B. 51). Kant's question and his proposed solution have given commentators on the *Critique of Judgment* a great deal of difficulty, in spite of the fact that Kant's solution is explicit: in the judgment of taste, the judging of the object must precede the feeling of pleasure; the pleasure in the object is a consequent of the judging of the object.

The first problem of interpretation is whether there is a distinction to be drawn between the "judging of the object" (*Beurteilung des Gegenstandes*) and the "judgment of taste" (*Geschmacksurteil*), and if so, what the distinction is. Walter Cerf, for example, takes the judging of the object and the judgment of taste to be one and the same; consequently, he claims that Kant maintains the paradoxical view that the judgment of taste determines the pleasure.[4] Cerf is quite correct in regarding this as a paradoxical view, for it contradicts Kant's analysis that the judgment of taste is aesthetic, since an aesthetic judgment by definition is one based on a feeling of pleasure. Cerf attempts to avoid this obvious inconsistency by distingishing two senses of "judgment of taste," the first a "tasting" and the second a "verdict." Edward Bullough was also puzzled by Kant's position in § 9, but he simply referred to it as "the asstounding theory of Kant—possibly one of the most inartistic persons who have ever speculated upon Art—that aesthetic judgment [Bullough means "verdict"] *precedes* appreciation, that we *judge* a flower to be beautiful and *therefore* like it (the famous judgment *a priori*)."[5]

If one takes the solution to the question of § 9 to be that the pleasure is a consequent of the judgment of taste, and the judgment of taste is thought of as a verdict that the object in question is beautiful, the meaning of Kant's conclusion is quite obscure and paradoxical. It is obscure because Kant nowhere explains *how* the pleasure could result from making such a verdictive judgment. It is paradoxical in that (1) Kant repeatedly and explicitly says that the defining characteristic of aesthetic judgments (of which the judgment of taste is an example) is that they relate a representation exclusively to the subject and to his feeling of pleasure or displeasure (see chapter 2, section 1); thus the existence of the feeling of pleasure is a precondition for making the verdictive judgment of taste. (2) Kant holds that the beautiful, the pleasurable, and the good indicate three different relations of representation to the feelings of pleasure and displeasure (§ 5.2, Ak. 209–10, B. 44), implying that the judgment that something is beautiful marks the relationship of what already exists—a feeling of pleasure. (3) In § 2.1 (Ak. 205, B. 39), Kant maintains that when the question is whether something is beautiful all one wants to know is whether the mere representation of the object is accompanied in me by satisfaction, indicating that the ground of the judgment of taste is a feeling of pleasure, and not vice versa. For these reasons alone one must conclude that in § 9 Kant is *not* maintaining that

4. Kant, *Analytic of the Beautiful*, trans. Cerf, pp. 84, 95, 105.

5. Edward Bullough, "The Modern Conception of Aesthetics" (1907), in *Aesthetics: Lectures and Essays*, ed. E. M. Wilkinson (London: Bowes and Bowes, 1957), p. 52.

the pleasure in the beautiful is a consequent of the judgment of taste, considered as a verdict, but that the "judging of the object," which Kant claims precedes the pleasure in the beautiful, is not the same as the judgment of taste.

Based on further features of Kant's analysis in and following § 9, a more complex argument is possible that similarly concludes that the judging of the object is not to be identified with the judgment of taste. One conclusion of § 9 is that the subjective ground of the judgment of taste must be the possibility of the universal communication of "the mental state in the given representation" (§ 9.3, Ak. 217, B. 51). Now if the judgment of the object (which has the pleasure in the beautiful as its consequent) is taken to be the judgment of taste, one cannot make intelligible Kant's conclusion that "the mental state in this representation must be one of a feeling of the free play of the powers of representation in a given representation with reference to a cognition in general" (§ 9.3, Ak. 217, B. 52). The mental state referred to must be the feeling (a consciousness or awareness) of the harmony of the cognitive faculties. Kant later identifies the pleasure with this consciousness: "The consciousness of the mere formal purposiveness in the play of the subject's cognitive powers, in a representation through which an object is given, is the pleasure itself" (§ 12.2, Ak. 222, B. 57–58). By substitution, the interpretation in question results in the basis of the judgment of taste being the consequent of it. In Kant's philosophy this is an impossibility, and the interpretation must be rejected. The judging of the object (*Beurteilung des Gegenstandes*) cannot be identified with the judgment of taste (*Geschmacksurteil*).

The argument giving the answer to the question posed in the title of § 9 and said to be the key to the critique of taste constitutes Stage I of the transcendental deduction of judgments of taste. It is completely contained in the second paragraph and the first sentence of the third paragraph of § 9. The remainder of § 9 is devoted to the further development of the transcendental deduction proper. The argument in § 9.2–3 (Ak. 217, B. 51) is deceptively simple, although Kant's language is characteristically obscure; a literal translation of the passage goes as follows:

If the pleasure in the given object precedes [the judging of the object], and it is only the universal communicability of this pleasure that is to be ascribed to the representation of the object in the judgment of taste, then such a procedure would be self-contradictory. For this pleasure would be nothing other than the mere pleasantness in sensation, and so in accordance with its nature could have only private validity, because it would depend immediately on the representation through which the object is given.

Hence it is the universal capability of communication of the mental state in the given representation which, as the subjective condition of the judgment of taste, must be the foundation of the latter [the judgment of taste] and must have the pleasure in the object as a consequent.

I shall set out the argument in steps, still mostly in Kant's own words but providing the assumptions and justifications in brackets:

(1) Suppose the pleasure in the given object precedes the judging of the object.

(2) Then the pleasure would be immediately dependent on the representation through which the object is given (that is, on sensation). [(1), and the assumption that there is nothing else for it to be immediately dependent upon.]

(3) And the universal communicability of *this* pleasure would be ascribed to the representation of the object in the judgment of taste; that is, this pleasure would be the pleasure related in the judgment of taste for which universal validity is claimed. [(1), (2), and the analysis of "judgment of taste."]

(4) Such a pleasure would be nothing but the mere pleasantness in sensation. [(2), and the definition of "pleasantness in sensation."]

(5) Such a pleasure, according to its nature, could have only private validity. [(4), and as everyone admits (as discussed in §§ 7–8).]

(6) Such a procedure would be self-contradictory; in the judgment of taste the universal communicability of that which has only private validity, and hence cannot be universally communicable, would be ascribed to the representation of the object. [(3) and (5).]

(7) The pleasure in the given object judged to be beautiful cannot precede, but must be consequent of the judging of the object. [(1) and (6).]

Thus at the end of only the first four sentences of § 9, Kant has answered the question which he claims is the key to the critique of taste. The argument is simply that if the judgment of taste is to make a legitimate claim to universal validity, the pleasure in the beautiful object must be a consequent of some as-yet-undetermined activity called "the judging of the object"; for if not, the pleasure in the beautiful would be no different from the pleasure in mere sensation, which can claim no universal validity. (The "judging of the object" will turn out to be the reflection and contemplation of the formal purposiveness of the object; in Kant's analysis, that constitutes the consideration of an object with respect to its beauty.)

The conclusion of Kant's argument is more complex than my step (7) indicates, and that complexity must be articulated in order to reach the conclusion that constitutes the end of Stage I of the transcendental deduction, that a universally communicable mental state is the ground of the pleasure in the beautiful. A slightly less cumbersome rendition of the final sentence yields:

Hence it is the universal capability of communication of the mental state in the given representation which must be the foundation of the judgment of taste, as its subjective condition, and must have the pleasure in the object as its consequent. (§ 9.3, Ak. 217; my translation, cf. B. 51)

A number of points are made in this conclusion. Firstly, underlying the transcendental deduction of judgments of taste, there is implied the major assumption that in order for a judgment to have universal validity there must be something at the basis of the judgment which is universally communicable or capable of being shared. Without this basis, judgments of aesthetic taste could not be distinguished logically from the merely privately valid judgments of sensuous taste. Secondly, the "mental state is the given representation" is Kant's way of referring to the state of the mind, as yet undetermined, that gives rise to the pleasure at the basis of the judgment of taste. This mental state is the harmony of the cognitive faculties (Stage II) resulting from the reflection and contemplation of the formal purposiveness of the object (Stage III). Thirdly, it is a *subjective* condition of the judgment of taste because it is a state of the mind or subject; an objective condition would have to be a characteristic of the object of contemplation. Fourthly, something must have pleasure in the object as its consequent. But what? A careful consideration of the text shows that Kant does not claim that the pleasure must be consequent to the judgment of taste. As both the literal and less cumbersome translations of the concluding sentence indicate, the second dependent clause, like the first, has as its subject "the universal capability of communication of the mental state in the given representation"; it is this which must be the foundation of the judgment of taste and have the pleasure in the beautiful as its consequent. The pleasure in the beautiful, in order to be distinguishable from mere sensuous pleasure, must itself be based upon a universally communicable mental state brought about by the reflection and contemplation (the reflective *judging*) of the beautiful object (or, in Kant's language, the representation through which it is given).

In summary, the judging of the object is that mental activity Kant elsewhere terms the reflective use of judgment; it is the contemplation of and reflection on the form of the object, the utilization of the powers of imagination and understanding to discern a significant organization of elements—a rule-governedness. If this way of judging the object is successful, there results a harmony of the cognitive powers (Stage II of the deduction). The consciousness of this harmony *is* the feeling of pleasure (§ 12.2, Ak. 222, B. 57–58). Thus the feeling of pleasure in the beautiful is a consequent of the activity of judging the object; it is the product of that activity. Kant himself summarizes: "this merely subjective (aesthetical) judging of the object . . . precedes the pleasure in the same and is the ground of this pleasure in the harmony of the cognitive faculties" (§ 9.6, Ak. 218, B. 52–53).

Precisely how the answer to the question posed in the title of § 9 provides the key to the critique of taste can now be explained. The key is the turning of the inquiry in the right direction. The universal validity implicitly claimed by our judgments of taste, their a priori character, can be justified only on the assumption that the feeling of pleasure in the beautiful does not rest immediately in sensation but is grounded in (a consequent of) some other mental state that is capable of universal communication. The legitimation of judgments of taste as a class of judgments (that is, their deduction) thus begins with the attempt to show how it is possible that the pleasure in the beautiful can itself be based upon a state of the mind that is universally communicable. The "key" may thus be considered Stage I of the deduction. Stage II is the further specification of this universally communicable mental state.

CHAPTER 4

Aesthetic Perception and the Cognitive Faculties

4.1 The Transcendental Deduction—Stage II: The Harmony of the Cognitive Faculties in Free Play

STAGE II of the transcendental deduction of judgments of taste is an argument showing the possibility of a universally communicable mental state which does not lead to a determinate concept and which is the basis of the pleasure in the beautiful. Kant has previously argued (Stage I) that the legitimacy of judgments of taste, with their import of universal validity, depends upon the possibility of such a universally communicable mental state. The pleasure on which a judgment of taste is based must itself be grounded in some activity of judging the object and not simply in immediate sense pleasure.

Kant distinguishes particular feelings in terms of their intensity, duration, and ground (cause). Pleasure in the beautiful is thus to be distinguished from other pleasures, such as the pleasure in mere sensation and the pleasure in the good, in terms of its grounds. The general question of the deduction is this: Is it possible for judgments of taste to be based on a pleasure which is universally communicable? The answer given in Stage I is: Yes, if that pleasure is itself based on a universally communicable mental state. The next question (Stage II) is thus: Is it possible for a pleasure to be based on a universally communicable mental state? The answer given in Stage II is: Yes, if that mental state is based on or bound up with cognition generally, namely, with the subjective state of the mind necessary for cognition in general—the harmony of the cognitive faculties (the imagination and the understanding). The harmony of the cognitive faculties occurs when they unite in subsuming a representation under a universal or concept. But, since the judgment of taste is an aesthetic and not a conceptual judgment, a representation is not subsumed under a definite (or determinate) concept in the judgment of taste. Thus the harmony of the cognitive faculties is possible in this case only if they are united in such a way as to fulfill the conditions for cognition in general, although no specific conceptualization is involved in the case of the experience of the beautiful.

Although the details of this argument are provided in a number of places in the *Critique of Judgment*,[1] the fullest statement of it occurs in § 9.3–4 (Ak. 217, B. 51–52), which I shall present in a stepwise fashion in a fairly literal translation, adding suppressed premises and justifications for the steps in brackets:

(1) The pleasure on which the judgment of taste is based must be grounded in a universally communicable mental state. [Conclusion of Stage I of the deduction; see chapter 3, section 5, above.]

(2) A representation can be objective and can have a universal point of reference with which everyone's faculty of representation is compelled to harmonize only insofar as it belongs to cognition (*Erkenntnis*). [Definition of *Erkenntnis*, B137, A320=B376.]

(3) Nothing can be universally communicated except cognition and representations, insofar as they belong to cognition. [(2).]

(4) The determining ground of the judgment for this universal communicability of the representation [that is, the judgment of taste] is merely subjective, that is, it is conceived without any concept of the object. ["The judgment of taste is aesthetic," § 1.]

(5) The determining ground of the judgment for the universal communicability of the representation [the universally communicable mental state] can be nothing else but the mental state found in the relation of representations to one another insofar as they relate a given representation to cognition in general. [(1), (3), and (4).]

(6) The powers required to turn a representation by which an object is given into knowledge (cognition) are imagination (to gather together the perceptual manifold) and understanding (to synthesize the representation into the unity of the concept). [Kant's account of the process of cognition; see chapter 1, note 17.]

(7) The universally communicable mental state in the judgment of taste must be one of feeling the free play of the powers of representation (that is, the imagination and the understanding) when a given representation is generally suited for cognition [that is, not leading to a definite concept]. [(4), (5), and (6).]

1. Intro. VII.3–5, §§ 9.3–4, 39.4, 57 Remark I.8; Ak. 189–91, 217, 292–93, 344; B. 26–28, 51–52, 134–35, 189.

(8) This state [that is, the mental state or the feeling] of free play of the cognitive faculties in a representation by which an object is given must be universally communicable, because cognition is the only kind of representation which is valid for everyone. [(3) and (7).]

The argument is then rehearsed in §§ 9.5 and 9.6 (Ak. 217–18, B. 52–53). Admittedly, the conclusion of Stage II is abstract and embedded in Kant's terminology and epistemology. I shall attempt to flesh it out and give it some content in two ways. Firstly, in the next section of this chapter I shall present a comprehensive summary of Kant's theory of cognitive perception, which I shall then compare with his views on aesthetic perception and experience. Secondly, in chapter 5 I shall pursue Kant's own attempt to explain the content of his theory through the next stage (Stage III) of the deduction, specifically through his doctrine of formal subjective purposiveness.

Kant's deduction of judgments of taste proceeds by linking aesthetic perception with cognitive perception. His insistence on the subjective nature of aesthetic judgments (judgments of taste) is consistently maintained by keeping the pleasure in the beautiful based on the subjective conditions for judgment in all men, which turn out to be the subjective conditions for the possibility of cognition in general. In other words, Kant is assuming that, since knowledge is communicable, the subjective state of the mind, when it has knowledge, is also communicable. In the experience of the beautiful, the subjective state of the mind is, in its general characteristics, the same as the subjective state of the mind when one has knowledge, and thus is universally communicable. Kant has argued that the pleasure in the beautiful must be so based if judgments of taste are to be legitimate. If we have reason to suppose that judgments of taste in fact are so based, Kant must explain how finding an object generally suitable for cognition can give rise to a pleasure which we feel we have a right to impute to others, to claim they ought also to find it pleasurable. Kant explicitly states in § 9.7 (Ak. 218, B. 53) that he has not so far answered that question. He raises the question again in § 12.1 (Ak. 221–22, B. 57) without answering it, nor is it dealt with in succeeding statements of the main part of the deduction (Stages I–IV). Kant raises the issue again, however, in § 40.7 (Ak. 296, B. 138), indicating that the complete deduction must go beyond simply showing how universally valid judgments of taste are possible. That we in fact have the right to make judgments of taste is not shown just by demonstrating that it is possible to base them on what is universally communicable. We are here anticipating Stage V of the deduction, the link between aesthetics and morality, which purports to show why we have a right to expect others to find pleasure in the experience of the beautiful. Stage V is discussed in detail in chapter 7.

4.2   Aesthetic and Cognitive Perception

... the ground of this pleasure [in the beautiful] is found in . . . the purposive harmony of an object (whether a product of nature or of art) with the mutual relations of the cognitive faculties (the imagination and the understanding), a harmony which is requisite for every empirical cognition. (Intro. VII.5, Ak. 191, B. 28)

... the aesthetical judgment contributes nothing toward the knowledge of its objects. . . . (Intro. VIII.4, Ak. 194, B. 31)

The quotations juxtaposed above indicate the paradoxical, close relation and yet the distance Kant sees between judgments of taste and cognitive judgments (knowledge claims): they are both grounded in the same general features of our mental faculties, but the aesthetic judgment does not result in knowledge. In judging whether an object is beautiful, the faculties are working just as if a knowledge claim is to be their product; all but the last stage of the conditions for knowledge are fulfilled, and that penultimate fulfillment is the source of the pleasure in the beautiful. It is as if the object were constructed for our faculties, for their harmonious interaction, that same harmonious interaction which in the ordinary (=nonaesthetic) situation results in perception and knowledge. Thus, both because Kant links the experience of the beautiful with knowledge (cognition) and because the experience of the beautiful is based on sense experience, a synoptic account of Kant's theory of perception and knowledge is appropriate.

Kant begins his Introduction to the *Critique of Pure Reason* by accepting the famous empiricist thesis that all knowledge begins with experience. He then qualifies this commitment to empiricism by insisting that it is a further question whether all our knowledge arises out of experience. Kant wants to answer this further question negatively because he believes we have knowledge of certain necessary ("synthetic a priori") truths such as the truths of mathematics, geometry, and the causal maxim, which cannot be justified empirically. Nonetheless, he criticizes traditional metaphysical philosophers for their mistaken belief that by mere thought (pure reason) we can arrive at knowledge of something transcending our experience. Kant attempts to show that if we have any knowledge that cannot be justified empirically, it must be justified *transcendentally*, that is, as being known a priori as a necessary condition of our experience. Thus the subject of transcendental philosophy, the object of transcendental knowledge, is not another realm; it remains the realm of experience, though the concern is with the conditions which make such experience possible.

If Kant's transcendental method can be said to result from his belief in the inability of either rationalism or empiricism to provide a firm foundation for human knowledge, his specific introduction of transcendental elements in his analysis of cognition is guided, if not determined, by his analysis of sense perception. The following brief account of Kant's theory of perception is an attempt to delineate the most consistent theory Kant presents, even though it is not in every respect the one he always presents. There are passages where Kant uses the key terms in more limited senses and others where he uses them in broader senses than in the following account. Such is to be expected in a large and difficult work whose composition took many years. It is often impossible to say precisely what Kant means even though one can be fairly clear on the major features of Kant's theory of perception and the basic concepts he uses in his discussions of perception and knowledge.

Sensibility and Intuition

Kant would have agreed with certain recent philosophers such as Ludwig Wittgenstein that it is misleading to say we are acquainted with our sensations or feelings. Rather, we simply have them. What we are acquainted with are the appearances of objects and their qualities: red balls, sharp knives, green sofas, and the like. We are acquainted with them by means of particular modifications of our physical and mental states, namely, through sensations *(Empfindungen)*. These modifications are the *content* of any awareness we might have; they are the "internal accusatives" of the verbs of sensing—sights, sounds, smells, tastes, and touches.

Kant accepts the Lockean representative theory of perception insofar as he holds that empirical objects have at least some qualities which correspond to the qualities we experience. But with respect to Kant, we do not by means of sensation, or by any other means, come to know the objects that ultimately affect us—things-in-themselves. However, through these modifications of our state we do come to know objects of the phenomenal world (the world of appearance, the world of empirical objects). These are the objects of our experience.

According to the faculty psychology Kant subscribed to, we must accordingly postulate a faculty that enables us to be affected by objects. This faculty Kant calls *sensibility (Sinnlichkeit)*. It is a passive faculty, the capacity to receive sensations or impressions. Sensations may be accompanied by feelings of pleasure and displeasure, and consequently we must also possess a capacity for such feelings—a faculty of the feeling of pleasure and displeasure. These feelings, for Kant, are also sense perceptions in an extended meaning of the term, of which there are two species: sensations *(Empfindungen)* and feeling-states *(Gefühle)*. Only sensations can be used as a basis for knowledge of the world of appearances external to the subject.

Although sensations are entirely passive, by means of them we have *intuitions (Anschauungen)* of empirical objects. An intuition is any presumed awareness or experience of an object. The object of an intuition Kant calls an *appearance (Erscheinung)*, to which a phenomenal object —an empirical object—may or may not correspond, as the case may be. One can have an intuition (and hence an appearance) of a pink elephant, although there is no phenomenal object to which such an appearance in fact corresponds. Our—the human—mode of intuition is sensibility; only through sensation can we humans be affected and have knowledge of objects. Although we can think objects through the understanding and imagine them through our power of imagination, these objects are nonetheless objects of sensible intuition. Kant thus comes very close to saying, as the logical empiricists said over a century later, that empirical objects are logical constructions from sense data. "All thought must, directly or indirectly, by way of certain characters, relate ultimately to intuitions, and therefore, with us, to sensibility, because in no other way can an object be given to us" (A19=B33). Every intuition (awareness or experience of an object) is thus in fact always sensible, relating either immediately or mediately to sensations. Although the content of intuitions is exhausted by reference to sensations, the form of our human intuitions (awareness of objects) is necessarily spatial and temporal. Space and time are thus said to be the pure forms of intuition.

Theoretically (in thought but not in experience), intuitions can be divided into the matter or content derived from the effect of objects on us (sensations) and the form imposed by the mind itself (the spatial and temporal relations—the a priori or pure forms of intuition). But it is misleading to say that the form is imposed or actively contributed by the mind, for two reasons: firstly, the mind does not impose or contribute the particular spatial and temporal relations the objects of the phenomenal world possess; the particular spatial and temporal relations of objects are discovered through sensation, like every other empirical fact. Kant is not an idealist in this respect, for he holds "that things as objects of our senses existing outside us are given, but we know nothing of what they may be in themselves, knowing only their appearances, that is, the representations which they cause in us by affecting our senses."[2] The mind may give laws to nature, but it does not give the whole of nature. Secondly, the form is not really imposed upon the objects of the phenomenal world. Empirical objects really are spatial and temporal, even though we can say nothing about those objects as they are in themselves. But the general form in which we are aware of these objects is not given in sensation; it is given in the relations between sensations, and the manner or mode in which sensations relate must be a function of the mind. Nonetheless, in our intuitions, appearances are necessarily presented in space and time.[3]

Imagination and Understanding

For a manifold of appearances to be experienced as an object, a further unification of the contents of one's experience must be achieved. The manifold of appearances (sense intuitions) must be unified in the concept of an object. This unity is not given in sensation; it must therefore be a function of the active faculties of the mind—the imagination and the understanding. We must be able to view the manifold as a unity, and this requires synthesis, which, Kant says, is the act of putting different representations together and of grasping what is manifold in them in one act of knowledge (A77=B103). Kant's discussions in the *Critique of Pure Reason* of the pure forms of intuitions, the forms of synthesis, the categories, concepts, the schemata, and the analogies of experience are all attempts to clarify the manner in which the mind must work in order to perceive, and yield knowledge of, empirical objects. They are all concerned with synthesis conceived in this broad sense. The aspect or treatment of synthesis of greatest concern to us here is that of the cooperative roles of the imagination and the understaning, because it is to these that Kant explicitly links the activities of the mental powers in the experience of the beautiful.

It must always be possible to apprehend a given manifold of intuitions as belonging to one apprehending conscious subject. This is a necessary condition for any experience whatsoever. But it must also be possible to apprehend it as a unity (as a manifold), and this requires (a) that the imagination keep in mind the previously given elements of the manifold —"reproduce them in imagination"—and (b) that the understanding recognize them as falling under a concept. Kant thus gives the imagina-

2. Kant, *Prolegomena* § 13. Remark II, Ak. 4:288–89, Beck 36.
3. In this account, I have tried to explicate Kant's theory without resorting to the seriously misleading language of the mind actively imposing or impressing the forms of space and time on a spaceless and atemporal manifold.

tion a central place in the activity of synthesis, but he is far from consistent in the precise respective roles he assigns to the imagination and the understanding in cognition. Consider this apparently straightforward summation of the roles of imagination and understanding in cognition: "[A] given object by means of sense excites the imagination to collect the manifold, and the imagination in its turn brings the understanding to bring about a unity of this collective process in concepts" (§ 21.1, Ak. 238, B. 75). Even this lucid statement presents difficulties. In the first edition of the *Critique of Pure Reason,* the collective role of the imagination includes "recognition in a concept," while the role of the understanding is limited to supplying the concept. Although consistently maintaining that the understanding supplies concepts, Kant vacillates whether the imagination or the understanding brings about the unity of the manifold by being the active faculty. Sometimes he seems to restrict the imagination to being "the faculty of representing in intuition an object that is not itself present" (B151), thereby relegating the active unification to the work of the understanding, as suggested in the above passage from the *Critique of Judgment.* This position characterizes the deduction of the second edition of the *Critique of Pure Reason.* But since cognition is supposed to result from the harmony of the equally active imagination and understanding, it is important to remember that the synthesis is a *single act.* "It is one and the same spontaneity, which in the one case, under the title of imagination, and in the other case, under the title of understanding, brings combination into the manifold of intuition" (B162n).

The unification of the synthesized manifold in a concept is supposed to occur through the recognition of similar marks or criteria (*Merkmale*) shared by manifold and concept. "The concepts of the understanding . . . are determinable through predicates of sensible intuition which can correspond to them" (§ 57.2, Ak. 339, B. 184). Through sense we experience a manifold of intuitions which the imagination then synthesizes ("holds together and runs through"—apprehends as a unity), whereupon it is recognized that the manifold possesses the marks that allow a certain concept to be applied by the understanding. These marks are the common characteristics possessed by all the particular intuitions which fall under the concept.

But there must be a means of connection between concepts, which are intellectual, and intuitions, which are sensible. The imagination is that which connects sensibility and understanding. The content of the manifold is supplied by sensibility; the unity of the imaginative synthesis depends upon the understanding. The mediating element brought in by the imagination is the image. It is through an image that the imagination reproduces intuitions, and it is through the image that intuitions are related to concepts.[4]

What is first given to us is an appearance, which is a manifold and thus requires a combination or synthesis such as it does not have in sense itself. Thus, according to Kant's faculty psychology, we must possess an active faculty for the synthesis of this manifold, namely, the imagination, which Kant defines as "the faculty of representing in intuition an object that is not itself present" (B151). Sense intuitions (perceptions) occur successively in time, the apprehension of the manifold is always successive, but "whether they also follow one another in the object is a point which calls for further reflection" (A189–90=B234–35).

Kant attempts to show that we must distinguish between the subjective order of appearances and the objective order in which the objects of appearances combine; thus we must synthesize appearances into an order (according to a rule) in which they become perceptions (of an object or event). Kant gives two examples to illustrate the distinction between the subjective and objective order of appearances. My apprehension of the appearances of a house is successive (for example, sides, door, roof), as is my apprehension of the successive positions of a boat moving downstream. This is the subjective time order. "In the previous example of the house my perceptions could begin with the apprehension of the roof and end with the basement, or could begin from below and end above; and I could similarly apprehend the manifold of the empirical intuition either from right to left or from left to right" (A192–93= B237–38). The question is whether the empirical object or event is to be judged successive in the manner in which the order of appearances is successive. In the case of the house, no one would claim that it is; the sides, roof, and door exist simultaneously in their ordered relations as parts of the house. In the case of the boat moving downstream, however, the successive appearances of the boat farther and farther away is in fact what has happened to the boat; I cannot reverse its actual course, although I can imagine its reversal. Kant argues that the subjective-objective time-order distinction is only possible if the mind reorganizes the representations in accordance with a rule for their necessary connection. Empirical concepts provide such rules for the synthesis of a manifold of intuitions. We synthesize the manifold of intuitions, reproduce

4. Actually, Kant finds need to postulate general products of the imagination to mediate between sensibility (intuitions) and understanding (concepts). These are the *schemata*, which Kant defines as the representations of universal procedures of imagination in providing an image for a concept (B179). A *schema* is not an image but a rule for producing images. But the precise distinction between a schema and a concept remains somewhat obscure.

them according to a rule if they admit of it, and thereby go beyond a mere order of appearances to an order of phenomenal objects to which a concept is applied. The point of Kant's examples of the house and the boat is to show that objectivity is a product of cognition, not of apprehension; whatever the order in which appearances enter consciousness, there are only certain orders in which they can be unified and hence thought.

Kant's and Hume's Theories of the Imagination

Since Hume, in both *A Treatise of Human Nature* and *An Enquiry concerning Human Understanding*, also claimed that the imagination plays an important role in the perception of empirical objects, the similarities and differences between their theories should bring Kant's theory into a clearer light.

Hume's epistemology consists of two parts: his critical or skeptical philosophy and his positive theories of the workings of the human mind. The latter are often interpreted as being void of philosophical content, as being the mere enunciation of Hume's psychological views. Hume says that reason cannot demonstrate the existence of objects external to the mind subsisting in space and time, it cannot prove the causal maxim, it cannot prove a necessary connection between particular causes and their effects or between past and future, nor can it prove the self's identity or existence. Reason is by itself unable to determine these matters. But neither, Hume claims, do the senses convey them as matters of fact.[5] Hume tries to show how in each case the mind goes beyond the evidence that is immediately present to the senses. He contends that knowledge in each of these areas is not possible and that, consequently, a description of how belief is generated is all we can have and all we should hope or strive for philosophically. In this connection, Hume's psychological theory of the imagination is time and again brought into play. Hume relies on a theory of the nature of the human mind for his positive account of the generation of our beliefs. This, he thinks, is the only task left for a nonskeptical philosophy. It is not reason or sensation, but the imagination, determined by experience through the laws of association, custom, and habit, that is the source (cause) of our beliefs.

With regard to empirical objects, what we are directly acquainted with, according to Hume, is a bundle of impressions. In fact, concerning

5. Hume's critique of the ability of either reason or experience to establish such truths does contain assumptions that are at least partly psychological in nature, namely, (1) that what is conceivable in the imagination is logically possible (and hence only empirically true or false), and (2) that what is separable in the imagination is logically distinct.

both Hume and Kant, it is misleading to say that there is a bundle (a unified manifold) of impressions apart from some activity of the imagination. To perceive empirical objects there must be a positive contribution of the mind: the imagination, working in accordance with the laws of association, is required to hold together the series of impressions into a bundle, and we feign their coherent, external, and enduring existence.

In contrast to Kant's distinguishing the imagination and the understanding as distinct faculties of the mind, Hume terms the understanding merely "the general and more established properties of the imagination."[6] The imagination is conceived as a source of ideas and a cause of beliefs, a purely empirical faculty of the mind. Kant, on the other hand, claims that the activities of synthesis by the imagination are necessary conditions of experience. Although it may appear Hume is putting forth a purely psychological theory while Kant is advancing a more philosophical one, this is an interpretation which needs further scrutiny.

Kant does claim a transcendental status for his theory of the role of the imagination and the understanding in the perception of empirical objects; he purports to have shown that these operations are necessary conditions for empirical knowledge or even for experience in general (he vacillates between these disjuncts). Hume at one point claims a similar status for his theory of mental activity, when he says:

In order to justify myself [in claiming that the imagination is the ultimate judge of all systems of philosophy], I must distinguish in the imagination betwixt the principles which are permanent, irresistable, and universal; such as the customary transitions from causes to effects, and from effects to causes: And the principles, which are changeable, weak, and irregular; . . . The former are *the foundations of all our thoughts and actions, so that upon their removal human nature must immediately perish and go to ruin.*[7]

Hume equates these "general and more established properties of the imagination" with the understanding; they are innate in human beings. But in his *Enquiry concerning Human Understanding* Hume seems to realize the threat this position poses to the consistency of his philosophical empiricism, for there he enunciates his more familiar and more consistently Humean view that the principles of human nature are obtained through philosophical and psychological reflection and have merely empirical validity:

By employing that word ["custom" or "habit"] we pretend not to have given

6. David Hume, *A Treatise of Human Nature*, bk. 1, pt. 4, Sec. 7; ed. L. A. Selby-Bigge (1888; reprint ed., Oxford: Clarendon Press, 1960), p. 267.

7. Hume, *Treatise*, bk. 1, pt. 4, sec. 4; ed. Selby-Bigge, p. 225. Italics added.

the ultimate reason of such a propensity. We only point out a principle of human nature, which is universally acknowledged and which is well known by its effects.[8]

Here the difference between Kant and Hume is simply the status each claims for the principles of the mind or the activities of the mental powers.

Nonetheless, to a large extent Kant and Hume share a positive theory of mental activity. Kant makes use of the theory of association to explain the empirical synthesis, which in turn requires the transcendental synthesis. A close examination shows that Hume's notion of the "propensities" of the mind (associationism in its more developed form) bears a strong resemblance to Kant's analysis of the synthetic activities of the mind.

This similarity between Kant and Hume has been elaborated by Robert Paul Wolff in his analysis of Hume's propensities and their relation to Kant's categories as second-order rules.[9] To ascertain how the two relate, we must first clarify the role of Kant's categories. Kant thinks he has shown that the categories are the a priori conditions of experience in general. But sometimes by "experience" Kant means "consciousness," while at other times he seems to mean "empirical knowledge." Kant's position progresses from the view that the categories are a priori forms of synthesis necessary for empirical knowledge, though not necessary conditions of all consciousness, to the notion that no representation could ever enter consciousness without undergoing synthesis and conforming to the categories. In other words, at first Kant says that an unsynthesized or unconceptualized manifold of perceptions (appearances) is possible, that synthesis or conceptualization in accordance with the categories is a necessary condition of empirical knowledge but not of intuition (see, for example, A89–91=B121–23). But in the deductions of the *Critique of Pure Reason* (A115–30, B129–69), Kant unambiguously states that we cannot be conscious of an unsynthesized manifold. The categories are thus the modes or forms of synthesis; they **are** second-order rules in that they are rules whereby empirical concepts are formed by the mind, and these empirical concepts are themselves rules for the reproduction and unification of representations (sense intuitions). The parallel in Hume is as follows: the innate propensities of the mind

8. David Hume, *An Enquiry concerning Human Understanding*, sec. 5, pt. 1, ed. L. A. Selby-Bigge, 2d ed. (1902; reprint ed., Oxford: Clarendon Press, 1961), p. 43.

9. Robert Paul Wolff, "Hume's Theory of Mental Activity," *Philosophical Review* 49 (1960):289–310; esp. pp. 292–95.

serve as rules whereby particular dispositions (not innate, but acquired) are formed by the mind, and these dispositions are themselves rules for the reproduction and unification of impressions and ideas in imagination.

In addition to relating the categories to the synthesizing activity of the imagination Kant gives a three-fold characterization of synthesis (A98–110): the synthesis of apprehension in intuition, the synthesis of reproduction in imagination, and the synthesis of recognition in a concept. Given the similarity between the roles of Kant's categories and Hume's propensities, one would expect to find a corresponding similarity between the particular dispositions in Hume's theory (the first-order dispositions and propensities) and Kant's three-fold synthesis. And important similarities can be found. Kant directly and specifically refers to the association of representations in his exposition of the synthesis of reproduction in imagination. "This subjective and *empirical* ground of reproduction according to rules is what is called *association* of representations" (A121). Kant appears to be fixing on just that feature of the mind Hume had found so important: the power to reproduce and the tendency to associate ideas which have often followed or accompanied one another.

Do the other aspects of synthesis have parallels in Hume's theory of propensities? The ambiguities in Kant's own account make it difficult to say conclusively. The synthesis of apprehension in intuition is the holding together of the manifold of distinct impressions or intuitions into a unity, and Kant does go on to say that this is accomplished by reproduction. It is increasingly plausible, as one proceeds in the *Critique of Pure Reason,* to view the three kinds of synthesis as merely different aspects of one mental activity; this synthesis is similar, to the extent that it is merely empirical, to Hume's account of the unification of impressions in objects as the result of past experience with their constancy and conjunction.[10]

Productive and Reproductive Imagination

In contrast to Hume, Kant does consistently maintain that one function of the imagination is more than simply empirical: the synthesis the imagination performs, or helps perform, is a necessary condition of cognition or experience and as such is known a priori. He thus calls it the "transcendental function of imagination" (A123), and it may be looked upon as having experience as its product. It is in this respect that Kant distinguishes the transcendental *productive* imagination from the empirical *reproductive* imagination. The latter works in accordance with

10. Hume, *Treatise*, bk. 1, pt. 4, sec. 2; ed. Selby-Bigge, pp. 192–218.

the merely empirical laws of association, while the former works only in accordance with the unity of apperception, that is, the understanding (A119). In the first edition (A121), Kant distinguishes between reproduction and association by saying that association is the empirical ground for reproduction while affinity is the transcendental ground. Kant several times argues that this empirical ground (reproduction in imagination by means of association) must itself rest on some objective ground ("affinity"); otherwise, experience could not be coherent and would be "a blind play of representations, less even than a dream" (A112; cf. A121). Kant asks upon what the empirical rule of association rests, how this association is itself possible, and claims that its objective ground (the affinity of the manifold) "is nowhere to be found save in the principle of the unity of apperception" (A122), that is, the law "that all appearances, without exception, must so enter the mind or be apprehended, that they conform to the unity of apperception" (ibid.).

How do the unity of consciousness and reproduction in imagination according to a rule (categories and concepts) necessitate an *objective* basis of such association? The rules of association must have an objective basis, Kant argues, or else there would be no unity to the manifold; it would not even be recognized as being bound up in one consciousness (the unity of apperception). Since the association of representations is dependent upon past experience, Kant reasons that, if the reproduction of representations through association is to result in empirical knowledge, there must be an objective "affinity of appearances" or "affinity of the manifold" on which such reproduction and association are based. This is merely to say again that empirical explanations in terms of association or anything else (Kant happens to hold the associationist view) can never be sufficient to justify the a priori knowledge we possess, nor to justify our empirical knowledge generally unless it can be shown that such reproduction or association rests on an objective basis. There must be some guarantee of constancy, some rule in accordance with which association and reproduction of appearances take place. This rule or principle Kant ascribes to the transcendental faculty or function of the imagination. He calls it the *productive* imagination to distinguish it from the empirical and psychological activity of the *reproductive* imagination and to make clear that it is a spontaneous faculty not dependent upon empirical laws but rather constitutive of them and hence constitutive of empirical objects.

That Kant never makes the details of this theory very clear is unfortunate for two reasons. Firstly, it is questionable whether this doubling of the faculties (transcendental and empirical) has any ultimate explanatory value. Kant's theory depends upon the two faculties, though distinct, engaging in exactly parallel activities, but the necessity of this view and the possibility of knowledge of its truth are left obscure. Secondly, in the *Critique of Judgment* Kant explicitly refers to the free play of the imagination as characteristic of the experience of the beautiful, and he links this free play to the productive imagination:

Now, if in the judgment of taste the imagination must be considered in its freedom, it is in the first place not regarded as reproductive, as it is subject to the laws of association, but as productive and spontaneous (as the author of arbitrary forms of possible intuition). (§ 22. G.R. 1, Ak. 240, B. 77)

This view of the productive and spontaneous faculty (function) of the imagination has an air of plausibility about it for the creative activity of the artist, but how the appreciator can be described as "the author of arbitrary forms of possible intuition" is not immediately clear. I suggest that this productive and spontaneous activity of the appreciator can be partially explained by relating it to the ordering of perceptions as discussed in the Second Analogy of the *Critique of Pure Reason*. The imagination has the ability to reorder the subjective spatial and temporal order of impressions or perceptions in its attempt to synthesize the manifold into a form to which a given concept can be applied by the understanding. In the case of the experience of the beautiful, however, no concept is forthcoming. Nonetheless, the imagination and the understanding engage in the same activities as does cognition, where there is a manifold but no concept given. Judgment is being used reflectively, not determinately. The faculty of judgment is used "reflexively" in that a unity in accordance with some rule is sought by reflection on the formal relatedness of the object's characteristics. One reflects on the manifold to discover a possible unity, rather than approach it with a specific rule of determinate organization to discover whether the specific rule is satisfied. What Kant terms the "free play of the imagination" thus can be viewed as the spatial and temporal ordering in the imagination of perceptions, the relating of parts (elements and complexes of elements) to each other in a variety of ways to determine whether a relatedness, a purposiveness of form, can be apprehended. "All appearances are consequently intuited as aggregates, as complexes of previously given parts" (B204).

Kant's model in the experience of the beautiful, as in experience in general, is the following: a mere succession of impressions cannot itself yield experience of an object. The experience of an object—an ordinary empirical object or a work of art—requires the synthesis of the manifold of intuition into a unity. In cognitive perception this synthesis is determined by rules; concepts determine the unification and the cognitive judgment is thus *determinate*. In aesthetic perception, a kind of reflective judgment, this synthesis is not determined by empirical rules or concepts, and hence it is free to relate the parts in whatever way it can to obtain a synthetic unity of the manifold. Pleasure in the beautiful results when such an ordering is achieved that the cognitive powers are in harmony; it is as if the manifold has a unity to which a concept ought to apply, even though there is no definite concept applicable.

A difficulty now arises. To be consistent with the doctrines of the *Critique of Pure Reason,* Kant must not completely exclude the reproductive function of the imagination from the experience of the beautiful. Kant himself says that "experience as such necessarily presupposes the reproducibility of appearances" (A102), and the experience of an object of art would seem to be no exception. Kant's doctrine of synthesis requires the reproduction in imagination of previously experienced perceptions; in no other way can the manifold of intuitions be held together in a unity. In excluding the reproductive function of imagination from his characterization of the activities of the mental powers in the experience of the beautiful, Kant was perhaps only casting aside a function of the mental powers which, though engaged, he did not think served to distinguish aesthetic perception.

Aesthetic Perception

Given this general account of Kant's theory of perception and cognition, the roles of the cognitive powers (imagination and understanding) in the experience of the beautiful must be interpreted as the reordering or relating of the various parts of the manifold of intuition to find an organization capable of being conceptualized—brought under a definite or determinate rule (law, concept). This is what takes place when we, in Kant's terms, "reflect upon" or "contemplate" (the form of) an object with respect to its beauty; it is what was referred to in § 9 as the "judging of the object."

But this is precisely where the difficulty arises in Kant's theory of aesthetic perception. For reflecting upon or contemplating the form of an object is what we do whenever we make a judgment, and, according to Kant, the making of judgments is what characterizes our ordinary perception of empirical objects. What would seem to be somewhat plausible in looking at or listening to something aesthetically Kant says occurs necessarily in perceiving objects and acquiring empirical knowledge.

What, then, is the difference between cognitive and aesthetic perception? In aesthetic perception the activity of relating the various parts of the manifold of intuition either ignores or does not result in an organization capable of being conceptualized according to definite or determinate rules (laws, concepts). In cases in which we are already know the kind of object, we abstract from that knowledge, disregarding it in our activity of contemplating the form of the object with respect to its beauty.[11] We do not concern ourselves with what kind of thing it is we are looking at; we do not relate what we see to the concept of an object (a conceptualized object). What we do concern ourselves with is the mere pleasure or displeasure of our contemplation or reflection. This contemplation or reflection is itself pleasureable and thereby gives rise to a positive judgment of taste when the cognitive powers harmonize with each other just as if a definite cognition (conceptualization) is to result. It is as if the object—its formal qualities and relations—were organized so as to result in a definite cognition, a cognitive judgment. As shown in Stage I of the deduction of judgments of taste (chapter 3, section 5, above), it is this reflection or contemplation which distinguishes the felt pleasure in the beautiful from the pleasures of mere sensation and which is necessary for the universal validity of judgments of taste.

The emphasis in looking at something with regard to its beauty is in the looking, not in the beauty. Kant is quite clear that the pleasure in the beautiful is not something apart from the reflection upon or contemplation of the object. "The consciousness of the mere formal purposiveness in the play of the subject's cognitive powers, in a representation through which an object is given, is the pleasure [in the beautiful] itself . . ." (§ 12.2, Ak. 222, B. 57–58). What distinguishes aesthetic perception from ordinary perception, then, is that we linger in the contemplation or reflection on the form of a thing (§ 12.2, Ak. 222. B. 58). The free play of the imagination and understanding in the experience of the beautiful achieves a stage where it is as if the object being contemplated were designed for our cognitive powers. This notion of the designedness or rule-governedness of the form of the object brings us to the next stage of the deduction of judgments of taste: formal subjective purposiveness.

11. §§ 14.5, 15.3, 16.2, 40.2; Ak. 224, 227, 229, 231, 294; B. 60, 63, 65, 67, 136.

CHAPTER 5

Kant's Aesthetic Formalism

5.1 The Transcendental Deduction—Stage III: Formal Purposiveness

KANT'S AESTHETIC theory is often cited as a clear example of aesthetic formalism—the emphasis of aesthetic form over or even to the exclusion of subject matter, ideas, and content. Attributing this view to Kant is largely due to Kant's claim that "beauty is the form of the purposiveness of an object" (§ 17.7, Ak. 236, B. 73), that the mere form of purposiveness is the determining ground of the judgment of taste (§ 11.2, Ak. 221, B. 56). Furthermore, since Kant maintains that the judgment of taste is not based on concepts, it might seem that Kant excludes subject matter or representational elements from being proper objects of attention with regard to beauty. In spite of these considerations, Kant ranks poetry as the highest form of art, and he maintains that "we may describe beauty in general (whether natural or artificial) as the expression of aesthetical ideas" (§ 51.1, Ak. 320, B. 164). An understanding of Kant's aesthetic theory thus necessitates a careful look at whether Kant is an aesthetic formalist, and if so to what extent.[1]

The formalistic aspects of Kant's theory are closely tied to his views on the process of acquiring knowledge and the possible content of knowledge claims. Kant's conception of form in aesthetics is bound up with some of his most basic epistemological assumptions and theses. One of

1. D. W. Gotshalk has argued that Kant's Third Critique contains two incompatible aesthetic theories, a formalistic one in the "Analytic of the Beautiful" and an expressionistic one in the "Deduction" and "Dialectic" of aesthetic judgment: "Form and Expression in Kant's Aesthetics," *British Journal of Aesthetics* 7 (1967): 250–60.

the contentions of this chapter is that the realization of those connections provides the basis for understanding, though not necessarily accepting, some of the less plausible aspects of Kant's aesthetic theory.

The entire *Critique of Judgment,* both the "Critique of Aesthetic Judgment" and the "Critique of Teleological Judgment," is unified by being a treatment of the aesthetic representation of the formal purposiveness of nature and art. The notion of purposiveness is logically tied to the notion of form. The linkage between these two notions (my hesitation to call them concepts will soon become clear) in art is dealt with explicitly in § 11, the title of which is: "The judgment of taste has nothing at its basis but the form of the purposiveness *[Zweckmässigkeit]* of an object (or of its mode of representation)" (Ak. 221, B. 56).

Kant defines "purpose" as "the object of a concept, in so far as the concept is regarded as the cause of the object (the real ground of its possibility)" (§ 10.1, Ak. 220, B. 55).[2] He defines "purposiveness" as *"Forma Finalis"*—"the causality of a *concept* in respect of its *object"* (ibid.). We think, Kant says, of a purpose where the object *itself* (not merely our cognition of it)—its form and existence—is regarded as an effect possible only by means of a concept of the object.

Purposes are tied to human motives and actions. An object is said to have a purpose when its form and existence is conceived as the result of a plan or rule (concept). Concepts are supplied by human beings. Thus, purposes (aims, goals, intentions) are linked to wills. An object made "on purpose" was made according to a purpose, that is, in accordance with a concept—a rule for its formal structure, the organization of its parts or matter; it is thus caused by a will. It is the result of a working of the faculty of desire through concepts. For example, the form and existence of a padlock is dependent, according to Kant, on a concept of that object in the mind of a being with a will; we conceive its very possibility as being based upon an idea in someone's mind.

Kant then makes an interesting and key move. He claims that we can call an object (or even a state of mind or an action) *purposive* on the basis of its formal organization (structure) even when we do not or cannot actually place the cause of this form in a will, that is, even when we do not actually conceive it as being made on purpose. An object's "purposiveness" is what we perceive in it—its form and organization—which leads us to say that it resulted from a concept. That is, we can talk about the formal pattern itself as being purposive, independent of whether in fact the object has a purpose. In such cases, however, it is simply as if the object were the result of the causality of a concept (or reason acting

2. Cf. First Intro. V.10, Ak. 215–16, H. 20; Intro. IV.4, § 15.3; Ak. 180, 227; B. 17, 63–64.

through will with respect to it); its possibility and existence are intelligible to us only in these terms, namely, "only so far as we assume for its ground a causality according to purposes, i.e., in accordance with a will which has regulated it according to the representation of a certain rule" (§ 10.2, Ak. 220, B. 55). In other words, although it is purposive in form and structure, we cannot conclude that it has a definite, objective purpose, even though the object is intelligible (explicable and conceivable) to us only in terms of purposes. We can observe a purposiveness of form, then, independently of a knowledge of actual or even possible purposes. Hence there can be "purposiveness without [any representation of a] purpose" (ibid.).

In the "Analytic of Teleological Judgment," Kant gives a helpful example, which, appropriately enough, reminds one of recent discussions in the philosophy of religion of the argument from design:

Suppose a man in an apparently uninhabited land perceived a geometrical figure, say a regular hexagon, inscribed on the sand. His reflection, working on such a concept, would attribute, although mysteriously, the unity of the principle of its genesis to reason, and consequently would not regard the sand, the neighboring sea, the winds, or beasts with familiar footprints, or any other unreasoning cause as the ground of the possibility of such a shape. For the chance of not encountering such a concept would seem so infinitely great that it would be just as if there were no natural law, no cause in the mere mechanical working of nature capable of producing it; but *it would be as if only the concept of such an object,* as a concept *which reason alone can supply* and with which it can compare the thing, *could contain the causality for such an effect.* This [figure], then, would be regarded as a purpose, but as a product of *art,* not as a natural purpose. (§ 64.2, Ak. 370, B. 216–17; my translation and italics, except for *"art"*)

The object, the regular hexagon in this case, is regarded as (having) a purpose because it is as if only the *concept* of this regular hexagon, supplied by reason and a will, could have brought about the existence of the hexagon in the sand. In existentialist terms, it is as if the essence of the hexagon preceded its existence and as if the conception of it in some mind with a will was the cause of its existence. The hexagon, being rule-governed, we understand in terms of a concept supplied by reason. That is how it is intelligible to us. Hence we tend to place the cause of this form—the hexagon in the sand—in a will; a will is supposed as a final cause of the hexagonal form. That the object in this case is conceived as having a purpose is owing to our apprehension of certain formal relationships exemplifying a rule; they are then conceived by us as the effects of the causality of a concept. By Kant's definition, this is simply the purposiveness of an object ("the causality of a concept in respect of its object"). If we go further and actually place the cause of this form (this purposiveness) in a will, we then attribute a purpose to the object. We say that it is the object of a purpose, that it was created on purpose, or, in Kant's terminology, that it is a purpose. But we need not go that far simply to say that the object—its form—is purposive.

No formal presentation of Stage III of the deduction is necessary, since it is really only an elaboration of Stage II in terms of the further details of Kant's theory of cognitive perception. In order for the cognitive faculties to be in harmony, there must be a formal unity of the manifold of intuition. These aspects of Kant's theory of synthesis in cognition have been previously discussed. But, since the judgment of taste is aesthetic and not a conceptual judgment, the unity cannot be the judgment that a definite concept is exemplified. Thus, the formal unity of the manifold that produces the harmony of the cognitive faculties can only be "the subjective purposiveness of the representations in the mind of the intuiting subject" (§ 15.3, Ak. 227, B. 63). The conclusion of Stage III is thus: "[The judgment of taste] simply refers the representation, by which an object is given, to the subject, and brings to our notice no characteristic of the object, but only the purposive form in the determination of the representative powers which are occupying themselves therewith" (§ 15.4, Ak. 228, B. 64–65).[3] In other words, if judgments of taste are to be legitimate, they must be based on the formal purposiveness (designedness, rule-governedness) of the object, without that object actually being judged to have a definite purpose, to be designed, or to be the exemplification of a concept.

The purposiveness of form (or formal purposiveness) at the basis of the judgment of taste Kant claims is *subjective*. If it were objective, it could "only be cognized by means of the reference of the manifold to a definite purpose, and therefore only through a concept" (§15.1, Ak. 226, B. 62), whereas the judgment of taste is aesthetic and thus cannot be based on a concept. "In order to represent objective purposiveness in a thing, the concept of *what sort of thing it is to be* must come first" (§ 15.3, Ak. 227, B. 63). In approaching an object aesthetically with respect to its beauty either we have no concept available or else we abstract from that concept in aesthetic perception; for in the aesthetic contemplation of an object the cognitive powers (imagination and understanding) must be completely free—they must be engaged in free play. Thus, the purposiveness of form in objects considered as to their beauty is merely subjective, in the sense that it is the purposiveness of an arrangement of

3. Cf. §§ 9.9, 21.1, 35.1, 38.1, 38.1n; Ak. 218–19, 238–39, 286–87, 289–90, 290n; B. 53–54, 75–76, 129, 132, 132n.

the manifold of intuition by the intuiting subject through the joint efforts of the imagination and understanding: we are able to see the formal characteristics of the object as being purposive. Since Kant believes that "the purposiveness of a thing, so far as it is represented in perception, is no characteristic of the object itself (for such cannot be perceived)" Intro. VII.2, Ak. 189, B. 26), it follows that the judgment of taste "brings to our notice no characteristic of the object, but only the purposive form" (§ 15.4, Ak. 228, B. 64). Stage III thus specifies further what is meant by Stage II: to say that the cognitive powers are in harmony but in free play is to say that the object's formal properties can be related in a purposive way, suitable for the application of a concept even though no concept is available or is being held up to judge the unity at this time.

Stage III of Kant's deduction is crucial for Kant's aesthetic theory, for it is the point at which the subjective experience of the appreciator is linked to qualities in the object of appreciation. Many of the details of Kant's philosophy of art, for example, his analysis of the nature and importance of the various arts, are derivable from this stage of the deduction, as will be shown subsequently. The judging of the object, demonstrated in Stage I of the deduction to be the key to the critique of taste and the basis for the pleasure in the beautiful, has been shown in Stage III to be the contemplation or reflection on the object with respect to the purposiveness of its formal qualities. In the following sections of this chapter, I shall attempt to show how Kant gives substance to his aesthetic theory as so far developed.

Stage III of the deduction is also the place to see the unique twist Kant has given to aesthetic theory. As noted earlier, the most general question of eighteenth century aesthetic theory was what qualities in objects occasion that particular pleasure or satisfaction we refer to as Beauty. Kant attempts to bridge the subjective-objective dichotomy in aesthetic theory in this way; he argues that the pleasure in the beautiful must be based on formal qualities of objects, thus maintaining an objective basis for judgments of taste; but at the same time he insists that the pleasure is based merely on the way in which we (through our cognitive powers) feel that those qualities are purposively related, thus maintaining a subjective basis for the experience of beauty.

5.2 Form, Content, and the Experience of the Beautiful

The Form-Content Distinction

The concepts of *form* and *content* (or matter) play a central role in Kant's theory of knowledge. H. J. Paton goes so far as to say that "the whole *Kritik of Pure Reason* may be described as an analysis of our experience into its formal and material elements."[4] Indeed, Kant's extensive use of the distinction tends to cause considerable difficulty, since he applies the distinction at several different levels in his analysis of experience and judgment; consequently, the material element of one application of the distinction may itself at another level of application be analyzed into its formal and material elements. For example, at the level of a given cognition or experience, the formal element consists of categories and concepts and the material element consists of the intuitions (particular awarenesses) given through the faculty of sensibility. But any one of these intuitions can itself be analyzed into formal and material components. Thus, what is said to be the formal or material element depends upon the level of application of the form-content distinction.

What follows is a summary of the various levels at which Kant applies the form-matter or form-content distinction in the *Critique of Pure Reason*.

(1) The form-matter distinction may be applied to judgments—the thinking of a particular as being subsumed under a universal or concept. The form of a judgment is what Kant calls its "logical form," by which he means the relation given by a copula (whatever in a given case links a subject and a predicate) to the two elements it connects—intuitions or concepts. The table of categories (A80=B106) gives the logical form that judgments can take. At this level of application, the matter or content of judgments is the experiential content underlying the judgment, the meaning of the judgment. This is the highest level at which Kant applies the form-content distinction. (A266=B322.)[5]

(2) As applied to a given cognition or experience—the content of judgments generally—the form is the activity of the understanding, the categories and concepts. The matter or content of a particular experience is the activity, or receptive product, of the faculty of sensibility— the intuitions given through it. (A51=B75, A86=B118.)

(3) Intuitions—which are the matter or content of particular experiences—may themselves be analyzed into form and matter. The formal component of intuition consists of the spatial and temporal relations which unify the matter of sensibility, consisting of particular sensations or *sensa*. (A20=B34, A42=B59, A223=B270, A723=B751.)

(4) Finally, sensations may be analyzed into matter and form: the

4. H. J. Paton, *Kant's Metaphysics of Experience*, 2 vols. (London: Allen & Unwin, 1951), 1:138.
5. Cf. §§ 35.1, 38.1; Ak. 287, 290; B. 128–29, 132.

matter of a sensation is its peculiar quality, while its form is its degree of intensity or magnitude. (A166–76=B207–18.)

In each of these four applications of the form-matter distinction, the matter or content consists of certain elements and the form is the manner in which, or the structure in terms of which, these elements are related to one another. "In every being *[Wesen]* the constituent elements of it *(essentialia)* are the matter, the mode in which they are combined in one thing the essential form" (A266=B322). In the various passages cited above, Kant repeatedly speaks of the form as ordering the matter, relating the elements in such a way as to give them a unity.

How, then, does this distinction, as elaborated in the *Critique of Pure Reason,* apply to the experience of the beautiful? Kant's position seems to be the following: In looking at, or listening to, something in an attempt to discover whether it is beautiful, what we (ought to) do is to reflect on or contemplate—somehow judge—the way in which the various sensations or *sensa* (sights, sounds) we have are, or can be, ordered or related into a purposive whole. "To *reflect [reflektieren]* (or to deliberate *[überlegen]*) is to compare and combine given representations either with other representations or with one's cognitive powers, with respect to a concept which is thereby made possible" (First Intro. V.1, Ak. 211, H. 16). The activity of experiencing art must be thought of as analogous to the exercise of the faculty of judgment in cognitive experience: the attempt is made on the part of the appreciator to organize (structure, order, relate) the manifold of intuitions into a meaningful unity, a formal purposiveness. This was the general conclusion of Stage III of the deduction. The following more detailed questions now arise: (a) Why does Kant consider the form (the relationships between, or structure of, the elements) to be so important? (b) Does the form of the intuitions we are supposed to consider in judging something aesthetically consist merely in their spatial and temporal relations? (c) What, in Kant's view, is the aesthetic relevance of nonformal qualities of the object of experience? In other words, what part, if any, do the sense elements play in the experience of the beautiful? Answers to these questions require more careful consideration of Kant's employment of the concept of form in the *Critique of Judgment.*

Form as Figure and Composition

"In painting, sculpture, and in all the formative arts ... the *delineation [Zeichnung]* is the essential thing; and here it is not what gratifies in sensation but what pleases by means of its form *[Form]* that is fundamental for taste" (§ 14.7, Ak. 225, B. 61). The word *"Zeichnung"* is used to refer to a drawing, sketch, or design in the sense of a presentation of figures or shapes by means of lines (rather than by color masses or planes). In other discussions of form, Kant speaks explicitly of figure and shape (which he seems to use interchangeably) as being what we are to contemplate or judge in the experience of the beautiful.[6] When he speaks of the beautiful forms in nature, Kant gives examples of regarding, and taking an immediate interest in, the beautiful *figure (Gestalt)* of wild flowers, birds, insects (§ 42.3, Ak. 299, B. 141). Kant's language and examples indicate that, in visual experience at least, by "form" he means "figure" or "shape." In such cases Kant analyzes form as the spatial relations of a given sensuous content.

The contrast Kant draws between the beautiful and the sublime also indicates that for Kant form in the visual aesthetic experience is identified with figure or shape. The sublime is characterized by its *formlessness*—the absence of definite perceivable boundaries or spatial or temporal limitations. A typical example of the experience of the sublime is our response to the infinite vastness of the ocean or of the heavens. "The beautiful in nature has to do with the form of the object, which consists in the boundary *[Begrenzung]*. The sublime, on the other hand, is to be found in a formless *[formlosen]* object, insofar as in it or by occasion of it *boundlessness [Unbegrenztheit]* is represented, and yet its totality is also present to thought" (§ 23.2, Ak. 244, my translation, cf. B. 82). The formlessness of the sublime is thus equated with being devoid of figure, having no boundary or limit (*ungestalt,* § 30.2, Ak. 279, B. 121), at least so far as our limited human perception of it is concerned. The sublime is considered formless because we cannot unify its elements spatially or temporally in sense intuition. When we gaze upon the starry heavens, for example, it is not that there are no spatial relations or that they have no unity, but rather that we have no sensible standards to fully apprehend them—they are of such a magnitude that we are immediately led beyond them to an idea which has no counterpart in our sense experience. We cannot unify the given sense content in intuition even though our intellect (reason) does comprehend a totality, that is, forms an idea of the spatially infinite (§ 25.7, 26.8; Ak. 250, 254; B. 88–89, 93). For this reason Kant claims that in the experience of the sublime the imagination and reason are in conflict (§§ 27.3, 29. G.R. 5; Ak. 258, 267; B. 97, 107), and the experience of the sublime thus involves a feeling of displeasure or pain *(Unlust)* brought about by the awareness of our incapacity to attain a sensible realization of an idea (§ 27). The things we call sublime

---

6. Figure [*Figur*]: § 17.7n, Ak. 235n, B. 73n. Shape [*Gestalt*]: §§ 14.8, 17.7n, 22. G.R. 2–3. 30.1, 42.3; Ak. 225, 232n, 241, 241–42, 279, 299; B. 61, 73n, 78–79, 120, 141.

do not have definite spatial relations (shape, figure) because they are ideas (for example, the vastness of the ocean, the magnitude of the heavens), and ideas, according to Kant, are never fully met with in intuition (sense experience). For this reason Kant says that "true sublimity must be sought only in the mind of the judging subject, not in the natural object" (§ 26.12, Ak. 251, my translation, cf. B. 95). Hence, one should not conclude that Kant believes some objects of (visual) intuition have form while others do not; the ocean is an object of sense experience, but its vastness is not. We are led to the idea of the vastness of the ocean (and thereby to the experience of the sublime) since in our perception it appears formless—it lacks definite figure or boundaries.

What about temporal relations? Traditionally, the arts have been divided into the temporal and the nontemporal. The nontemporal are the plastic arts (sculpture, ceramics), painting, drawing, and architecture; the temporal arts consist of drama, music, poetry, and other literary forms, the dance, and the film. Kant analyzes music as a purely temporal art form—the composition of sensations (tones) in time.[7] The dance he recognizes as more complex: its time-related elements are not mere sensations but human figures, and the dance thus involves spatial as well as temporal relations (§ 52.1, Ak. 325, B. 170). Kant's analysis of form in terms of spatial and temporal relations is clearly summarized in the following passage:

Every form of the objects of sense (both of external sense [space] and mediately of internal [time]) is either *figure* [*Gestalt*] or *play* [*Spiel*]. In the latter case it is either play of figures (in space, viz. pantomime and dancing) or the mere play of sensations (in time). The charm [*Reiz*] of colors or of the pleasant tones of an instrument may be added, but the *delineation* [*Zeichnung*] in the first case and the composition [*Komposition*] in the second constitute the proper object of the pure judgment of taste. (§ 14.8, Ak. 225, B. 61)

Thus, for Kant, form consists of the spatial and temporal organization of elements: figure, shape, or delineation in the one case, composition in the other. In the parts of the *Critique of Judgment* in which form is emphasized as the essential aspect of beauty, Kant is consistently a pure formalist, in the sense that every nonformal feature of an object is completely irrelevant to its beauty and is usually, as we shall see, also a positive distraction and interferes with the aesthetic experience of beauty.

7. §§ 14.8, 51.10, 53.2–4; Ak. 225, 324–25, 328–30, 331; B. 61, 168–69, 172–74, 176.

5.3 The Epistemological Basis for Kant's Aesthetic Formalism

Space and Time as the (Pure) Forms of Intuition

As noted in chapter 4, section 2, Kant holds that for human beings *intuitions* (the apprehension and awareness of objects of experience) are based upon *sensibility* (the capacity to receive sensations or impressions). Only through sensation, or what is ultimately based upon sensation, can we be affected by objects and gain knowledge of their existence and nature. We can think about objects through our powers of understanding, and we can imagine objects through our powers of imagination, but these are always objects of potential sensible awareness. In his *Critique of Pure Reason,* Kant argues that there is no means by which human powers of reason alone can gain knowledge of objects. The legitimate use of pure reason is restricted to deriving knowledge of the conditions necessary for human experience and knowledge in general. One of Kant's most famous and influential conclusions on this score is the status of space and time. He argues that all objects of experience whatsoever necessarily exist and are presented to us within a temporal framework, and all objects of experience external to us necessarily exist and are presented to us within a spatial framework. Space and time are thus said to be the pure forms of intuition; they are the forms in which intuitions necessarily are given to us.

Kant believes that by a process of thought (namely, analysis) we can distinguish the formal and material components of our intuition of objects. His method in the "Transcendental Aesthetic" of the *Critique of Pure Reason* is to "isolate" the components of intuition:

In the transcendental aesthetic we shall, therefore, first *isolate* sensibility, by taking away from it everything which the understanding thinks through its concepts [substance, force, divisibility, etc.] so that nothing may remain save empirical intuition. Secondly, we shall also separate off from it everything which belongs to sensation [impenetrability, hardness, color, etc.], so that nothing may remain save pure intuition and the mere form of appearances, which is all that sensibility can supply *a priori*. In the course of this investigation it will be found that there are two pure forms of sensible intuition, serving as principles of *a priori* knowledge, namely, space and time. (A22=B36)

This isolation of the matter of intuitions (that is, sensations) and the form of intuitions (that is, space and time) can only be done in thought, since what we experience is *presented in* space and time. Space and time are conditions of sense-experience. Space is "the form of all appearances of the external world, that is, the subjective conditions of sensibility, under which alone external intuition is possible for us (a26=b42), while time is the a priori and the immediate condition of inner appearances and hence the mediate condition of outer appearances. "Just as I can say *a priori* that all outer appearances are in space, and are determined *a priori* in conformity with the relations of space, I can also say, from the principle of inner sense, that all appearances whatsoever, that is, all objects of the senses, are in time, and necessarily stand in time relations" (a34=b51). Sensations, modifications of our state, necessarily occur in time related to past and present inner states of consciousness; since our intuitions and hence our knowledge of things in the world of phenomena are dependent upon sensibility (our capacity to be affected by objects in terms of sensations), time is also a condition of outer experience.

The a priori character of space and time in part determines the kinds of qualities relevant to the judgment of taste, if that judgment is to lay claim to universal validity and hence be a pure judgment of taste. The manner in which this determination takes place may be seen by examining the modified version of the primary-secondary quality distinction which Kant held.

Primary and Secondary Qualities

Since the primary-secondary quality distinction is not usually associated with Kant, it may be helpful to compare his views with the traditional Lockean presentation of the distinction and arguments advanced in support of it.

Locke characterizes the primary-secondary quality distinction in two ways; his dual characterization involves him in two separate claims:

(1) *Inseparability.* Primary qualities (solidity, bulk, extension, position, figure, mobility, and number) are "utterly inseparable from the body in what estate soever it be; such as, in all the alterations and changes it suffers, all the force can be used upon it, it constantly keeps."[8] Locke must mean that certain determinable (but not determinate) qualities are necessary for anything to be a body; as long as a body remains in existence, in whatever form it may take, it possesses some determinate quality or other of each of the primary qualities. The "inseparability" Locke refers to must, therefore, be a logical or conceptual inseparability: our concept of a body necessarily involves the concepts of extension, mobility, and so forth. Locke is claiming that the so-called primary qualities are the defining qualities of bodies or material objects, that, for example, some determinate position or other is inseparable from any

---

8. John Locke, *An Essay concerning Human Understanding,* bk. 2, chap. 8, sec. 9.

given candle. Secondary qualities are then by implication separable from a body, in the sense that we can imagine a body without color, taste, smell, heat, cold. Given the above interpretation of Locke's inseparability criterion, he must claim that it is possible (conceptually) for something to be a body or material object without possessing any secondary qualities.

(2) *Resemblance.* Our ideas of primary qualities are said to be resemblances of the qualities of external bodies themselves, while our ideas of secondary qualities (colors, sounds, tastes, smells, heat, and light) do not in any way resemble the qualities of external bodies themselves. Locke holds that what causes our ideas of primary qualities are the primary qualities of bodies (extensional, finite particles in space-time), while it would be a mistake to suppose, in an exactly similar way, that what causes our ideas of secondary qualities are the secondary qualities of bodies. Secondary qualities are nothing more than the powers of certain arrangements and propensities of primary qualities to affect us in certain ways. "There is nothing like our idea [of any secondary quality] existing in the bodies themselves."[9] In the context of this claim Locke produces examples of (a) variations in our ideas of secondary qualities where the primary qualities of the object have undergone no change, and (b) changes effected in secondary qualities by modification of primary qualities (such as pounding an almond, where by changing its texture we produce changes in both its color and taste). One looks in vain through Locke's writings for specific support for the resemblance thesis.[10] Indeed, it is not clear that he ever attempts to prove it. Rather, it seems to be an assumption Locke thought the great scientific achievements of his day justified. He subscribed to Boyle's modification of Descartes's corpuscularism: all sensation is produced by motions, which are transmitted by impulse.[11] Hence, our ideas of qualities capable of or involved in such transmission resemble their causes.

In the *Prolegomena*, Kant criticizes Locke for assuming we can know the nature of objects completely external to ourselves, things-in-themselves.[12] Thus, insofar as primary qualities are said to be qualities of things-in-themselves while secondary qualities are not, Kant rejects the distinction made by Locke. Where Locke proposed a two-fold distinction between things as they appear and things-in-themselves, Kant proposes a three-fold distinction between (a) things-in-themselves,

9. Locke, *Essay*, bk. 2, chap. 8, sec. 15.
10. See E. M. Curley, "Locke, Boyle, and the Distinction between Primary and Secondary Qualities," *Philosophical Review* 81 (1972):438–64.
11. Locke, *Essay*, bk. 4, chap. 2, sec. 11.
12. Kant, *Prolegomena* § 13, Remark II; Ak. 4:289; Beck 36–37.

(b) the qualities of things-as-they-appear, and (c) the qualities we attribute to things-as-they-appear, even though these qualities are merely modifications of our individual sense organs.[13] The natures of things-in-themselves are in no way knowable to us. The qualities of things-as-they-appear are common to all who experience them; they do not depend upon the individuality of our sense organs although they do depend upon the constitution of the human mind and its faculties of cognition; thus, they are not properties of things-in-themselves. These qualities are the forms of intuition, namely, their spatial and temporal relations. The third classification, the qualities we attribute to things-as-they-appear even though these qualities are merely modifications of our individual sense organs, consists of the *matter of intuitions*—what corresponds to the particular sensations of color, taste, sound, smell, heat, and cold (A20). In other words, the primary-secondary quality distinction, as modified by Kant, is a distinction not between things as they really are and things as they appear, but a distinction within the realm of appearance, the phenomenal world. In summary, Kant's position is that "all the properties which constitute the intuition of a body belong merely to its appearance."[14]

Kant retains two of Locke's considerations in support of the distinction between primary and secondary qualities:

(1) *Inseparability of primary qualities.* In abstracting the merely empirical features from our concept of body, figure and extension still remain (B5–6, A20–1=B35), as do motion (alteration of place) and rest, the latter two possible only through the representation of time (A32=B48–49).

(2) *Variability of secondary qualities.* The other qualities, such as color, tone, touch, taste, smell, heat, and cold, must be regarded as mere changes in experiencing subjects, because they appear differently to different individuals; they are relative to "a particular standpoint or to a peculiarity of structure in this or that sense" (A45=B62; cf. A29–30= B45, A46=B63).

Given Kant's historical position after the severe criticisms of the primary-secondary quality distinction by both Berkeley and Hume, one might be surprised that Kant maintained the distinction even in this modified form. Kant's distinction between primary and secondary qualities parallels his distinction between the form and matter of intuitions,

---

13. Kant completely ignores Locke's notion of substance, the something-I-know-not-what, and thus fails to consider whether it corresponds to his notion of things-in-themselves.

14. Kant, *Prolegomena* § 13, Remark II; Ak. 4:289; Beck 36–37.

between objective and subjective sensations. Kant analyzes the primary qualities into relations of a spatial or temporal character, the forms of intuition, which he takes to be the necessary manner in which bodies appear to us. Hence, Kant claims that "All bodies are extended" is an analytic judgment, while "All bodies are heavy" as a synthetic judgment (A7=B11).

Secondary Qualities and Communication

In holding his modified form of the primary-secondary quality distinction, Kant commits himself to the view that colors, tastes, smells, and tones, while modifications of the state of the experiencing subject, always remain subjective in that they cannot themselves yield knowledge of (phenomenal) objects. Although we attribute secondary qualities to objects, these qualities really "belong to the subjective constitution of our manner in sensibility" (B44). Colors, tastes, tones, "cannot rightly be regarded as properties of things, but only as changes in the subject, changes which may indeed, be different for different men"; for example, "a rose . . . in respect of its color, can appear differently to every observer" (A29–30=B45).

Communication and, hence, empirical knowledge are dependent, in Kant's view, on the forms of our experience, that is, on the relations between sensations. In fact, according to Kant, concepts govern how sensations, as vehicles of intuition, can be related and ordered. The criteria, in terms of which the particular orderings are accomplished, are (constitutive of objects) and hence the same for each individual. Not only the pleasure we take in a given sensation, but also the matter or content of intuitions, is private and incommunicable.

[A sensation's] specific quality may be represented as universally communicable in a uniform way, if we assume that each person has a similar sense to our own. But this cannot be presupposed at all of any single sensation. To a man who is deficient in the sense of smell, this kind of sensation cannot be communicated; and even if he is not deficient in it we cannot be certain that he gets exactly the same sensation from a flower that we get. But additionally we must represent men as differing in respect of the *pleasantness* [*Annehmlichkeit*] or *unpleasantness* involved in the sensation from the same object of sense, and it cannot possible be required that every man should take pleasure in the same objects. (§ 39.1, Ak. 291, my translation, cf. B. 133–34)

On the other hand, the relations or orderings of appearances in space and time are alleged to be objective because they are conditions for experience in general—they are the a priori forms of intuition.

Difficulties arise. Even if one were to agree with Kant's doctrine that space and time are the necessary forms of appearances, it is a further and stronger claim to say that any particular set of spatial or temporal relations (that is, a set of determinate relations) is *objective* in any way that colors, tones, tastes and smells are not. Kant's general position is that any appearance must have *some* spatial and temporal properties, not that any given appearance has determinate spatial and temporal properties which can be ascertained a priori. Hence, even if it can be said that spatial and temporal properties (as opposed to colors, tones, and the like) are really possessed by empirical objects, there is still the problem of determining whether a given spatial relation is true of the given object. The fact that space and time are the a priori forms of intuition does not show that determinate spatial and temporal properties are any more communicable than the secondary qualities. Kant attempts to avoid this difficulty through his analysis of concepts as rules for the unification or ordering of appearances spatially and temporally. He carries over this attempted solution to aesthetics by maintaining that when we find an object beautiful we have discovered a purposive relationship among its forms—a "rule-governedness" has been observed, as if a concept were to apply to the manifold.

The form-matter distinction and the primary-secondary quality distinction thus provide an epistemological basis for Kant's analysis of the experience of the beautiful and of pure judgments of taste. The pure judgment of taste must be based on the reflection and contemplation of the spatial and temporal relations of sensations, for in no other way can the claim to universal validity be justified. But, as shown above, the communicability of determinate spatial and temporal relations is not insured by the epistemological basis. Kant must appeal to the ordering of specific sensations by means of concepts to provide a basis for specific cases of empirical knowledge. The difficulty is that Kant claims that concepts are not relevant to looking at or listening to something aesthetically. Thus, to claim a similar objectivity in aesthetics Kant must maintain that, in the experience of the beautiful, spatial and temporal properties are related in a lawlike way. He does this by means of his doctrine of "conformity to law without a law" (§ 22. G.R. 1, Ak. 241, B. 78) or "purposiveness without a purpose" (§§ 10–12, Ak. 219–22, B. 54–58). Experienced qualities are related, ordered, unified, as if the whole were designed for a determinate purpose; but either we cannot say what this purpose is, or we prevent ourselves (through abstracting the formal relations from the purpose) from thinking what it is.

5.4 Secondary Qualities in the Experience of the Beautiful

Stages II and III of the deduction of judgments of taste both may be considered attempts to point out how the process of cognition in general underlies the judging of the object on which the pleasure in the beautiful is based. The manner in which Kant's theory of knowledge partially determines Kant's aesthetic theory has been shown above to be explicable in terms of the form-matter and the primary-secondary quality distinctions. The role of the primary (formal) qualities in Kant's theory is clear, but the precise role of the secondary qualities (the matter)—or indeed whether they even have a role in the process of judging an object aesthetically—is not so clear. What role does the matter of intuition—the particular (secondary) qualities of color, taste, sound, and smell—play in this experience?

Kant continually emphasizes the subjective character of these qualities or sensations and what appears to him to be their intrinsic sensuous appeal (charm). "A smell which one man enjoys gives another a headache" (§ 32.2, Ak. 282, B. 123). "To one, violet color is soft and lovely; to another, it is washed out and dead. One man likes the tone of wind instruments, another that of strings" (§ 7.1, Ak. 212, B. 47). The very fact that colors and tones are themselves pleasing or displeasing, he believes, often results in their detracting from attempts to contemplate the form of an object. They may lure someone whose taste is crude and untrained to consider a work of art he might otherwise ignore, but "they actually impair the judgment of taste if they draw attention to themselves as the grounds for the judgment of beauty" (§ 14.6, Ak. 225, my translation, cf. B. 61).

In his discussion of the visual arts, Kant speaks of the aesthetic importance of drawing or delineation and figure or shape without reference to colors. He speaks of the colors being added to the drawing but not contributing to the beauty of the work: "The colors which light up the sketch belong to the charm; they may indeed enliven the object for sensation, but they cannot make it worthy of contemplation and beautiful" (§ 14.7, Ak. 225, B. 61). Kant also rules out the aesthetic relevance of color to the arts of painting and landscape gardening; he remarks that insofar as landscape gardening is a "free beauty" (that is, presupposes no concept of what its object ought to be) it "involves merely the free play of the imagination in contemplation," being thus like "mere aesthetical painting, which has no definite theme (which arranges sky, land, and water so as to entertain us *by means of light and shade only*)" (§ 51.9n, Ak. 323n, B. 167n; italics added).

On other occasions, however, Kant admits that colors and tones may make a positive contribution to the aesthetic value of the art object. But they do so not because of their own nature or any (aesthetic) pleasure we may take in them, but only insofar as "they make the form more exactly, definitely, and completely intuitible, and besides, by their charm awaken and fix our attention on the object itself" (§ 14.8, Ak. 225–26, B. 61). Kant's mention of the "the object itself" in this context confirms the preceding analysis of the importance of Kant's epistemologically grounded form-matter and primary-secondary quality distinctions for his views on aesthetic experience and judgment. The phenomenal "object itself" (not to be confused with the thing-in-itself) is given by form (relations of primary qualities) alone (B66–67).

Kant consistently maintains that mere sensations neither add nor contribute to the beauty of a thing; any pleasure resulting only from sensation (of color, tone, taste, smell, or touch) is not a legitimate basis for judging something to be beautiful. Kant is not altogether clear, however, on whether the experiences of colors and tones are mere sensations, and thus he is ambiguous on the issue of whether the pleasure we take in them is relevant to the beauty of the object being considered.

Forms can be beautiful. But can colors or tones be beautiful? On at least two occasions, Kant answers this question in the negative, using the following argument: If colors or tones are pleasing to us, *and if* colors and tones are simple sensations (that is, not formal determinations of a manifold of sensations), then colors and tones cannot be beautiful *in themselves;* for if they are simple sensations they would merely be pleasant to sense, and such pleasure, unlike the pleasure in the beautiful, can have only private validity. On the assumption, then, that music and the art of color are the play of pleasant sensations, Kant concludes that, strictly speaking, they are not beautiful arts (§§ 14.3–5, 51.10; Ak. 224, 324–25; B. 59–60, 168–69).

But on another occasion Kants answers the question in the affirmative, presenting the opposing view that colors and tones may themselves be beautiful. On the assumption that colors and tones are isochronous vibrations of the ether and air, and on the assumption that the mind not only perceives by sense their effect in exciting the appropriate sense organ but also perceives by reflection the regular play of impressions (that is, the vibrations themselves), then insofar as given colors or tones are pure (that is, have no admixture of any foreign sensation) they can be beautiful. In support of the assumptions of this second argument, Kant remarks (a) that there is a "mathematical [element] which enables us to pronounce on the proportion between these oscillations in music and thus to judge of them; and by analogy with which we easily may judge of the distinctions between colors" (§ 51.10, Ak. 324–25; B. 169); and (b) that there are people who have excellent vision or hearing but cannot distinguish particular colors or tones. Kant recognizes that this argument rests on two assumptions: the first a physical one concerning the nature of colors and sounds (apparently advanced by Leonhard Euler [1707–1783]); the second a psychological one concerning the nature of our sense awareness. On the initial assumptions of this second argument, Kant concludes that music and the art of color are the beautiful play of sensations, not merely the play of pleasant sensations.

In spite of their differing conclusions, these two arguments have a common assumption: for an object of experience to be beautiful it must possess form, and to have form, it must have two or more elements related in some spatial or temporal manner. On the assumption that colors and tones are simple sensations which we find pleasant or unpleasant—a view apparently held by Kant through the first two editions of the *Critique of Judgment*—colors or tones cannot be beautiful because they are mere elements (matter) with no internally perceptible (Kant says "intelligible") relations of parts. But on the second assumption—that of Euler, and apparently that held by Kant in the third edition (1799)—they are isochronous vibrations of the ether and air, and hence they can be beautiful because we can reflect on their inner relations—their form.

In his two most extensive discussions of the arts of color and tone (§§14, 51; Ak. 223–26, 320–25; B. 59–62, 164–69), Kant seems to overlook the fact that both music and the art of color are based on the composition of a variety of tones and colors, respectively, and that for the composition to be beautiful on the basis of its form the elements themselves need be neither beautiful nor not beautiful. That is, even if Kant's first argument is granted, it only shows that a single color or tone cannot be beautiful; it does not show that a composition of tones or colors cannot be beautiful. And even if the epistemological basis of Kant's formalism is accepted, there is no reason why the play of pleasant sensations (such as tones) cannot be beautiful on Kant's own terms because of the formal characteristics (namely, "purposiveness without a purpose") of their play (in time).

This misconception of the requirements of his own theory seems to underlie Kant's views on music, which he relegates to a low position among the various arts because of its overwhelming sensuous appeal. He casts aspersions on music as a significant art medium since it "merely plays with sensations" (§ 53.4, Ak. 329, B. 174). The same misconception interferes with his analysis of the art of painting, insofar as he fails to allow a gradation or contrast of colors to be aesthetically significant (§ 14.8, Ak. 225–26, B. 61), even though he grants that sensations have form in their degree of intensity or qualitative magnitude (A166–76= B207–18). However, one must be cautious in criticism on this point, since sometimes Kant does seem to hold a position more consistent with his theory, as when he says that form is either figure or play and then analyzes play as either play of figures or play of sensations (§ 14.7, Ak. 225, B. 61). And in § 53.2 (Ak. 329, B. 173) he says that, insofar as the art of tone can be brought under mathematical rules (relations), there is form in music. But even here he feels that these mathematical rules must relate to the vibrations themselves, a position which seems to make the psychological assumption mentioned above a condition for the art of music.

In summary, there are two major difficulties in Kant's form-matter distinction as he applies it to the various arts. Firstly, he too readily (but understandably, given his epistemological assumptions) identifies form with geometrical figure or mathematical proportion; he thinks form must be susceptible to measurement in order to be objective and provide a foundation for universal communicability. Secondly, he seems to think that the sensations themselves are irrelevant, whereas by his own characterization of the form-matter distinction the two are inseparable in experience. By opting for the abstraction of form in thought or reflection, Kant fails to recognize that the character of a composition or a visual representation is determined by the sense qualities as they are related, not by the relations alone. What is left of the form without that which is formed? Kant seems to think that figure or shape is left, but in his own analysis of these as relations there must be some content in terms of which figure, shape, and composition are presented. In the *Critique of Pure Reason*, Kant does speak of space and time as being pure objects of intuition (as well as the a priori forms that intuitions take), but in that context he is not speaking of determinate spatial and temporal relations. And in the experience of an object of beauty, such as a painting, what counts are the determinate relations, not spatial relatedness in general.

Perhaps an example will serve to make Kant's theory and these criticisms simultaneously clear. There are innumerable Pietà paintings in which the total effect of the work is partially the result of an intense contrast between the deathly pale white of the body of Christ and the warm browns of the earth below him. Apart from Kant's view on primary versus secondary qualities, which is a view independent of the form-content distinction, there is nothing in Kant's theory of formal purposiveness as the basis of the judgment of taste that is inconsistent with considering the contrast of these two colors a formal feature of the painting. Thus, Kant's exclusion of the so-called secondary qualities from the realm of the aesthetic is based partly on a hasty application of the form-content distinction, but mostly on an independent view concerning the inferior epistemological status of secondary qualities.

5.5   Formal Purposiveness and Representation in Art
The Aesthetic Surface and Representational Elements

Form is often opposed to content in the sense of representational content or subject matter. Considering that the pure judgment of taste must be based on mere formal purposiveness and not in any way on concepts, one is easily led to an interpretation of Kant's aesthetic theory in which form is opposed to representational or conceptualized subject matter. The issue involves the manner in which the form-content distinction is applied by Kant to what we may call representational art in the broadest sense—any art form or genre or individual work in which we are led through a perception or consideration of the elements of the work to respond to more than the mere sensual qualities of the work in their determinate relations. When we experience representational art, we are led to respond to what determinate sense qualities (surface qualities of tones, lines, shapes, surfaces, figures) in determinate relations represent, symbolize, suggest, or communicate. Sometimes this representation occurs naturally, as when the surface qualities are organized so that they are seen as images; at other times the deeper level of experience is achieved conventionally, such as through the organization of the surface qualities into symbols. Into the latter division of the arts fall, for example, the plastic arts, painting, and drawing (insofar as they specifically include themes or subject matter); prose, poetry, drama, and the theater; and music when combined with words or a program.

All works of art, with the possible exception of so-called conceptual art, are presented in a sensuous, public medium, and thus may be said to have surface qualities; in a given work, we can regard the sum total of surface qualities as its "aesthetic surface."[15] The artist may be looked upon as a director modifying the perceptual elements on which our experiences are based. The artist makes decisions in terms of which he organizes or instructs others to organize a public medium—an aesthetic surface; when we experience an object as a work of art, we let this public medium control our experience. Kant insists that to judge an object with respect to its beauty one must judge it freely, and that means that with respect to the aesthetic surface one does not approach the work with any prior decision as to what elements are important. The organization of the aesthetic surface is judged entirely by how one is able to see it at the time, not as the result of previously acquired concepts or presuppositions (about what is charming, perfect, and so forth). What is important in

15. The locution, "aesthetic surface," originates, I believe, with D. W. Prall in *Aesthetic Judgment* (New York: Crowell, 1929).

treating an object aesthetically is simply how it appears to one in the act of judging it (contemplating, reflecting upon it). According to Kant's theory, as we have seen, in judging the beautiful one contemplates the formal purposiveness of the qualities of the object as they appear to one. Kant's analysis is fairly easily interpreted with respect to the aesthetic surface, for it is here that a pure formalism is most easily understood. Prior to the presentation of Stage V of the deduction—beauty as the symbol of morality—one would say that in Kant's theory the significance of any beautiful object whose elements are exhausted by the aesthetic surface is equivalent to the formal purposiveness of those surface elements and their formal relations.

But for purposes of analysis, two distinct levels of experience can be described. A painting may present us with various lines and surface areas which we see as no more than that (=nonobjective or totally abstract art). But some other painting may present us with a given combination—ordered relationship—of lines and colored planes which relate in such a way that they are seen as a bowl of fruit, a seascape, or a portrait. In such cases we experience objects as represented or depicted, not simply surface qualities as presented. These representational elements, which may be called "depth elements" (as opposed to surface elements), can be experienced when the work's surface elements are seen to be related in a certain way; the aesthetic surface of the work "thickens."[16] The surface-depth level distinction, which is descriptive and not evaluative, may be made in other art media as well. In listening to poetry, for example, we are presented with an aesthetic surface of sounds and silences in a temporal composition; these same elements, however, with the sounds heard as phonemes, may become elements of meaning and hence depth elements. Images, ideas, concepts—depth elements—are achieved through organizations of aesthetic surfaces. Painting without subject matter, sounds without meaning, moving forms in abstract patterns, are all examples of art forms whose aesthetic totality is wholly constituted by surface qualities and their relations. But subject matter, representation, ideas, images, conceptualized elements —what in the broadest sense goes by the name of "content" in art— comprise a level of experience that is not identical with the mere composition of surface qualities.

In the above distinction, as applied to Kant's theory, depth elements

16. E. F. Kaelin develops this view in a fine example of phenomenological description of surface and depth elements in selected representational, abstract, and completely nonobjective paintings: "The Visibility of Things Seen," in M. Edie, ed., *An Introduction to Phenomenology* (Chicago: Quadrangle Books, 1965); reprinted in E. F. Kaelin, *Art and Existence* (Lewisburg, Pa.: Bucknell Univ. Press, 1970), with color reproductions.

are concepts or the representation of concepts or conceptualized objects. For Kant, to see a colored orange blotch as (a representation of) an orange in a bowl of fruit is to subsume it under a concept, to make a cognitive judgment. Thus, for Kant, any experience of a work of art in which attention is directed to depth elements cannot be an experience leading to a pure judgment of taste, since a judgment dependent upon concepts is not a pure judgment of taste. The crucial question here is complex: Do Kant's strict formalism, his insistence on the non-conceptuality of pure judgments of taste, and his thesis of the necessary free play of the cognitive faculties in the experience of the beautiful, separately or together, require him to exclude all subject matter or representation, any depth elements, from the realm of the proper object of pure formalism of taste? In other words, is Kant's formalism a formalism which confines the aesthetic to the aesthetic surface?

Free and Dependent Beauty

As noted in chapter 2, section 3, Kant's distinction between free and dependent beauty is a consequence of his analysis of pure judgments of taste as based on disinterested pleasure. Kant characterizes "free beauty" (*pulchritudo vaga*) as selfsubsistent beauty: it "presupposes no concept of what the object ought to be" (§ 16.1, Ak. 229, B. 65). "Dependent beauty," on the other hand, is characterized as conditioned beauty: it "does presuppose such a concept and the perfection of the object in accordance therewith," that is, it is "ascribed to objects which come under the concept of a particular purpose" (ibid.). Now that we have explored the reasoning behind Kant's claim that "beauty . . . properly speaking ought merely to be concerned with form" (§ 13.2, Ak. 223, B. 59), the distinction between free and dependent beauty takes on a new significance in his aesthetic theory. It may provide the basis for answering the important question of the nature of Kant's aesthetic formalism.

As examples of free beauties, Kant mentions both natural and artificial (that is, man-made) objects. Flowers, birds such as the parrot, the hummingbird, and the bird of paradise, and seashells can be free beauties, since when we judge them to be beautiful there is, Kant says, "no perfection of any kind, no internal purposiveness" (§ 16.2, Ak. 229, B. 65–66) which is appealed to in making the judgment; they please freely in and of themselves. Kant is suggesting a logical distinction between judging that something (which happens to be a rose) is beautiful and judging that something is a beautiful rose. In the former case, the fact that the object is a rose does not enter into the basis for making the judgment, while in the latter case it does.

Although Kant's discussion of the distinction between free and de-

pendent beauty is very brief, evidently he places considerable importance on it. For example, he remarks on the obvious usefulness of employing the distinction to settle certain disputes in matters of taste, where
the disputing individuals are making different logical types of judgments. The implication is that the nature of their experience is cor-
respondingly different: "By means of this distinction we can settle many
disputes about beauty between judges of taste, by showing that the one
is speaking of free, the other of dependent, beauty—that the first is making a pure, the second an applied, judgment of taste" (§ 16.8, Ak. 231,
B. 67–68). But Kant's comment is easily misunderstood; one is tempted
to restate the point by saying that a judgment of taste must be free in
order to be pure and hence in order to have a basis for universal validity.
This way of putting Kant's view is misleading because, even though they
are not pure judgments of taste, judgments of dependent beauty may
still claim universal validity; since they are conceptual judgments in
disguise, they may claim whatever validity ordinary empirical generalizations may claim. In judgments of dependent beauty, "This is beautiful"
is to be analyzed as an assessment of close approximation to the perfection or ideal of the kind. It should be recalled that freedom from concepts is a necessary but not a sufficient condition for a judgment of taste
to be pure. To be a pure judgment of taste, a judgment that something is
beautiful must be devoid of all appeal to charm, emotion, and sense
pleasure as well.

Kant's examples of free beauties in nature (flowers, birds, seashells)
indicate that the mere presence of a concept or represented object (a
depth element) does not entail that the judgment of an object which
may be subsumed under a concept is necessarily a judgment of dependent beauty. The distinction is not in terms of what is present; the
distinction between free and dependent beauty is one concerning how
the object is judged. A Siamese cat or a conch shell may be judged in
terms of the extent to which it exemplifies the perfection of the species,
or it may be judged simply in terms of its free beauty (formal subjective
purposiveness). In considering free beauty, we are not to consider the
object with regard to whether or to what extent the marks which comprise the criteria of the concept are exemplified in the form before us;
we are to judge the purposiveness of the form itself apart from any
conceptualization. If the distinction is to be interpreted in terms of how
one judges, however, it may seem puzzling that Kant gives general examples of free and dependent beauty according to kinds of objects. But
Kant's notion of abstraction allows the admission of these examples; they
are consistent with the above interpretation that the main point concerns

the kind of attention paid to the object. In the case of a flower, for example, "hardly anyone but a botanist knows what sort of thing a flower ought to be; and even he, though recognizing in the flower the reproductive organ of the plant, pays no regard to this natural purpose if he is passing judgment on the flower by taste" (§ 16.2, Ak. 229, B. 65). Kant consistently singles out the kind of attention for the distinction between free and dependent beauty. Attention to the formal purposiveness is regard for an object's free beauty; attention to the extent to which the object manifests those characteristics that are the criteria for the application of a concept constitutes regard for an object's dependent beauty. Kant does, however, assume throughout that these two kinds of attention are mutually exclusive for any given act of judging the object, and he implies that some objects are more naturally considered as free beauties and others as dependent beauties.

The most far-reaching statement of the extent of dependent beauty occurs in Kant's discussion of the relation of genius to taste in § 48. Genius has been analyzed as the talent for producing beautiful or "fine" art (*schöne Kunst*), and Kant then turns to the distinction between natural and artistic beauty: "A natural beauty is a *beautiful thing;* artificial beauty is a *beautiful representation* of a thing" [*Eine Naturschönheit ist ein* schönes Ding; *die Kunstschönheit ist eine* schöne Vorstellung *von einem Dinge]* (§ 48.3, Ak. 311, B. 154). Then follows the curious argument the conclusion of which seems to be that all artistic beauty is dependent beauty. Kant argues that art always presupposes a purpose in the cause of an object; hence "if the object is given as a product of art and as such is to be declared beautiful, . . . there must be at bottom in the first instance a concept of what the thing is to be" (§ 48.4, Ak. 311, B. 154). Furthermore, "it follows that in judging of artificial beauty [*Kunstschönheit]* the perfection of the thing must be taken into account" (ibid.), whereas there is no question of a purpose or perfection in judging of natural beauty as such. In short, the artist creates a beautiful representation of a conceptualized object; thus, artistic beauty "is properly only the form of the presentation of a concept, by means of which this latter is communicated universally" (§ 48.6, Ak. 312, B. 155).

Nonetheless, Kant seems to hold that the free-dependent beauty distinction is one between kinds of judgment and not between kinds of objects of judgment. The botanist in the example given in § 16.2 (Ak. 229, B. 65) may "pay no regard" to the concept of the object (the reproductive function of the flower). Interpreted in this way, the free-dependent beauty distinction depends upon Kant's notion of *abstraction:* "A judgment of taste, then, in respect of an object with a definite internal purpose, can only be pure if either the person judging has no concept of this purpose or else abstracts [abstrahierte] from it in his judgment" (§ 16.8, Ak. 231, B. 67; and see § 15.3, Ak. 227, B. 63). Kant's remarks here seem to indicate that just as we can abstract from charm and emotion, and *must* so abstract if our judgment of taste is to be pure (§§ 14.5, 40.2; Ak. 224, 294; B. 60, 136), so we can abstract from any concept of a purpose determining the form of what we are considering. Thus to judge a church, palace, arsenal, or summerhouse as a beautiful church, palace, arsenal, or summerhouse is always an impure judgment of taste, a judgment of dependent beauty (§ 16.4, Ak. 230, B. 66). But this does not exclude the possibility that the same object on some other occasion can be considered as a free beauty and the judgment on it a pure judgment of taste; to do so we must consider it not as a church, for example, but simply as a sensuous manifold in terms of the purposiveness of its form.

If the above line of reasoning is correct, Kant's distinction does not seem to be equivalent to that drawn earlier between (1) works of art or natural objects wholly constituted by surface qualities and relations and (2) works of art or natural objects whose qualities also include depth or representational elements. Firstly, a judgment of the beauty of an object which possesses depth or representational elements does not entail that it is a judgment of dependent beauty, in Kant's terms. The distinction is in terms of what one considers rather than in terms of the kind of object being contemplated. Secondly, a judgment of dependent beauty is a judgment in terms of a concept of what the object ought to be; it is thus a judgment in terms of actual purposes ("this is a beautiful knife") or in terms of the idea or the perfection of a species or kind ("this is a beautiful Boston bull"). Kant's examples of dependent artistic beauty do not cover the spectrum of representational work *generally*, but are confined to those works where the representation is considered as an ideal of a species, as in a sculpture of a human being.

Further examples given by Kant lead to the conclusion that he may not be entirely clear precisely what distinction he is attempting to draw. He says free beauties include delineations à la grecque, all music without words, foliage for borders, wallpapers—things that he says "mean nothing in themselves; they represent nothing—no object under a definite concept—and are free beauties" (§ 16.2, Ak. 229, B. 66). In his analysis of fine art as the beautiful representation of a thing (§ 48.3, Ak. 311, B. 154), Kant implies that to consider an object as a work of (fine) art, that is, as a beautiful representation of a thing, one must always consider it as a purpose—there must be a concept of what the thing is to be at the basis of the representation. But elsewhere what he says implies that not all the arts presuppose a concept in this same sense. When he discusses landscape gardening as akin to painting, he remarks that "it also has no concept of the object and its purpose (as in architecture) conditioning its arrangements, but . . . agrees with mere aesthetical painting, which has no definite theme (which arranges sky, land, and water so as to entertain us by means of light and shade only)" (§ 51.9n, Ak. 323n, B. 167n). In these cases the distinction does seem to be between kinds of works of art or between methods of artistic creation rather than between ways of apprehending and judging them. Also, Kant's discussion of sculpture suggests he thought that one cannot abstract from a conceptualized object therein represented, at least in cases where the sculpture would be said to be a such-and-such (e.g., human) sculpture.

It may be possible to reconcile Kant's remarks with our earlier interpretation of the free-dependent beauty distinction by noting that, whenever Kant presents the distinction as if it is between kinds of objects, his examples are of those art media or genres which he seems to think could not contain depth elements—they could not be other than free beauties. But in cases in which dependent beauty is possible, he sometimes leaves the question open as to what kind of beauty the object can possess. Throughout, he is consistent in his view that "the judgment of taste upon whatever is beautiful in these various arts is always determined in the same way, viz. it only judges the forms (without any reference to a purpose) as they present themselves to the eye, either singly or in combination, according to the effect they produce upon the imagination" (§ 51.9, Ak. 324, B. 168).

Form and Representation

Kant's example of what he calls "aesthetic painting" provides the key to his view on the relevance of representational elements to the pure judgment of taste. He claims that a painting which has no definite theme, such as a painting which arranges sky, land, and water so as to entertain us by means of light and shade only, is a free beauty and hence the proper object of a pure judgment of taste (§ 51.9n, Ak. 323n, B. 167n). Such a painting contains recognizable depth elements (sky, land, trees, water), and no indication is given that we abstract from these elements, even though, in Kant's view, the aesthetic pleasure results from the relationships between these elements (the formal purposiveness). These paintings are not abstract, nonobjective paintings; they are representational paintings. In the language of the time, they are limitations of nature (natural beauty). The paintings with which they are to be contrasted are of two main types: portraits and story paintings. Portraits are indeed usually judged conceptually, either in terms of the accuracy of depiction of a known personage or in terms of the degree of perfection in the realization of a type of object (e.g., a peasant or king). Story paintings were usually judged in terms of thematic accuracy to the event represented. These theories of evaluation or judgment were well developed by earlier writers such as Hutcheson, Addison, and Burke. Thus, Kant's view is less innovative and less peculiar than it seems; he makes a distinction which allows him to capture the significance of an experience in which art is judged, like the beauties of nature when such beauties are not judged as species-specific in terms of perfection (a beautiful, i.e., perfect speciment of a lion). Free beauty is the beauty of an object, whether of nature or art, judged simply as to its form; and although some such objects are describable wholly in terms of surface qualities and relations, others quite obviously contain depth elements; in these cases, however, our attention is to be directed to the formal aspects of those elements (for example, the light of the clouds and the dark water, contrasting yet blending together through the rising forms of the trees).

The mere presence of representational or depth element does not prevent the object from becoming a free beauty; it does not preclude one's experience from being an experience of free beauty or the judgment from being a pure judgment of taste.[17] Kant's doctrine of formal purposiveness, then, is not a strict formalism which deprecates representational elements. But Kant's aesthetic theory does circumscribe a realm of experience that specifies a particular way of judging such elements and works of art that contain them.

5.6   Art as the Expression of Aesthetic Ideas

Kant's conception of and emphasis upon form may give the impression that his aesthetic theory is "formalistic" in the more modern sense in which aesthetic value is strictly identified with formal considerations, as in the theory of Significant Form. In the last section I attempted to show how Kant's aesthetic formalism did not entail the total exclusion of representational elements as such, even though it is true that Kant at least claims that (a pure) aesthetic experience is based upon the apprehension of and satisfaction taken in beautiful forms in art or in nature. Independently of those considerations, however, it would be misleading

17. The interpretation presented in this section avoids the paradoxical but understandable interpretation of M. C. Nahm, who argues that all of Kant's examples of pure beauties degenerate into dependent beauties. M. C. Nahm, "Kant and Some Problems of Criticism and Taste," *Proceedings of the Fifth International Congress of Aesthetics* (Amsterdam, 1964), p. 125.

to say that Kant believes aesthetic experience to be no more than the apprehension of and satisfaction taken in beautiful forms, since this would give insufficient weight to his more thorough attempt to justify the existence of art as a significant human activity and to legitimize the full import of our judgments of taste.

Left at the level of the pleasure in experiencing mere purposive form (formal subjective purposiveness), even given the conclusion of Stage III of the deduction that such pleasure can be universally communicated, the creation and experience of the beautiful in art and in nature has not been shown by Kant to be any more than an interesting (though disinterested) diversion from other more important human activities. And we have independent reasons for thinking that, if the experience of the beautiful cannot be shown to serve any higher and peculiarly human end than a diversion, Kant personally would have considered it merely a nuisance at best. In § 52.1, (Ak. 326, B. 170), Kant claims that charm and emotion, which he previously said may add to the pleasure and enjoyment of art, dull the spirit, while by contrast pure pleasure in the form "disposes the spirit to ideas." Here is an indication of the value placed on the pleasure in the beautiful other than simply the inherent satisfaction of the experience of it. This section considers the more specific function Kant sees for artistic beauty—the expression of aesthetic ideas. Chapter 7 deals with the value Kant sees in the experience of the beautiful and sublime in nature, and the connections between artistic and natural beauty in their linkage to morality. The general interpretation here is that Kant confronts the question of the significance of the experience of the beautiful. With respect to artistic beauty, he answers it partially by linking art with morality through genius and the expression of aesthetic ideas.

The beautiful or fine arts must be considered as arts of *genius* (§ 46.2, Ak. 307, B. 150); genius is the talent for producing beautiful or fine art (*schöne Kunst*) (§ 46.4, Ak. 307–8, B. 150–51). "For *judging* of beautiful objects as such, *taste* is requisite; but for beautiful art, i.e., for the *production* of such objects, *genius* is requisite" (§ 48.1, Ak. 311, B. 153). Since no determinate rule can be given for an object's being beautiful, as reflected in the fact that the judgment of taste is aesthetic and not conceptual, the first property of genius must be originality (§ 46.4, Ak. 307–8, B. 150). Genius consists in originality in producing exemplary products, which others then imitate; thus, genius "gives the rule to art" (§ 46.1, Ak. 307, B. 150). Genius itself is therefore opposed to the spirit of imitation and is not, strictly speaking, teachable (§ 47.1, Ak. 308, B. 151); it is not a skill which can be communicated, but rather is a natural gift—a talent. The artistic genius is mentally animated. He has an extraordinary imagination. Genius shows itself therefore through *Geist*, roughly translated as "spirit," the animating principle of the mind; it is the faculty of presenting *aesthetic ideas* (§ 49.2–3, Ak. 313–14, B. 157)— representations of the imagination which lie beyond the bounds of sense experience and for which, consequently, no concept is ever fully adequate. The artistic genius creates beautiful things, and thus "we may describe beauty in general (whether natural or artificial) as the expression of aesthetical ideas" (§ 51.1, Ak. 320, B. 164). (How Kant's doctrine applies to natural beauty will be discussed in chapter 7).

Aesthetic ideas are presented by virtue of the faculty of *Geist*—spirit. (Kant gives an interesting grammatical exposition of the concept of *Geist* in terms of artistic products, a poem, a history, a festal discourse, conversation, and even a woman (§ 49.1, Ak. 313, B. 156).) An aesthetic idea is characterized as a "representation of the imagination which occasions much thought, without however any definite thought, i.e., any *concept*, being capable of being adequate to it; it consequently cannot be completely compassed and made intelligible by language" (§ 49.3, Ak. 314, B. 157).

Kant briefly attempts to explain why he calls what art expresses aesthetic ideas. Because his views are bound up so closely with his other philosophical views, it is difficult to avoid using much of his technical terminology (much of which was explained in earlier chapters; see the Index for specific technical terms). What a work of art expresses is called an aesthetic idea because it is the sensible counterpart to a rational idea. A rational idea is a concept for which no sensible intuition or representation of the imagination is or can be adequate (A327= B383–84, § 57 Remark I.2, Ak. 342, B. 187). An aesthetic idea is a counterpart to a rational idea, since it is a sensible representation of that for which no concept is or can be adequate, whereas a rational idea is a concept of that for which no sensible representation is or can be adequate. An idea, in general, is a representation of the imagination. Empirically the imagination, so to speak, creates a surrogate for nature out of the material nature provides the imagination to work with, but its activities exceed the creation of new materials by means of the mere association of ideas, since its products—imaginings—can surpass existing nature. These representations of the imagination are called ideas (as opposed to intuitions or concepts) because (1) like rational or intellectual ideas such as Freedom, God, and Immortality, they strive after something which lies beyond the bounds of possible experience and thereby seek to present a concept of reason (a rational or intellectual idea) to sense and give it the appearance of objective reality; and (2) no concept can be fully adequate to them as intuitions—whatever we are aware of apprehending cannot be fully conceptualized.

Our awareness of aesthetic ideas (as expressed by the beautiful in art or nature) is related to formal purposiveness in the following way. Aesthetic ideas are defined as representations referred to an intuition according to a merely subjective principle of the mutual harmony of the cognitive powers (the imagination and the understanding), but in a way that they can never become a cognition of an object (§ 57. Remark I.1, Ak. 341–42, B. 187). An aesthetic idea can never become a cognition of an object because it is an intuition of the imagination for which an adequate concept can never be found (§ 57. Remark I.2, Ak. 342, B. 187); all cognition, according to Kant, involves conceptualization. For this reason Kant epigrammatically calls an aesthetic idea "an *inexponible* representation of the imagination" and a rational idea "an *indemonstrable* concept of reason" (§ 57. Remark I.3, Ak. 342, B. 187).

The artist, because of his unique powers of imagination and his technical skills in working with a given art medium, attempts to make aesthetic ideas sensible. He attempts to communicate through sensuous representation that which goes beyond the world of sense. For example:

The poet ventures to realize to sense rational ideas of invisible beings, the kingdom of the blessed, hell, eternity, creation, etc.; or even if he deals with things of which there are examples in experience—e.g., death, envy, and all vices, also love, fame, and the like—he tries, by means of the imagination . . . to go beyond the limits of experience and to present them to sense with a completeness of which there is no example in nature. (§ 49.5, Ak. 314, B. 157–58)

Kant does place poetry in a special position among the arts, since it lends itself more readily than the other arts to the process of communication and the expression of aesthetic ideas. He maintains, however, that the expression of aesthetic ideas is not confined to poetry but is the mark of all the fine arts and of the beautiful in nature as well.

The artist, who combines genius and taste, plays for big stakes. He tries the impossible: the achievement through the free play of his imagination of the sensuous presentation of a rational idea, such as love or envy. He can never attain this, however, since an idea is "a necessary concept of reason to which no corresponding object can be given in sense-experience" (A327=B383); an idea cannot be fully represented to actual sense perception or to the imagination in images. In Kant's view, however, the great artist in this attempt to do the impossible (make real and, hence, objective an idea of reason), does succeed in expressing an aesthetic idea, though he does not present it. What he does present to sense is a specific image or representation of the manifestations of the idea, such as love or envy. Kant explains this doctrine in terms of the notion of an *aesthetic attribute*. The poet, for example, can express an aesthetic idea, such as "the mighty king of heaven" (Jupiter) by presenting "Jupiter's eagle with the lightning in its claws" (§ 49.7, Ak. 315, B. 158), or the queen of heaven (Juno) by presenting a peacock. Kant says that the peacock is an attribute of Juno, but not a logical attribute; we would call it a symbol of Juno. Jupiter's eagle with the lightning in its claws is a case of synecdoche and symbolism; a symbolic part of Jupiter's might is presented as standing for the whole of his might. Kant's rhetorical concepts are not sophisticated enough to allow him to give a very complete or convincing description of what he has in mind. But his general point is that whatever the artist does, he does not present the idea itself but only something that gets us to think about the idea. "Aesthetical attribute" is the general term Kant uses to refer to what the artist does present. Aesthetic attributes "do not constitute the presentation of a given concept itself but only, as approximate representations of the imagination, express the consequences bound up with it and its relationship to other concepts"; thus "they furnish an *aesthetical idea*" (§ 49.7, Ak. 315, B. 158). Aesthetic attributes allow the imagination to spread itself over a number of kindred representations that arouse more thought than can be expressed in a determinate concept. In this way the artist gets the mental powers of his audience into full, imaginative activity centering around what has been presented and leading to the reflection on ideas.

In a lucid article, Gotshalk argues that this apparent shift from a formalist aesthetics in the "Analytic of the Beautful" to an expressionist aesthetics in the later sections of Part One of the *Critique of Judgment* (§§ 43–60) can best be explained in terms of the general problem in Kant's critical philosophy which generated his consideration of beauty and pleasing designs in art and nature in the first place. Kant's interest, Gotshalk states, was "in discovering evidence of an *a priori* congruence between Nature and moral aspiration," since the first two Critiques "had interpreted each realm in terms of *a priori* or universal and necessary principles absolutely distinct and independent."[18]

Something more natural than the obviously artificial and man-made forms in the fine arts must be found to furnish a priori evidence for a harmony between nature and moral aspiration. This something more natural Kant finds in Genius, the mark of which is the production of rich, exciting content surpassing the limited and relative concepts of the scientific mind. Thus, Gotshalk rightly concludes that in Kant's aesthetic theory, "while form is absolutely essential for Beautiful Art, it is not

18. Gotshalk, "Form and Expression," pp. 257, 256.

sufficient and is indeed the lesser necessity so far as satisfying aesthetic value in art. If art were merely the elegant manipulation of sensory materials according to standard forms, it would be a negligible and even annoying pursuit."[19]

R. K. Elliott pursues the latter point in more detail to argue that Kant's attempt to establish the validity of judgments of taste cannot end with the deduction or the postulation of a Common Sense, but is only achieved through linking the experience of art with moral feeling. Only in this way, he suggests, can judgments of taste be fully legitimized, since part of their meaning is the *demand* that all other men *should* share our judgment, in full recognition that this demand will never be satisfied empirically.[20] That we impose our pleasure in the beautiful on every other man as a duty (§ 59.5, Ak. 353, B. 198–99) requires that art be an expression of aesthetic ideas, that art be linked to morality. Other-wise, the judgment of taste violates the autonomy of others and is incon-sistent with the moral realm. (Precisely how Kant attempts this linkage is discussed in detail in chapter 6, section 2, and in chapter 7.) Kant's aesthetic theory thus endeavors to be complete: an analysis of our key aesthetic concepts, a justification of the implications of these concepts in terms of the experience on which their use is based, and a theory as to the ultimate importance of such experiences—their place in the human condition of attempting to make the entire realm of experience (the phenomenal world) intelligible to man.

What happens to the concept of form in Kant's aesthetics, given this linkage? Form retains its central role as the means by which art com-municates, and hence the means by which it achieves this significance. Kant makes this point explicitly when he says that "the pleasing form that is given to [a work of fine art] is only the vehicle of communication and a mode, as it were, of presenting it, in respect of which we remain free to a certain extent, although it is combined with a definite purpose" (§ 48.7, Ak. 313, B. 156). The great artist is not simply an imaginative genius; he is a creative genius who himself must exercise taste (judgment on the formal purposiveness of the elements under his control) in the very course of creating. "Taste, like the [faculty of] judgment in general . . . brings clarity and order into the multitude of the thoughts [of genius], it make the ideas susceptible of being permanently and, at the same time, universally assented to, and capable of being followed by

. 19. Ibid., p. 259.
    20. R. K. Elliott, "The Unity of Kant's 'Critique of Judgment,' " *British Journal of Aesthetics* 8 (1968):244–59.

others, and of an ever progressive culture" (§ 50.2, Ak. 319, B. 163). In completing his aesthetic theory in the later sections of the "Critique of Aesthetic Judgment," Kant is in effect arguing that the justification of art must lie not simply in the fact of communication or shared response by itself, but in what is communicated or shared in aesthetic experience. Pleasing forms are not enough; form is a means to significant experience. "Pleasant arts [*Angenehme Künste*] are those that are directed merely to enjoyment" (§ 44.3, Ak. 305, B. 148). "On the other hand, beautiful art [*schöne Kunst*] is a mode of representation which is purposive for itself and which, although devoid of [definite] purpose, yet furthers the culture of the mental powers in reference to social communication" (§ 44.4, Ak. 306, B. 148).

CHAPTER 6

A Common Sense and the Supersensible

6.1 The Transcendental Deduction—Stage IV: A Common Sense

THE POSTULATION of a common sense (*sensus communis*) is Stage IV of Kant's deduction of judgments of taste, but it is pertinent to precede a discussion of this stage with a review of the deduction up to this point. In the "Analytic of the Beautiful," Kant found upon analysis that when one asserts something to be beautiful one implies that the judgment is valid for everyone and necessarily follows from the contemplation of the object considered with respect to its beauty. His justification of our right to make such judgments—his deduction of judgments of taste—has proceeded as follows: Kant has argued, first, that the universal communicability of a sensation or a feeling is postulated or presupposed by the judgment of taste because in no other way, given the analysis of judgments of taste as nonconceptual and aesthetic, could the universal validity claimed by the judgment of taste be justified (Stage I). Such universal communicability, Kant argued in Stage II, can be grounded only in the conditions which make possible cognition in general—the harmony of the faculties used for cognition (the imagination and the understanding). In Stage III, Kant argued that this harmony of the cognitive faculties must rest on the formal subjective purposiveness of the object being considered. In Stage IV, Kant argues that the universal communicability of the mental state or feeling of pleasure based upon the experience of this formal purposiveness presupposes a common sense. This condition we must assume to be present in all men, for otherwise there would be no basis, and hence no justification, for the communication and knowledge we do actually possess. Stages III and IV of

125

the deduction, in inverse order, are summarized by Kant in a footnote to § 38:

In order to be justified in claiming universal assent for an aesthetical judgment that rests merely on subjective grounds, it is sufficient to assume: (1) that the subjective conditions of the judgment, as regards the relation of the cognitive powers thus put into activity to a cognition in general, are the same in all men. This must be true, because otherwise men would not be able to communicate their representations or even their knowledge. (2) The judgment must merely have reference to this relation (consequently to the *formal condition* of the judgment) and be pure, i.e., not mingled either with concepts of the object or with sensations, as determining grounds. (§ 38n, Ak. 290n, B. 132n)

The doctrine of the presupposition of a common sense occurs in three distinct places in the *Critique of Judgment*. In § 8, long before the notion of a common sense itself occurs, Kant says that in making judgments of taste we postulate a "universal voice," which seems to play the same role as a common sense. The notion of a common sense itself is hinted at in § 19, and then explicitly postulated and discussed in §§ 20–22. In the "Deduction," it is suggested in § 35 and discussed explicitly in §§ 38–40.

A Common Sense Presupposed in All Judgment

The discussion of Kant's theory of cognition and perception noted that, for Kant, judgment is the basis of empirical knowledge; sometimes, however, Kant goes so far as to claim that it is the basis of all consciousness of objects or experience in general. Insofar as Kant refers to a raw material, or to what is given, as the basis for experience and knowledge, it is not experienced raw material which is then combined or related in judgments; the basic building blocks of experience and knowledge, insofar as these are elements of experience, are themselves the components of judgments. Space, time, the categories, and the causal maxim, each conceived by Kant as necessary conditions for an experience, are simultaneously necessary conditions for making judgments. Awareness of empirical objects, for Kant, is categorical and conceptual.

Kant calls a common sense the subjective principle of judgments of taste (§ 20), but he also considers it the necessary subjective condition of universal communication in general and therefore of all judgments, not just judgments of taste. Universal communicability "is presupposed in every logic and in every principle of knowledge that is not skeptical" (§ 21.1, Ak. 239, B. 76). It is the only alternative to solipsism. Thus Kant says that "the principle of taste is the subjective principle [the faculty of] judgment in general" (title to § 35, Ak. 286, B. 128).

The general role played by a common sense in Kant's aesthetics is thus clear: it is a necessary subjective condition for the universal validity of judgments of taste. Kant therefore says it is postulated or presupposed in every judgment of taste, and there is reason to believe that he would say it is postulated or presupposed in other judgments as well. Specifying the alleged role of a common sense in Kant's aesthetic theory is thus relatively easy. Although the complete deduction requires a final stage which shows that the pleasure related in the judgment of taste may be necessarily imputed to others, such that their experience of it upon contemplation of the beautiful object may be demanded, the doctrine of a common sense may be considered the final stage in the deduction of judgments of taste, insofar as that deduction is viewed simply as justifying the universal communicability of such judgments. It thus shows the kind of objectivity judgments of taste can possess: the objectivity of shared feeling-responses.[1]

In § 22, however, Kant is unwilling to commit himself on the detailed status of the "indeterminate norm of a common sense." There he remarks that "whether there is in fact such a common sense, as a constitutive principle of the possibility of experience, or whether a yet higher principle of reasons makes it only into a regulative principle for producing in us a common sense for higher purposes . . . we have neither the wish nor the power to investigate as yet" (§ 22.2, Ak. 240, B. 77). Thus Kant indicates that his argument is not complete at this stage of the *Critique of Judgment*. Later he claims that "the principle of taste is the subjective principle of judgment in general" and that "the subjective condition of all judgments is the faculty of judgment itself" (§ 35.1, Ak. 286–87, B. 128–29). Since in § 20 Kant explicitly claimed that a common sense is the subjective principle of judgments of taste, it follows that the subjective principle of all judgments is a common sense. Hence it follows that a common sense, as the subjective principle of all judgments, is thus the subjective principle of moral judgments as well. We shall return to this point later. As to the ultimate status Kant gives a common sense, we must

1. Kant's argument is virtually repeated by D. W. Prall: "But it is through men's common nature, not through their differences, that they know and serve one another, as Spinoza long ago taught. It is only by their like ways of functioning that communication is possible at all, and hence that science is a general possession. Aesthetics, like all other knowledge, makes its generalizations on the assumption that human organisms in perceptual-affective response are not totally various, but largely alike. Since the one test of communication is response, content in any given case must be for all men sufficiently resembling to be amenable to generalization, if there is any full communication among men at all. Formal symbolic communication itself, whether linguistic or logical or mathematical, rests on this same basis. Hence if no aesthetic generalizations are possible, no scientific knowledge is communicable," pp. 176–77 in his *Aesthetic Analysis* (New York: Crowell, 1936).

remember that it is only an idea, an ideal, and a norm. It is a subjective principle, and it is directed to that which also is subjective—the formal purposiveness of an object. As such and consistent with Kant's philosophy, it must remain and function as a regulative principle.

A Common Sense as a Principle and as a Feeling

Although the role of a common sense may be relatively clear, the exact nature of it is not. Two competing interpretations emerge, each capable of being supported by the text. The first interpretation is that a common sense is a universally communicable mental state or feeling; the second is that it is a principle underlying the exercise of the faculty of judgment; it is a principle we all have in common, or must have in common, for there to be objective knowledge or judgments at all.

There are several passages in which Kant identifies a common sense with a *feeling* or with the effect of the free play of the cognitive faculties in the contemplation (judging) of an object of art:

. . . by [a common sense] we do not understand an external sense, but the effect resulting from the free play of our cognitive powers. (§ 20.2, Ak. 238, B. 75)

In all judgments by which we describe anything as beautiful, we allow no one to be of another opinion, without, however, grounding our judgment on concepts, but only on our feeling, which we therefore place at its basis, not as a private, but as a common feeling. Now this common sense cannot be grounded on experience, for it aims at justifying judgments which contain an *ought*. (§ 22.1, Ak. 239, B. 76)

I say that taste can be called *sensus communis* with more justice than sound understanding can, and that the aesthetical judgment rather than the intellectual may bear the name of a sense common to all, if we are willing to use the word "sense" of an effect of mere reflection upon the mind, for then we understand by sense the feeling of pleasure. (§ 40.4, Ak. 295, B. 137–38)

There is no denying Kant's claim that (1) a universally communicable mental state or feeling and (2) a common sense are, in his theory, necessary conditions or presuppositions for judgments of taste having universal validity. The question is whether the two are identical—whether, that is, Kant means anything more than a universally communicable feeling by "common sense."

There are also passages in which Kant explicitly links the common sense with a *faculty of the mind,* namely, with the ability to have or experience a mental state or feeling common to all mankind—one capable of being universally shared or communicated:

But under the *sensus communis* we must include the idea of a sense *common to all,* i.e., of a faculty of judgment which, in its reflection, takes account (*a priori*) of the mode of representation of all other men in thought. (§ 40.2, Ak. 293, B. 136)

Now this operation of reflection [abstracting from the limitations which contingently attach to our own judgment] seems perhaps too artificial to be attributed to the faculty called *common sense,* but it only appears so when expressed in abstract formulae. (ibid.)

Further support for the interpretation of a common sense as a principle underlying the exercise of the faculty of judgment can be found in Kant's characterization of taste itself as the faculty of judgment. Indeed, the title of § 40 (Ak. 293, B. 135) is "Of Taste as a Kind of *Sensus Communis.*"

The definition of "taste" which is laid down here is that it is the faculty of judging of the beautiful. (note to title of First Moment, Ak. 203, B. 37)

We could even define taste as the faculty of judging of that which makes *universally communicable,* without the mediation of a concept, our feeling in a given representation. (§ 40.4, Ak. 295, B. 138)

Taste is then the faculty of judging *a priori* of the communicability of feelings that are bound up with a given representation (without the mediation of a concept). (§ 40.6, Ak. 296, B. 138)

[W]e cannot escape from regarding taste as a faculty for judging everything in respect of which we can communicate our *feeling* to all other men. . . . (§ 41.2, Ak. 297, B. 139)

Taste is thus viewed as a faculty of judgment which is dependent for its exercise as well as for its existence upon an a priori principle. This principle is a common sense, the capacity for experiencing a feeling that is universally communicable.

A common sense is not simply a feeling but rather the capacity for a feeling just because it is a principle, rule, idea, or norm. As such, it can never be fully exemplified in actuality. But the failure of exemplification does not negate either the force or the meaning of judgments of taste (§ 38n, Ak. 290n, B. 132n). In making a judgment of taste, we do not assume, postulate, or presuppose that the feeling of pleasure or displeasure on which the judgment is based will in fact be shared by every other human being who contemplates the object. Yet this would be required if we interpret a common sense as a feeling, since in making each judgment of taste Kant says we presuppose a common sense. Kant insists that neither the sense, the point or force, nor the truth of a judgment of taste depends upon empirical concurrence; but the sense, the point or force, and the truth of any judgment of taste do rely on the possibility or capability of sharing the mental state or feeling on which the judgment is grounded and hence on the capacity for such universal communication or sharing in all men. This principles underlies all our communication—cognitive and moral judgments as well as our judgments of taste. A common sense is thus the objective principle of the faculty of judgment.

A Common Sense as a Postulate

Interpreting a common sense as a capacity for experiencing a feeling that is universally communicable seems to leave us in the middle of a confused faculty psychology. Kant insists, however, that psychological observations are irrelevant to establishing a common sense, because it is a principle presupposed by all knowledge and judgment. Kant disclaims that he is making an empirical, psychological postulate and denies that the assumption of a common sense relies upon psychological observations (§ 21, Ak. 239, B. 76). But he consistently claims that we do (or must) postulate this universal voice or common sense as an idea. What kind of a postulate is it?

The three postulates of practical reason—the immortality of the soul, the existence of God, and the freedom of the will—are said to be practical presuppositions of morality.[2] Similarly, it seems plausible to say that the idea of a universal voice or a common sense is a postulate in the sense that it is a practical presupposition of pure judgments of taste. In making a moral decision or choice, I act as if I were free. Analogously, in making a judgment of taste with its implication of universal validity, I act as if I am being supported by a universal voice or a common sense. I believe that in my judgment I, so to speak, judge for all men. In other words, my judgment of taste itself indicates that I believe there is something—some underlying principle, a common sense or universal voice—which supports my judgment and makes it hold for everyone.

Kant characterizes both the universal voice and the common sense as ideas.[3] The common sense is an idea, in Kant's terminology, because it can never be adequately met in experience. An idea is neither abstracted from sense experience nor fully applicable to sense experience. An idea has its origin in the understanding alone and transcends the possibility of experience; nonetheless, it serves as a foundation for some form of

2. For the distinction between mathematical and Kantian postulates and a clear discussion of the role and status of the postulates of practical reason, see Lewis White Beck, *A Commentary on Kant's Critique of Practical Reason* (Chicago: Univ. Chicago Press, 1960), pp. 251–55, 264–65.

3. §§ 8.7, 20 (title), 22.1, 40.2; Ak. 216, 237, 239, 293; B. 51, 74, 76, 136.

human experience. In the *Critique of Judgment,* the idea of a universal voice or a common sense serves as the foundation for the claim to universal validity on the part of judgments of taste. A common sense is the subjective ground of the necessity we feel our judgments of taste possess. In § 40, Kant identifies a common sense with the faculty of judgment in taking account of "the mode of representation of all other men in thought, in order, as it were, to compare its judgment with the collective reason of humanity, and thus to escape the illustration arising from the private conditions that could be so easily taken for objective, which would injuriously affect the judgment" (§ 40.2, Ak. 293–94, B. 136). In other words, by abstracting from our own limitations and the idiosyncrasies that contingently attach to our own judgment, we put ourselves in the place of any other person and base our judgment on what can be common to all men—the formal purposiveness of the way the object appears. Thus the principle of taste is just a common sense—the ability to limit one's powers of judgment to a feeling based on what is universally communicable—the form—and abstract from all other factors. In this way a common sense is postulated by the judgment of taste. Since this procedure of the power of judgment must also be exercised in all judgments, including cognitive judgments, we are justified in assuming a common sense.

A Common Sense and Morality

There are two major ways in which the notion of a common sense relates to morality. First, if a common sense is presupposed in all judgments, a notion similar to, if not identical with, a common sense should be expected to appear in Kant's moral philosophy. In the *Critique of Practical Reason,* Kant's position is that the very possibility of universal and necessary moral judgments is conditioned by our freedom and our common or universal feeling of respect or reverence for law. Here, too, the possibility of universally communicating a feeling or mental state is a presupposition—a postulate—of our making a certain kind of judgment, in this case a moral judgment. Thus, pure moral judgments also presuppose a common sense—a subjective principle of moral judgment that allows us to restrict the subjective basis of our moral judgment to the feeling of respect for law. If other human beings were not capable of feeling respect for law, moral judgments could not be viewed as universal and necessary commands (categorical imperatives) and could not have the point they do have. Kant's analysis of moral judgments as categorical imperatives requires the postulation of a universally communicable mental state or feeling (of respect for law), just as he claims his analysis of judgments of taste requires the postulation of such a feeling which a faculty or principle—a common sense—allows us to isolate as the subjective basis of the judgment of taste.

Thus the general notion of a common sense does not seem to be peculiar to the realm of the experience of the beautiful and the judgments made thereupon, even though to my knowledge Kant does not refer to a common sense elsewhere in his writings. The notion of a common sense underlies his entire philosophy, however, because Kant assumes that universal validity depends upon universal communicability, which, in turn, depends upon something each of us possesses or can possess—a subjective state or feeling that is universally communicable; and this, in turn, depends upon our common ability to restrict the subjective grounds of judgment to that universally communicable mental state or feeling.

Another way of putting this connection between a common sense and morality is to point out that judgments of taste, like moral judgments, have as a necessary condition of the supposition of their truth (and hence of their universal validity) the fact that they are disinterested judgments. Although we can never know for certain whether our judgment of taste is in fact based on the formal conditions of judgment, there are steps we can take in attempting to insure the purity of our judgment and hence of its being exemplary for all men. Kant's central concept in this regard is *abstraction*. We can abstract from the impure elements accompanying our experience of the beautiful: we can abstract from any merely private appeal the object might have for us, such as charm and emotional qualities, and we can abstract from any concept of the purpose of the object which might interfere with the purity of our judgment.[4] There is a striking similarity here between what Kant says concerning abstraction in judgments of taste and abstraction from the private considerations which could interfere with making a moral judgment in accordance with the Categorical Imperative. Kant goes so far as to compare the exercise of the faculty of a common sense with relating our judgment to the "collective reason of humanity" (*gesammte Menschenvernunft*) (§ 40.2, Ak. 293, B. 136), putting ourselves in the place of any other man. This is very much like what Kant says about moral judgments, and it lends further support to the view that a common sense is the subjective principle of all judgments, including those of morality.

The notion of a common sense relates to morality in a second way: the postulation of a common sense as the basis of judgments of taste (Stage IV of the deduction) leads to Stage V, which consists in linking the beautiful with morality. The doctrine of a common sense may be considered the final stage in the deduction of judgments of taste insofar as

4. See note 11, chap. 4.

that deduction is viewed simply as justifying the universal communicability of such judgments. There are convincing reasons, however, for maintaining that the complete deduction does more than show the grounds on which intersubjective judgments of taste are possible. Kant's analysis of pure judgments of taste goes beyond his claims that they are nonconceptual, aesthetic, disinterested, and have universal validity. He holds that "the feeling in the judgment of taste comes to be imputed to everyone, so to speak, *as a duty*" (§ 40.7, Ak. 296, B. 138; italics added). At the end of his discussion of a *sensus communis* in § 40, taste is defined as "the faculty of judging of that which makes *universally communicable*, without the mediation of a concept, our feeling in a given representation" (§ 40.4, Ak. 295, B. 138; cf. § 40.6, Ak. 296, B. 138), whereas previously it had provisionally been defined as "the faculty of judging the beautiful" (note to title of First Moment). This is the conclusion of Stage IV of the deduction. But in the last paragraph of § 40, Kant indicates that a complete explanation of the judgment of taste has not been given:

If we could assume that the mere universal communicability of a feeling must carry in itself an interest for us with it (which, however, we are not justified in concluding from the character of a merely reflective judgment), we should be able to explain why the feeling in the judgment of taste comes to be imputed to everyone, so to speak, as a duty. (§ 40.7, Ak. 296, H. 138)

If the complete deduction must go beyond showing the possibility of an intersubjective response and fully justify the force of our judgments of taste and their implications for others, then there must be a link between the beautiful and the moral realms. In other words, the legitimation of the complete force of judgments of taste goes beyond showing that they are grounded in that which is universally communicable. The transition to Stage V of the deduction thus becomes the problem of the relationship between the doctrine of a common sense and morality. That relationship is best approached through a discussion of the single most difficult aspect of Kant's aesthetic theory to make intelligible—aesthetics and the supersensible.

6.2   Aesthetics and the Supersensible

The puzzling notion of the supersensible is raised frequently but disjointedly in the *Critique of Judgment*. In this section I will attempt to tie together Kant's diffuse references to the notion and clarify the role it plays in Kant's aesthetic theory. Of course, the notion itself is inherently obscure, since the supersensible is unknown and unknowable by human beings. Still, we can come to understand how, according to Kant, certain of our experiences presuppose that there is a realm of the supersensible and how we can have an idea of it, even though we cannot come to know it. Understanding Kant's references to the supersensible is essential to grasping Kant's attempted transition from the realm of aesthetics to the realm of morality—the final stage in the transcendental deduction of judgments of taste.

Aesthetic Ideas and the Supersensible

All ideas are supersensible in that no sensible intuition or set of sensible intuitions is adequate for them—they are not empirically knowable and hence, by definition, are supersensible. More specifically, however, aesthetic ideas are supersensible in that they are the attempt to present for our sense experience that which is beyond the bounds of sense experience. For example, the poet, in dealing with ideas of hell, eternity, creation, death, envy, and love, "tries, by means of imagination . . . to go beyond the limits of experience and to present [ideas] to sense with a completeness of which there is no example in nature" (§ 49.5, Ak. 314, B. 158). But the expression of aesthetic ideas is not restricted to art: "We may describe beauty in general (whether natural or artificial) as the expression of aesthetical ideas" (§ 51.1, Ak. 320, B. 164). Obviously, it cannot be literally true that nature, through its beautiful products, expresses aesthetic ideas in the same sense that the artist, through his products, expresses them. Rather, the contemplation of a beautiful natural object "is sufficient for the awakening and communicating of the idea of which that object is regarded as the expression" (ibid.). Kant's view is that the contemplation of the beautiful brings about certain ideas in us. But natural beauty cannot express ideas of hell, death, envy, and the like. What, then, are the aesthetic ideas that natural beauties express? In Kant's view, all natural beauties ultimately express the same idea aesthetically—it is the indeterminate idea of the supersensible in general. This idea of the supersensible is the "concept of the general ground of the subjective purposiveness of nature for the judgment" (§ 57.5, Ak. 340, B. 185), i.e., the idea that nature was designed for our powers of cognition. Artistic beauty also symbolically expresses the supersensible in this sense because it presents in a microcosm the harmony between a formal ordering of nature as intelligible to us and our cognitive faculties.

Thus, somewhat paradoxically, natural beauty pleases us ultimately because it is like art—it seems designed for our contemplation of it; and artistic beauty pleases us ultimately because it is like nature—it presents a formal purposiveness akin to the organic unity in nature, which gives rise in us to the idea of the supersensible substrate in nature. "Natural beauty . . . brings with it a purposiveness in its form by which the object seems to be, as it were, preadapted to our judgment, and thus constitutes in itself an object of satisfaction" (§ 23.3, Ak. 245, B. 83). The supersensible idea expressed by all beautiful objects, natural and artistic alike, is the idea of the purposiveness of forms in the phenomenal world being adapted to our powers of cognition and judgment.

The Sublime and the Supersensible

The rationale for having delayed a detailed discussion of Kant's theory of the sublime is that, although certain aspects of it are clearly and straightforwardly explicated by Kant, other aspects are very puzzling, if not obscure, and can best be clarified in the context of the final stages of the deduction of judgments of taste. The concern in this section is with the manner in which the experience of the sublime, in Kant's analysis, relates to the experience of the beautiful through the idea of the supersensible. Chapter 7 considers the relationship between the deduction of judgments upon the sublime and the final stage of the deduction of judgments of taste.

In ordinary language we call certain natural objects or phenomena "sublime," for example, the vast oceans, the starry heavens, great waterfalls, grand canyons and rock formations, even a raging, torrential storm (provided we are in safety from it). Kant, however, believes that we actually speak incorrectly if we call an object of nature sublime.[5] Strictly speaking, he thinks, the sublime is only a state of our mind brought about by the contemplation of the natural phenomena that we (grammatically) call sublime. Analogous to his analysis of judgments of taste, Kant claims that the logical form of judgments on the sublime is not the same as their grammatical form. An exposition, or what Kant calls an "analytic," of the sublime must answer three major questions: (1) What natural objects or phenomena bring about the experience of the sublime? (2) How do they do so? (3) What precisely is the state of mind that constitutes the experience of the sublime? Kant begins to answer these questions by dividing the sublime into two divisions, the *mathematically sublime* and the *dynamically sublime*.

Nature is considered mathematically sublime in those of its phenomena that evoke the idea of its infinity (either spatial or temporal) (§ 26.10, Ak. 255, B. 94). "We call that *sublime* which is *absolutely great*," that is, "*what is great beyond all comparison*" (§ 25.1, Ak. 248, B. 86), "*that in comparison with which everything else is small*" (§ 25.7,

5. §§ 23.4–6, 26.12, 28.10; Ak. 245–46, 256, 264; B. 83–84, 95, 104.

Ak. 250, B. 88). But to cognize how great something is (in intuition) always requires some other magnitude as a measure (§ 25.1, Ak. 248, B. 86), and nothing in sensible intuition is adequate as a standard for the infinitely great. The application of any measurable, sensible standard simply leads to greater and greater wholes (§ 26.13, Ak. 256, B. 95), but never attains the realization of the absolutely great. Nonetheless, reason can form the idea of the infinite. The human mind can think it, but our powers of imagination (sensible intuition) are inadequate to apprehend the infinite as thought (§§ 25.7, 26.12; Ak. 250, 256; B. 88, 95). Thus the contemplation of a natural phenomenon which is very great produces a conflict in the operation of our faculties: an idea of reason (the infinite) is generated for which the imagination is inadequate. The resulting state of mind, described in terms of feeling, is that of pain or displeasure (*Unlust*):

The feeling of the [mathematically] sublime is therefore a feeling of pain arising from the want of accordance between the aesthetical estimation of magnitude formed by the imagination and the estimation of the same formed by reason. (§ 27.2, Ak. 257, B. 96)

But this feeling of displeasure at the inadequacy of all sensible standards to measure what is absolutely great, "the impossibility of ever arriving at an absolute totality, by means of the progress of the measurement of things of the sensible world in time and space, i.e., as an impossibility of *thinking* the infinite as entirely given" (§ 27.6, Ak. 259, B. 98), at the same time produces a pleasure in finding our power of reason holding sway over the sensible faculties, legislating their activities for them toward a goal which, however, they cannot attain. The sublime "makes intuitively evident the superiority of the rational determination of our cognitive faculties to the greatest faculty of our sensibility" (§ 27.1, Ak. 257, B. 96), since it legislates for that faculty. The feeling of pleasure involved in the mathematically sublime paradoxically results from the unpleasant conflict between the imagination and the reason—the former being inadequate to the latter. This conflict indicates to us the superiority of the reason and the dominion it has over the sensible imagination, thereby providing a pleasurable experience. Thus, "this very inadequateness for that idea in our faculty for estimating the magnitude of things of sense excites in us the feeling of a supersensible faculty" (§ 25.7, Ak. 250, B. 88). Kant concludes that "*the sublime is that, the mere ability to think which shows a faculty of the mind surpassing every standard of sense*" (§ 25.8, Ak. 250, B. 89).

The *dynamically sublime* in nature is that which has might or power but, from the standpoint of our experience, has no dominion over us. It is fearful without our actually being afraid of it. Natural phenomena, such as a raging storm at sea, make nature appear almighty, but the sublime experience of its might under certain circumstances can be pleasurable. Kant again claims that this pleasure results from a displeasure. In the dynamically sublime we experience a displeasure caused by the realization of the inadequacy of our powers in comparison with nature's might. And yet, under circumstances when nature's might is fearful but not actually causing fear in us, the experience is pleasurable because it arouses in us the feeling of there being something in us which is supersensible and thus superior to nature and outside her dominion. When we do not actually fear it, the (supersensible) idea of nature having no dominion over us may be excited in us; it is the idea of our reason exerting dominion over sensibility by drawing our attention to the infinite, the supersensible realm, the realm of ideas.

Thus the sublime in general relates to the supersensible in two ways. First, though marked by a feeling of pleasure (brought about by a displeasure), it is itself an idea and thus is supersensible in the same sense that any idea is supersensible. But the sublime is, more specifically, the idea of a supersensible faculty of our mind being more important than, and having dominion over, our sensible faculties. It is the faculty of the mind that surpasses every standard of sense, and that has as its object a supersensible reality. The object, which in ordinary language we call "sublime," leads us to the idea of the supersensible:

But this idea of the supersensible, which we can no further determine—so that we cannot *know* but only *think* nature as its presentation—is awakened in us by means of an object the aesthetical judging [*Beurteilung*] of which strains the imagination to its utmost bounds, whether of extension (mathematical) or of its might over the mind (dynamical). (§ 29. G.R. 9, Ak. 268, my translation, cf. B. 108)

The object we call "sublime" forces us to think of nature as a presentation of the supersensible, though we cannot objectively arrive at this presentation. Thus the judgment on the sublime has "its root in human nature, even in that which, alike with common understanding, we can impute to and expect of everyone, viz. in the tendency to the feeling for (practical) ideas, i.e., to what is moral" (§ 29.3, Ak. 265, B. 105). Consequently, the beautiful and the sublime end up having a common basis which allows us to legitimately demand that others agree with our judgments, specifically a link to the basis of morality. Precisely how this linkage is achieved is discussed in chapter 7.

Formal Purposiveness, Morality, and the Supersensible

In section 1 of this chapter, the principle of a common sense was shown to be the subjective principle underlying judgments of taste and all other judgments. A common sense is an ability to restrict subjectively the basis of one's judgment to formal considerations or their subjective effects (for example, the feeling of respect for law). It is an ability to restrict one's judgment to a universally communicable mental state or feeling, and so is a principle underlying all judgments—cognitive, aesthetic, and moral. In aesthetic judgments, a common sense is formal subjective purposiveness seen as a principle for the operation of the faculty of judgment. A common sense is, as a principle, only an idea; it is the idea of our ability to legislate the basis for a judgment—in the case of aesthetic judgments, this is formal subjective purposiveness. It is thus supersensible in a double sense: in terms of its form, it is supersensible because it is an idea or principle; and in terms of its content, it is supersensible because it is the idea of a supersensible faculty of human awareness and judgment. More specifically, it relates to morality in that it is the source of the ability to legislate universally for human beings, to lay down a universal law. It thus is the presupposition of morality as well—a supersensible basis for a decision of free choice being effective in the empirical world.

We can approach this same point via a different path, the Antinomy of Taste. The Antinomy of Taste is solved "by showing that the concept to which we refer the object in this kind of judgment is not taken in the same sense in both maxims of the aesthetical judgment" (§ 57.1, Ak. 339, B. 184). The judgment of taste must refer to some concept, or else it could make absolutely no claim to universal validity; but it cannot refer to a definite or determinate concept, or else it would be capable of proof (which it is not). Thus it must refer to an undetermined and indeterminate concept—a concept not determinable through predicates of sensible intuition. Interpreted in terms of the alleged concept of Beauty, Kant is saying (as he has consistently said) that Beauty is not a (determinate) concept; there is no determinable set of properties in virtue of the possession of which something can be said to be beautiful. In more modern terms, we might be inclined to say that Kant's position is that Beauty is not a general term the application of which has necessary and sufficient empirical conditions. This, however, is misleading. In Kantian terms, the concept upon which the judgment of taste is based is not a determinate concept, but an indeterminate one.

Kant makes some observations in his "Lectures on Logic" that gloss his position.[6] A concept, according to Kant, is a general or universal representation of that which is common to many objects; an empirical

6. Ak 9:91–100, from which the following account is taken.

concept arises out of sense experience through the comparison of objects of experience. An empirical concept thus has as its content the common properties or characteristics (called "partial concepts" by Kant) of the individuals falling under it; what Kant calls the content of an empirical concept is thus its intention. The content of a concept may also be considered as a series of marks (*Merkmale*), which are the criteria for determining whether a given object falls under the concept. These marks or criteria are the determinations of the concept. The application of an empirical concept is thus determined by the presence of these marks; if they are present in the synthesized manifold of intuition, the concept is applicable to the manifold; if not, the concept is inapplicable. In saying that Beauty is not a concept and that the judgment of taste is not based upon a determinate concept, Kant is saying that there are no marks or criteria for the application of the term "beautiful" in terms of determinate properties or qualities of objects. The statement that "the judgment of taste is not based upon *determinate* concepts" (§ 57.7, Ak. 340, B. 186) just means that there are no empirical determinations for the notions of Beauty and the Sublime.

The above account must be tempered somewhat in light of a lengthy and tightly argued passage in the *Critique of Pure Reason* (A727–32=B755–60), in which Kant denies that either empirical or a priori concepts, with the sole exception of mathematical concepts, allow precise definition. We are never certain, Kant argues, that we are using the same criteria or marks in applying concepts. Completeness of definition ("clearness and sufficiency of characteristics," A727=B755) is restricted to those concepts that are arbitrarily invented or stipulated, though even this kind of definition Kant rejects in that it "may be better described as a declaration of my project than as a definition of an object" (A729=B757). Kant concludes that "there remain, therefore, no concepts which allow of definition, except only those which contain an arbitrary synthesis that admits of *a priori* construction" (ibid.), namely, mathematical concepts. All we can do with all other concepts—empirical, philosophical, and a priori concepts alike—is to give an exposition, explication, or explanation (*Erklärung*) of them; we cannot give strict definitions of them. Therefore, since Kant is making a special claim for Beauty, that claim is not equivalent to saying that Beauty cannot be precisely defined, for that is true of any nonmathematical concept. Rather, Kant's claim is that one cannot specify, in advance, the successful exemplification of the concept in terms of empirical characteristics. In just this way, a beautiful object is unlike a dog.

What, then, is the indeterminate concept that underlies the judgment of taste—the concept which cannot be determined through sensible intuitions, through which we know nothing, and which consequently can supply no proof for the judgment of taste (§ 57.4, Ak. 340, B. 185)? In his solution to the Antinomy of Taste, Kant explicitly identifies that concept with the supersensible, and he identifies the supersensible as the ground of the subjective purposiveness of nature for the judgment. In other words, the beautiful is judged "by the purposive attuning of the imagination to agreement with the faculty of concepts in general" (§ 57. Remark I.8, Ak. 344, B. 189)—formal subjective purposiveness. The principle of so restricting the judgment is a common sense, and that general ability—the ability of the human mind to legislate for itself—is a supersensible idea:

It can only be that in the subject which is nature and cannot be brought under rules or concepts, i.e., the supersensible substrate of all his faculties (to which no concept of the understanding extends), and consequently that with respect to which it is the final purpose given by the intelligible [part] of our nature to harmonize all our cognitive faculties. (ibid.)

At this point, one should read in full § 57 and the two Remarks following it; they are not easily summarized or paraphrased. Kant's general point is clear: Kant believes that the supersensible substrate we discover when we analyze the judgment of taste to bedrock is the same as that which we discover when we analyze moral judgments to their bedrock.

The idea (indeterminate concept) of the supersensible is therefore what is ultimately expressed by natural and artistic beauty, in the form of the principle of the subjective purposiveness of nature for our cognitive faculty (§ 57. Remark II.4, Ak. 346, B. 191). But this is the same as the idea of the supersensible in general as the substrate of nature (the noumenal world—things-in-themselves); and it is also the same as the "principle of the purposes of freedom and of the agreement of freedom with its purposes in the moral sphere" (ibid.). Thus, as we shall explore further in chapter 7, section 2, the ultimate ground of the experience of the beautiful is also the ground of the basis of morality—our supersensible ability to legislate for our faculties and make real moral choices, which are decisions to follow a law we set for ourselves. And consequently, because of its ultimate basis, the beautiful becomes the symbol for morality in that it expresses the necessary supersensible basis for morality.

The idea of the supersensible underlying the sublime is thus the same as that underlying the beautiful, though we become aware of it in a different way. In the case of the sublime, we become aware of it through an ability to think of that for which our cognitive faculties are inadequate but in terms of which they function and towards which they strive, giving us the idea of the powers of legislation of our faculty of reason. Similarly, in cognition in general the human faculties presuppose a principle of organic relatedness in terms of which the phenomenal world is made intelligible to us. That principle is formal purposiveness, and our ability to restrict our judgment to such formal purposiveness is a common sense, the subjective principle underlying all judgment— here seen from the standpoint of gaining knowledge (cognition). This principle is in some sense legislated by the mind itself, since we cannot objectively determine it to be a characteristic of things (purposiveness without an objective purpose); it is nonetheless a condition of our cognitive inquiry (perception, experience).

What we discover when we uncover the principle underlying aesthetic experience is a result that makes it seem as if the world of our experience—the empirical world—were designed for our faculties. Our own legislation of principles of judgment results in a seeming adaptation of the natural world to our faculties (and hence our purposes). This leads to the idea of the supersensible substrate of humanity, our faculties, and morality. As will be discussed in more detail in chapter 7, section 2, the beautiful in this way becomes the symbol of morality, because it gives us a glimpse of what must underlie moral judgments— the supersensible, which underlies all judgment, including the judgment of taste.

CHAPTER 7

Aesthetics and Morality

7.1 Interest in the Beautiful

KANT'S IMPORTANT thesis of the disinterestedness of judgments of taste was interpreted in chapter 2, section 2, in terms of the basis of the pleasure that, in the judgment of taste, is related to the object judged to be beautiful. The pleasure in the beautiful, in contrast to the pleasure in the good (either the good for something or the good in itself—the morally good) and the pleasure of the senses in sensation, is not an interested pleasure. It is not bound up with the actual existence of an object; rather, it is a satisfaction in the mere reflection on or contemplation of the object. Kant states categorically in numerous places that "the judgment of taste by which something is declared beautiful must have no interest *as its determining ground*" (§ 41.1, Ak. 296, B. 138); furthermore, "judgments of taste . . . do not in themselves establish any interest" (§ 2.1n, Ak. 205n, B. 39n). Pleasure in the beautiful "is merely contemplative and does not bring about an interest in the object" (§ 12.2, Ak. 222, B. 57).

Thus Kant claims that no interest is at the basis of the judgment that an object is beautiful nor is it a direct consequence of finding an object beautiful. The first point is clear from Kant's deduction of judgments of taste; since the judgment of taste is aesthetic and not conceptual, if the judgment of taste is legitimately to claim universal validity, the pleasure in the beautiful must be based on the free play of the cognitive faculties in reflection on the form of an object and thus cannot be determined by any interest whatsoever. But the second point, that the pleasure in the beautiful does not in itself directly bring about any interest in an object, is not so clear. Kant's claim is that one cannot derive from the character of a judgment of taste (as a reflective judgment on the formal purposiveness of an object) any conclusion concerning an interest in beautiful objects themselves or an interest in finding objects beautiful.

Consequently, any connection between the pleasure in the beautiful and an interest in beautiful objects or in judging the beauty of objects must be indirect. Kant is fully aware when he advances the thesis of the disinterestedness of judgments of taste that people desire (the existence of) beautiful objects, that they are in fact interested in their existence, wish to possess them and create them in actuality. How do such interests come about? How is the pleasure in the beautiful linked to interests? This turns out to be an important question for Kant's aesthetic theory, because as that theory has been presented up through Stage IV of the deduction the full implication of our judgments of taste has not been explained and hence they have not been fully justified or "deduced." Stage IV, the postulation of a common sense, ends with the definition of taste as "the faculty of judging of that which makes *universally communicable*, without the mediation of a concept, our feeling in a given representation" (§ 40.4, Ak. 295, B. 138); "taste is then the faculty of judging *a priori* of the communicability of feelings that are bound up with a given representation (without the mediation of a concept)" (§ 40.6, Ak. 296, B. 138). But why should we demand the agreement of others when we judge something to be beautiful? Why do we say they ought also to find the object beautiful? Why do we say they are somehow lacking and condemn them for having "bad taste" if they do not find the object beautiful? Why should we care for a moment that others agree with us? The mere fact that we believe our judgment to be based on that which is universally communicable is not enough to justify these implications of judgments of taste. Kant explicitly recognizes the incompleteness of his argument as developed through Stage IV:

If we could assume that the mere universal communicability of a feeling must carry in itself an interest for us with it (which, however, we are not justified in concluding from the character of a merely reflective judgment), we should be able to explain why the feeling in the judgment of taste comes to be imputed to everyone, so to speak, as a duty. (§ 40.7, Ak. 296, B. 138)

In other words, the full import of a judgment of taste is not justified simply by the deduction that the basis of the judgment is universally communicable (Stages I–IV).

The link to an interest must, however, be indirect. In §§ 41–42, Kant examines the possibility of this indirect linkage. The model for his analysis is provided by the other types of judgment which are bound up with interests. The interest in the good-in-itself, the morally good, is derived from a concept of reason; it is thus an intellectual interest.

Kant considers whether the pleasure in the beautiful can be indirectly linked to such an intellectual interest in § 42. The interest in the useful and the interest in the pleasing to sense are what Kant calls "empirical interests"; they depend or are conditioned upon certain desires, wants, and inclinations of individuals or of human nature. In § 41, Kant considers whether the pleasure in the beautiful can be indirectly linked to these interests. The remainder of this section considers the latter topic; the former is discussed in section 2 of this chapter.

In what respect can taste (as a faculty of judging the beautiful) be indirectly related to "an inclination proper to human nature" (§ 41.1, Ak. 296, B. 139)? Kant's answer is that man's natural impulse to sociability leads him both to refine and to communicate his taste. We, as social beings, naturally desire to share our knowledge and our feelings, and since the pleasure in the beautiful is universally communicable (when based on what is universally communicable), we desire to share and communicate it. Consequently, according to Kant, in terms of an empirical interest the beautiful is of interest only in society.[1] Compatible with this empirical interest is the possibility, Kant thinks even the likelihood, that outside of society it would never occur to a man to create or acquire beautiful objects (§ 2.1, 41.3; Ak. 204–5, 297; B. 39, 139); the empirical interest in existing beautiful objects and in the judging of them is the result of our social natures. There are social pressures and sanctions on us to have taste and to communicate our tastes.

In § 41.4 (Ak. 297, B. 140), Kant declares that this empirical interest in the beautiful is irrelevant to the question at issue, namely, whether an interest indirectly attaches to the beautiful sufficient to justify our demand that others agree with our judgments of taste and have taste themselves. This is the question posed in § 40.7 (Ak. 296, B. 138). The empirical interest in the beautiful, dependent upon our inclination to sociability, is insufficient because it does not justify our right to demand the agreement of others; it is an empirical justification (deduction), not a transcendental one (see chap. 3, sec. 1). Kant puts it this way:

But this interest that indirectly attaches to the beautiful through our inclination to society, and consequently is empirical, is of no importance for us now, because we have only to look to what may have a reference, although only indirectly, to the judgment of taste *a priori*. (§ 41.4, Ak. 297, B. 140)

In other words, "the *beautiful* we think as having a *necessary* reference to satisfaction" (§ 18.1, Ak. 236, B. 73), and no merely empirical explanation can justify the necessity thereby attributed. The empirical inter-

1. §§ 2.1n, 29. G.R. 21, 41.2; Ak. 205, 275, 296; B. 39, 116, 139.

est in the beautiful is subservient to our inclination toward sociability, and such subservience can never justify our right to legislate over other human beings, which we implicitly do in the judgment of taste. Questions of rights are questions of morality, and Kant concludes:

> . . . the interest in the beautiful, if it is grounded thereon [that is, on our interest in sociability], can only furnish a very ambiguous transition from the pleasant to the good. But whether this [that is, the transition from the pleasant to the good] can or cannot be furthered by taste, taken in its purity, is what we now have to investigate. (§ 41.4, Ak. 298, B. 140)

Thus, the empirical connection between the pleasure in the beautiful and the empirical interest in society and the communication of feelings is not sufficient to justify our claim to the pleasure at the basis of the judgment of taste being necessary (a priori). That justification requires a further inquiry into the possible indirect relationship between the form of the judgment of taste and interest. The only other possibility for such a linkage is an intellectual interest, namely, "the property of the will of being capable of *a priori* determination by reason" (§ 41.1, Ak. 296, B. 139). Thus, Kant explicitly declares that what he is after—what the complete deduction requires—is "a means of passing from sense enjoyment to moral feeling" (§ 41.4, Ak. 297, B. 140). This transition constitutes the final stage—Stage V—in the transcendental deduction of judgments of taste.

7.2 The Transcendental Deduction—Stage V: Aesthetics and Morality

The complete deduction of judgments of taste requires a transition from the enjoyment of the sensible representation of objects (aesthetic experience) to moral feeling. Although consideration of the object in the experience of and judgment upon the beautiful must be suitably restricted to formal purposiveness and the free play of the cognitive powers, the pleasure in the beautiful and the sublime—the aesthetic experience generally—is basically a pleasure in objects as represented to sense. Previous stages of the deduction have shown how it is possible for such a pleasure to be universally communicable and thus how the judgment of taste can legitimately claim to be universally valid. The final stage of the deduction must show the legitimacy of the implication of the necessity of experiencing such pleasure and thereby justify our right to demand the agreement of others and find fault with them if they show no taste. One way Kant attempts to make the transition between the aesthetic and the moral is to ask whether there is any legitimate connection, however indirect, between one's aesthetic and one's moral dispositions, between moral virtue and the appreciation of the beautiful and the sublime. The first two parts of this section consist of a discussion of these attempts. Kant does reach some interesting conclusions on this topic, but they are insufficient. The complete transition between the moral and aesthetic realms is not achieved until Kant advances his doctrine of the beautiful (both in art and in nature) as the symbol of morality; this doctrine is the topic of the third part of this section.

Moral Virtue and Aesthetic Sensitivity

Kant makes two points in his attempt to establish an indirect linkage between aesthetics and morality in terms of the characteristics of the aesthetic experience. The first point is that the experiences of the beautiful and the sublime are instrumental in influencing the creation and maintenance of a moral disposition:

Both [the beautiful and the sublime] . . . are purposive in reference to the moral feeling. The beautiful prepares us to love disinterestedly something, even nature itself; the sublime prepares us to esteem something highly even in opposition to our own (sensible) interest. (§ 29. G.R. 6, Ak. 267, B. 108)

Moral feeling is, for Kant, the feeling of respect for law or the conformity to law. It is a feeling that satisfies independently of any interest, desire, or inclination of the agent. The aesthetic experience disposes us to the moral feeling since it, too, is a totally disinterested pleasure and "cultivates us, in that it teaches us to attend to the purposiveness in the feeling of pleasure" (§ 29. G.R. 2, Ak. 266, B. 107). But this transition by means of instrumental value between aesthetics and morality is insufficient for Kant's purposes, because the experience of the beautiful (or the sublime) is not a necessary instrument in the establishment or maintenance of a morally good disposition, however useful it may be in that regard. There is no justification for claiming that a person ought to cultivate moral feeling in this way.

Kant's next attempt to link aesthetic sensitivity and moral virtue seems more promising, though ultimately it, too, is insufficient for the complete transition between the two realms. The second point is that the taking of an immediate interest in the beautiful in nature is a symptom of a morally good person:

. . . I maintain that to take an *immediate interest* in the beauty of *nature* (not merely to have taste in judging it) is always the mark of a good soul [*Seele*]; and that, when this interest is habitual, it at least indicates a frame of mind favorable to the moral feeling if it is voluntarily bound up with the *contemplation of nature.* (§ 42.2, Ak. 298–99, B. 141)

Kant is speaking, for example, of an individual "who by himself (and without any design of communicating his observations to others) regards the beautiful figure of a wild flower, a bird, an insect, etc., with admiration and love" (§ 42.3, Ak. 299, B. 141), who takes an immediate delight not merely in the form but also in the presence of the object— and hence an interest in its existence.

A more detailed example may serve to illustrate Kant's point. Suppose a person learns that a very striking bird—say, a pileated woodpecker— occurs in his area. He might make an effort to see one, and this effort might involve fairly elaborate preparations: positioning himself near a dead tree containing woodpecker excavations, wearing dark clothing to reduce the chances of frightening the bird, obtaining binoculars, a bird identification book, and learning to recognize the bird's call. His reason for doing all these things might be interested in the sense that his motive is to advance his social status as an acute bird watcher ("I saw a pileated woodpecker this morning. Have you ever managed to see one?"). But he might have made the effort and had the desire and the interest for none of these social reasons. The experience of seeing the pileated woodpecker may be self-gratifying; its very presence may please him, making his efforts well worth the labor and trouble (inconvenience, financial outlay, discomfort from insect bites). What are we to say of this satisfaction in the existence of an object, this immediate interest in a natural beauty?

Kant argues that the satisfaction cannot be explained simply by reference to the beautiful form of the natural object. If another person were to place an artificial pileated woodpecker (and perhaps mechanically activated, complete with sound) on the trunk of a tree, however accurate the formal representation might be, discovery of the artificiality would have the effect that "the immediate interest that he previously took in [it] would disappear at once" (§ 42.4, Ak. 299–300, B. 142). The immediate interest in the beautiful in nature previously described is an interest in the presence and existence of an object that nature has produced. Indeed, the example can be pushed even further to illustrate Kant's point. The immediate interest taken in and pleasure received from observing a beautiful natural object is reduced if the naturalness of its presentation (and existence) is diminished in any way. Seeing the same pileated woodpecker in a zoo setting, however natural it may be made to look, is not quite the same, but even that is better than seeing it in the same setting with a metal band around one leg; and even the latter is better than seeing the same beautiful bird in a cage or stuffed in a taxidermic exhibit. So what seems crucial to Kant's point—his insight—is that the immediate interest is in natural beauty as nature.

How is it that this immediate interest in natural beauty is an indication or symptom of moral interest? Kant's reasoning on this point in § 42.6–7 (Ak. 300–301, B. 142–43) is somewhat obscure. His extended analogy in § 42.6 between the faculties of aesthetic judgment and moral judgment does not seem to the point (though it is to the point of the topic of beauty as the symbol of morality), or at least its point in this context is not clearly made. His argument in § 42.7 seems to be that the intellect (reason) has an interest in any trace or indication of nature exhibiting a correspondence (harmony, fittingness) between its products and our faculties, because morality—the human legislation of universal laws—presupposes the possibility of man actually exerting influence (causality) upon the natural, phenomenal world. Thus there is a moral interest in the subjective purposiveness of nature for human faculties, since that in itself, when it is the result of the human faculties functioning disinterestedly, is an indication of the possibility of an actual influence of the human faculties on the natural world.

But even given Kant's analyses of the nature and presuppositions of morality and the experience of the beautiful, the most this argument shows is that a moral interest results in an interest in the presence or existence of the beautiful forms of nature, as if they were designed for our faculties. It does not follow that an immediate interest in the beauties of nature implies a moral interest or the possession of moral feeling. To be fair to Kant, he does not say that an immediate interest logically entails a moral interest; he only says that interest in the beauties of nature, if habitual, "indicates a frame of mind favorable to the moral feeling if it is voluntarily bound up with the *contemplation of nature*" (§ 42.2, Ak. 299, B. 141). And in § 42.8 (Ak. 301, B. 143), he is careful to indicate that the kind of immediate interest in the beauty in nature to which he is referring is indeed rare; in fact, it turns out to be a metaphysical contemplation of the relation between the beautiful forms in nature and the human faculties. The most Kant can claim, then, is that there is one kind of contemplation of natural beauty which is consistent with a concern for the metaphysical basis of morality—the supersensible. This is a tenuous link between the aesthetic and the moral, simply because this contemplation does not itself seem to be any firm indication of a morally good disposition.

Even if Kant could make out the more general claim that in his restricted sense an immediate interest in natural beauty is the mark of a morally good disposition, this linkage between moral virtue and sensitivity to the beauties of nature as products of nature is still insufficient for Kant's purposes, for two reasons. Firstly, as Kant makes perfectly clear, this sensitivity is only an *indication* or a *symptom* of a morally good person in that it merely satisfies one of the necessary conditions for a morally good disposition (§§ 42.2, 42.7–8; Ak. 298–99, 300–301; B. 141, 143–44). It provides us with a basis sufficient to conclude that a necessary condition for a morally good disposition is fulfilled, though it itself is not a necessary condition for moral virtue or sensitivity. Thus we cannot rightfully demand that others take an immediate interest in natural beauty. Secondly, as Kant is himself aware, the conclusions reached about this linkage do not apply to artistic beauty. Kant does not accept the general presumption of his time that taking an interest in the beautiful is a mark of good moral character; "the interest in the *beautiful of art* (under which I include the artificial use of natural beauties for adornment and so for vanity) furnishes no proof whatever of a disposition attached to the morally good or even inclined thereto" (§ 42.2, Ak. 298, B. 141). Indeed, Kant thinks that "connoisseurs in taste not only often, but generally, are given up to idle, capricious, and mischievous passions, and that they [can] perhaps make less claim than others to any superiority of attachment to moral principles" (§ 42.1, Ak. 298, B. 141).

That Kant did not say the same for connoisseurs of natural beauty clearly shows the assumption underlying his argument, which is brought out into the open in the final stage of the deduction of judgments of taste. Kant failed to condemn connoisseurs of natural beauty because basically he links an awareness of and concern for the basis of morality with a morally good person. Thus, Kant's reasoning in § 42.6–7 (Ak. 300–301, B. 142–43) contains the basis of the important argument that constitutes the concluding stage of the transcendental deduction of judgments of taste, that the beautiful in both nature and art is the symbol of morality. If the beautiful is able to be seen by any normal being as such a symbol, then there is a basis for implying that others ought to agree with our judgments of taste, because they ought to be morally sensitive. The Kantian assumption is clearly that moral sensitivity is the same as, or at least implies, a sensitivity to the basis of morality. Hence, to complete the deduction, Kant must argue or assume that moral sensitivity implies a sensitivity to that which symbolizes the basis of morality. Where is this symbol to be found?

The Experience of the Sublime and Moral Feeling

Kant claims that there is a strong empirical connection between being able to experience the pleasure in the sublime and being of a moral disposition. "That the mind be attuned to feel the sublime postulates a susceptibility of the mind for ideas" (§ 29.2, Ak. 265, B. 104). "In fact, a feeling for the sublime in nature cannot well be thought without combining therewith a mental disposition which is akin to the moral," in that the mind is engaged "in that law-directed *occupation* which is the genuine characteristic of human morality, in which reason must exercise dominion over sensibility" (§ 29. G.R. 10, Ak. 268–69, B. 109). And the experience of the sublime is instrumental in moral development; the sublime is purposive in reference to moral feeling because it "prepares us to esteem something highly even in opposition to our own (sensible) interest" (§ 29. G.R. 6, Ak. 267, B. 108). Still, the strong inference required to make the bridge from the realm of aesthetics to morality is not forthcoming. For the above considerations, if true, show at most that the two capacities (for experiencing the sublime and of having a moral disposition or a susceptibility to moral ideas) go hand in hand. The moral demands we feel justified in imposing on others do not, at least not obviously, extend to displaying the symptoms of the moral disposition or to all those things which may lead one to possess moral feeling or sensibility. Hence this way of attempting to make the connection between the two realms is no better in the case of the sublime than it was in the case of the beautiful.

But Kant's argument becomes more complex. We have shown how, in Kant's analysis of the sublime, the feeling of pleasure in the experience of the sublime results from an awareness of a supersensible faculty of the mind. This awareness is attractive or pleasurable because it brings to us the idea that "reason exerts a dominion over sensibility in order to extend it in conformity with its proper realm (the practical) and to make it look out into the infinite, which is for it an abyss" (§ 29.2, Ak. 265, B. 105). The pleasure in the sublime arises because "we can become conscious that we are superior to nature within, and therefore also to nature without us (so far as it influences us)" (§ 28.10, Ak. 264, B. 104). Since the reality of this idea is a necessary presupposition of morality, the final stage of the deduction, the justification for our demand that others agree with our judgments upon the sublime, would seem to be close at hand. Thus it seems plausible that the key to the completion of the deduction of judgments of taste could lie in the deduction of judgments on the sublime.

Here, however, a major difficulty arises. Although, in the middle of the "Analytic of the Sublime," Kant says that an examination of the idea at the basis of the sublime must be reserved for the "Deduction" (§ 25.6, Ak. 250, B. 88), there is no separate deduction for judgments on the sublime. The title of § 30 reads: "The deduction of aesthetical judgments on the objects of nature must not be directed to what we call sublime in nature, but only to the beautiful." The reason, we learn, is that the "exposition of judgments concerning the sublime in nature was at the same time their deduction" (§ 30.3, Ak. 280, B. 121). Kant does not say that no deduction is required; he simply believes he has already given it in his exposition (or "analytic") of judgments on the sublime. His summary of that earlier deduction is presented in a very succinct, if not obscure, passage in § 30: the claim of judgments on the sublime to universal and necessary validity was justified in the exposition of judgments on the sublime because "when we analyzed the reflection of the [power of] judgment in such acts, we found in them a purposive relation of the cognitive faculties, which must be ascribed ultimately to the faculty of purposes (the will), and hence is itself purposive *a priori* (§ 30.3, Ak. 280, B. 121). Thus, to understand Kant's deduction we must backtrack to see how purposiveness is involved in the sublime.

The subjective purposiveness at the basis of judgments of taste is the fittingness of the form of the object (as experienced, of course) for our powers of cognition (imagination and understanding). The subjective purposiveness at the basis of judgments on the sublime must be different however, because the objects we call sublime may be formless. "No purposiveness of the *form* of the object lies (as in the case of the beautiful) at the basis of the judgment [of the sublime]" (§ 26.6, Ak. 253, B. 92). Rather, the subjective purposiveness at the basis of judgments on the sublime is based on the unsuitability of all sensible standards for the powers of reason as the source of ideas (§ 27.6, Ak. 256–57, B. 98–99). In the experience of the sublime, we extend our faculties to their limits: reason "generates the unsuccessful effort of the mind to make the representation of the senses adequate to these [ideas]" (§ 29. G.R. 8, Ak. 268, B. 108), and "strains the imagination to its utmost bounds" (§ 29. G.R. 9, Ak. 268, B. 108). The feeling, in the case of the sublime, is that the imagination "is purposively determined according to a different law from that of its empirical employment" (§ 29. G.R. 11, Ak. 269, B. 109). Thus we are led by the experience of the sublime to the supersensible:

This effort—and the feeling of the unattainability of the idea by means of the imagination—is itself a presentation of the subjective purposiveness of our mind in the employment of the imagination for its supersensible destination and forces us, subjectively, to *think* nature itself in its totality as a presentation of something supersensible, without being able *objectively* to arrive at this presentation. (§ 29. G.R. 8, Ak. 268, B. 108)

In this way Kant reaches the conclusion, stated earlier, that "the *sublime*

consists merely in the *relation* by which the sensible in the representation of nature is judged available for a possible supersensible use"
(§ 29. G.R. 2, Ak. 266–67, B. 107).

How does this relate to moral feeling? A satisfaction independent of
mere sense enjoyment is created by the imagination, regarded as the
instrument of reason, exercising a dominion over sensibility (§ 29.
G.R. 10, Ak. 269, B. 109). In morality, reason must exercise dominion
over sensibility. Thus the idea at the basis of the sublime is the idea of
what constitutes the basis of morality.

But how does Kant get from this fact to a justification of the necessity
we attribute to others agreeing with our judgments on the sublime?
His argument is presented succinctly in § 29, in his exposition of the
modality of the judgment upon the sublime in nature. That modality is
that judgments upon the sublime are necessary judgments (§ 24.1, Ak.
247, B. 85). The judgment upon the sublime in nature "has its root in
human nature, even in that which, alike with common understanding,
we can impute to and expect of everyone, namely, in the tendency to
the feeling for (practical) ideas, that is, to what is moral" (§ 29.3, Ak.
265, B. 105). The use of the imagination in the judgment upon the
sublime is purposive—that is, it is an instrument of reason directed
toward ideas, the supersensible. It is this use which, Kant claims, we
are authorized to impute to everyone (§ 29.4, Ak. 266, B. 106).

But the argument, though an admirable attempt, is invalid as presented. Kant's major premise is that we believe we are authorized to
impute to, and expect of, everyone moral feeling, a tendency to the
feeling for (practical) ideas, that is, to what is moral. The sublime is
not itself a practical idea. In Kant's analysis, the feeling of the sublime
is a feeling of pleasure resulting from an awareness of the mind's supersensible powers, which are a necessary condition of morality. In being
moral, we become conscious of a power of the mind which must be
exercised. But how can we demand of others that they become conscious of what is at the basis of morality? Suppressed premises must be
introduced to allow us to conclude that we can rightfully demand that
others agree with our aesthetic judgments, that persons who fail to
respond to the beautiful or the sublime are deficient in some significant
way. These premises are best brought out in conjunction with the more
comprehensible final stage of the deduction of judgments of taste proper, that is, judgments of an object's beauty.

Beauty as the Symbol of Morality

The final stage of the transcendental deduction of judgments of taste,
the link between the aesthetic and the moral realms, has been treated

from a variety of standpoints in the preceding chapters, each time with some indication of the way in which that linkage is intended by Kant to advance or complete the deduction. An enumeration follows of those discussions of Kant's attempts to link the aesthetic with the moral: (1) a summary of the extended transcendental deduction, concluding with a discussion of Stage V: aesthetics and morality (chapter 3, section 4); (2) beauty as the expression of aesthetic ideas in anticipation of the linkage to morality (chapter 5, section 6); (3) the idea of a common sense as the subjective principle of all judgments, including moral judgments (chapter 6, section 1); (4) the idea of the supersensible underlying the experience of the beautiful and the sublime, as well as morality (chapter 6, section 2); and (5) Kant's attempt to draw a connection between aesthetic sensitivity and a morally good disposition was examined in the immediately preceding section of this chapter. The present section will endeavor to bring the above points together and to stress the major line of argument of the *Critique of Judgment* reflected in each of the above attempted linkages.

In analyzing the development of Kant's argument after the completion of Stage IV, we find that Kant himself recognizes that the deduction of judgments of taste is not concluded with that stage's postulation of a common sense, but requires a linkage to morality in terms of what art expresses. Kant concludes his extended discussion of a common sense as a necessary postulate for the universal validity of judgments of taste with the following remark:

If we could assume that the mere universal communicability of a feeling must carry in itself an interest for us with it (which, however, we are not justified in concluding from the character of a merely reflective judgment), we should be able to explain why the feeling in the judgment of taste comes to be imputed to everyone, so to speak, as a duty. (§ 40.7, Ak. 296, B. 138)

In this passage, Kant clearly indicates that the hypothesis or postulate of a common sense (as the subjective principle of all judgment) is insufficient to complete the deduction, that is, to legitimize the general claims (the logic) of our judgments of taste.

Kant next considers whether the experience of the beautiful can carry an interest with it by being indirectly linked with an empirical interest, that is, with "an inclination proper to human nature" (§ 41.1, Ak. 296, B. 138–39). But he argues that, since the beautiful interests us empirically only in society and does not have any force or sanction on us outside of society, this linkage between aesthetics and morality fails:

But this interest that indirectly attaches to the beautiful through our inclination to society, and consequently is empirical, is of no importance for us now, because we have only to look to what may have a reference, although only indirectly, to the judgment of taste *a priori*. For if an interest should also be detected as bound up with this form [that is, with the judgment of taste taken as universally and necessarily valid], taste would detect for our faculty of judging a means of passing from sense enjoyment to moral feeling. (§ 41.4, Ak. 297, B. 140)

Our interest in the beautiful based on our social inclination "can only furnish a very ambiguous transition from the pleasant to the good" (§ 41.4, Ak. 298, B. 140). It is insufficient to explain the necessity bound up with judgments of taste, and it cannot complete their deduction.

Kant then turns to another possibility. He shifts from a discussion of certain inclinations bound up empirically with human nature to the possibility of reason determining an interest in the beautiful. Kant's conclusion, as discussed earlier, is the following: "If, therefore, the beauty of nature interests a man immediately, we have reason for attributing to him at least a basis for a good moral disposition" (§ 42.7, Ak. 300–301, B. 143). But this interest of reason—an intellectual interest of practical reason—in the beautiful as a basis for a morally good disposition was shown above (chap. 7, sec. 1) to be insufficient to complete the deduction for two reasons. (1) Because it is only a mark or indication of a good man (it provides just a basis and not the only or a necessary basis), it is not sufficient to legitimize our demand that others have taste. (2) Because the immediate interest in the beautiful *in art* does not provide a similar indication of a morally good person (as Kant clearly states several times in § 42), the observation is again insufficient to complete the deduction of judgments of taste.

At this point in the *Critique of Judgment*, Kant shifts to a lengthy analysis of art in general and the fine arts in particular. His discussion extends from § 43 through § 54, to the beginning of the "Dialectic of the Aesthetic Judgment" (§ 55). The explanation of Kant's argumentative procedure here is fairly obvious. Only by a detailed examination of the nature of art (and not just beauty) can the question which follows Stage IV of the deduction be adequately answered. Kant's analyses of art generally, the fine arts in particular, genius, aesthetic ideas, the comparative aesthetic worth of the fine arts, all provide the material to explain how the experience of the beautiful in art can carry an interest with it and so justify the fact that "the feeling in the judgment of taste comes to be imputed to everyone, so to speak, as a duty" (§ 40.7, Ak. 296, B. 138). Universal communicability of the feeling of pleasure on which the judgment of taste is based is insufficient. The key to the solution has already been given, that an immediate intellectual interest in natural beauty provides a reason for attributing to someone a *basis* for a morally good disposition, though precisely how that point becomes generally applicable has not yet been explained.

Thus we reach the "Dialectic of the Aesthetic Judgment," where the solution to the remaining question of the deduction, if it is to be discovered at all, must be found. The dialectic is introduced by the famous Antinomy of Taste (cf. chap. 3, sec. 3), the solution to which is an indeterminate concept, namely, "the concept of the general ground of the subjective purposiveness of nature for the judgment" (§ 57.5, Ak. 340, B. 185). "The indefinite idea of the supersensible in us" is declared to be "the sole key to the puzzle of this faculty [that is, the faculty of judgment] whose sources are hidden from us" (§ 57.8, Ak. 341, B. 186). This indeterminate concept was partially explored in chapter 6, section 2, where its preliminary linkage to morality was noted. Before elaborating on that point, let us continue the interpretation of Kant's extended argument from § 41 on to the end of the first part of the *Critique of Judgment*.

In Remark I following § 57, Kant returns to his analysis of the beautiful as the expression of aesthetic ideas, argues that the rational concept of the supersensible substrate of all phenomena is an idea, and that it is this idea as the basis of the formal purposiveness and harmony of the cognitive faculties (upon which the judgment of taste is based) which legitimizes judgments of taste as a class of judgment, thus completing the deduction:

Thus alone is it possible that there should be *a priori* at the basis of this purposiveness, for which we can prescribe no objective principle, a principle subjective and yet of universal validity. (§ 57. Remark I.8, Ak. 344, B. 189)

Remark II following § 57 reviews in four paragraphs the complete deduction in the form advanced in the Antinomy of Taste. It concludes with a comprehensive statement of the idea of the supersensible being the same thing described in three different ways: (1) as the general substrate of nature; (2) as the principle of the subjective purposiveness for our cognitive faculties; and (3) as the principle underlying morality ("the principle of the purposes of freedom and of the agreement of freedom with its purposes in the moral sphere" [§ 57. Remark II.4, Ak. 346, B. 191]).

In § 58, Kant argues that the principle or idea of the purposiveness of nature is only ideal. The beautiful objects of art or nature appear to us as if they are purposive, but we cannot know that they are. The purposiveness is simply a feature of our experience of the objects. Kant then explicitly shows how the argument from § 41 up to this point amounts to the conclusion that beauty is the symbol of morality. His

explicitly made claim also involves the categorical assertion that this is
the conclusion of the transcendental deduction of judgments of taste:

Now I say the beautiful is the symbol of the morally good, and that it is
only in this respect (a reference which is natural to every man and which
every man postulates in others as a duty) that it gives pleasure with a claim
for the agreement of everyone else. (§ 59.5, Ak. 353, B. 198–99)

The most succinct statement of Kant's reasoning in support of this claim
is given in the last sentence of § 59:

Taste makes possible the transition, without any violent leap, from the charm
of sense to habitual moral interest, as it represents the imagination in its freedom as capable of purposive determination for the understanding, and so
teaches us to find even in objects of sense a free satisfaction apart from any
charm of sense. (§ 59.7, Ak. 354, B. 200)

The structure of Kant's argument from § 41 on should now be clear.
Our judgments marking the pleasure in the beautiful (and the sublime,
too) can rightfully demand universal assent, not simply because they
can be based on what can be universally communicated, but because
they mark an experience of that which symbolizes morality.

How, precisely, is beauty a symbol of the morally good? Kant provides two suggestions, only the second of which is really adequate in
terms of his argument. The first suggestion is that beauty is the symbol
of morality in that the beautiful expresses moral ideas, that is, that the
aesthetical ideas expressed by the beautiful are particular moral ideas:

If the beautiful arts are not brought into more or less close combination
with moral ideas, which alone bring with them a self-sufficing satisfaction,
this latter fate [dulling the spirit] must ultimately be theirs. They then serve
only as a distraction. . . . (§ 52.2, Ak. 326, B. 170)

It is for this reason that Kant, from one point of view, found the highest
aesthetic worth in poetry, the lowest in music (§ 53). And the last
paragraph of the first part of the *Critique of Judgment* reiterates this
suggestion when Kant claims that "taste is at bottom a faculty for judging of the sensible illustration of moral ideas" (§ 60.4, Ak. 356, B. 202).
One interpretation is that what Kant has in mind is the expression in
art of certain moral ideas such as love, honesty, and charity. But this is
inadequate for two reasons. Firstly, our belief that others ought to agree
with us is not confined to those works of art that express such ideas.
(It is possible, of course, that Kant believed that all works of art do, or
ought to, express such ideas [cf. § 17.6, Ak. 235–36, B. 72].) Secondly,
there is no ready explanation in terms of this interpretation how the
beautiful in nature expresses moral ideas in this sense. Still, it cannot

be dismissed. It would be consistent with his theory and extended argument for Kant to claim that those works of art which express moral ideas through their formal purposiveness and are thereby beautiful rightfully demand our agreement, since sensitivity to moral ideas is legitimately demanded of all men.

Kant's second suggestion of the way in which beauty acts as the symbol of morality is that what beauty expresses generally (though symbolically) is the idea of morality (rather than specific moral ideas) or, more precisely, the idea at the basis of morality. According to this suggestion, which better serves Kant's overall argument but which is not inconsistent with the first one, the beautiful in nature and in art, and the sublime as well, symbolizes the basis of morality by leading us to the contemplation of the supersensible. The sublime does this by exposing our supersensible faculty (imagination, as the agent of reason) as if it could dominate the sensible. The beautiful in nature accomplishes this by presenting nature as if it were designed for our purposes, thus symbolizing the idea of our dominion over it. And the beautiful in art does this by being a microcosmic presentation of the same formal purposiveness experienced in natural beauty.

The morally good is the good-in-itself, a good will. A good will is motivated subjectively (that is, in terms of feeling) out of respect for law and objectively (that is, through the use of reason) out of duty, which is given by the Categorical Imperative. The Categorical Imperative is the supreme law of morality; it is not a law given in nature but a law legislated by man—the supreme law legislated by man. The meaning and point of morality require the supposition of man's free will, that the principles guiding his legislation and his choices can be effective. This presupposition of morality, the idea of freedom, is merely an idea; it is not met with in experience. Thus there is a gulf between the sensible realm of the concept of nature and the supersensible realm of the concept of freedom (Intro. II.7, Intro. IX.1; Ak. 175, 195; B. 12, 32). But the point of morality requires the assumption that freedom be effective in the world:

The concept of freedom is meant to actualize in the world of sense the purpose proposed by its laws, and consequently nature must be so thought that the conformity to law of its form at least harmonizes with the possibility of the purposes to be effected in it according to laws of freedom. There must, therefore, be a ground of the *unity* of the supersensible, which lies at the basis of nature, with that which the concept of freedom practically contains. (Intro. II.7, Ak. 175, B. 12)

This ground, then, is the basis of morality, and it is what, in the present interpretation, is symbolized by the beautiful (and the sublime).

Natural beauty is an object of satisfaction and indirectly produces an interest because it "brings with it a purposiveness in its form by which the object seems to be, as it were, preadapted to our judgment" (§ 23.3, Ak. 245, B. 83), *as if* it were designed for our purposes. Like the couplet from the poem alleged to have been found on the wall of a shack in the desert,

> Mornin' on the desert, and the air is like a wine,
> And it seems like all creation has been made for me and mine.

Rodgers and Hammerstein did not express the idea much more eloquently in the various verses to "Oh, What a Beautiful Morning." The same designedness holds for artistic beauty as well; in Kant's view, art is made to look like nature (§ 45.3, Ak. 306–7, B. 149). Thus the conclusion holds generally for judgments of taste: "a judgment of taste consists in calling a thing beautiful just because of that characteristic in respect of which it accommodates itself to our mode of apprehension" (§ 32.2, Ak. 282, B. 123).

But the principle underlying judgments of taste (and, indeed, all judgments) is a subjective principle: it is simply the way in which our minds order the manifold of experience so as to make it intelligible to us. Beauty is thus the symbol of the basis of morality because the experience of the beautiful is a result of ourselves (supersensibly) legislating a principle that determines how we experience the world. And, for Kant, the empirical world, the natural or phenomenal world, is just the world as we experience it. Thus, our legislation of a principle is or, more precisely, appears to be effective in the sensible world, the world of our experience. In this way the beautiful and the sublime symbolize the basis of morality.

The conclusion of Kant's deduction, however, is that this analogy somehow justifies the implication of our judgments of taste and judgments of the sublime that others ought to agree with us, that they are to be blamed if they do not also find the object beautiful (or sublime). If we grant the above interpretation of the way in which beauty is the symbol of morality, Kant's final conclusion can be drawn, but only with the addition of two suppressed premises. Kant does not himself argue for these assumptions, but it is possible to show why he might accept them without undue hesitation.

The first necessary assumption is that the moral demands which we have a right to make of other human beings include the demand that they be sensitive to and cultivate an interest in the basis of morality. Kant surely accepts this view. For Kant, doing the right thing is not enough to attain moral worth. To have moral worth, one must have a good will, and a good will is attained by consistently acting out of, and not merely in accordance with, duty. This requires being able to recognize or determine what is one's duty; this in turn means understanding the basis of morality.

The second necessary assumption is that our legitimate moral demands on others extend to their recognizing and taking an interest in what symbolizes the basis of morality. There is less to be said for the plausibility of this assumption, though in Kant's philosophy it seems a natural extension of his concept of rationality. Furthermore, Kant seems to think that the cultivation of a response to the beautiful (as the symbol of the basis of morality) generates a strong susceptibility for moral feeling itself by cultivating a satisfaction independent of mere sensible enjoyment and by making the mind more susceptible to moral ideas.

Viewed from the perspective of its concluding stage, Kant's transcendental deduction of judgments of taste takes on some of the important characteristics Kant indicated in both versions of the Introduction. In particular, Kant has attempted to link the cognitive faculties of understanding and reason through judgment and the a priori determination of a feeling of pleasure (Intro. VIII–IX, Ak. 192–97, B. 29–34). The complete deduction also has the virtue of being an explanation of the nature and value of aesthetic experience generally, and hence it is more than a justification for forms of speech or uses of words such as "beautiful" and "sublime." Consequently, as a theory it has implications for several other problems of philosophical aesthetics. In the next and final chapter we turn to four of these problems: the relevance of exercising the power of critical judgment in (a) aesthetic appreciation and (b) artistic creativity, (c) whether Kant's aesthetic theory contains or is consistent with an account of reason-giving and critical discourse, and (d) the theoretical analysis of the arts and the resulting possibility of ranking them in terms of their significance.

CHAPTER 8

Kant's Aesthetic Theory and Art Criticism

8.1 Criticism and Appreciation

EVEN THOUGH the extended line of argument presented above has been interpreted as uniting the major elements of Kant's aesthetic theory, there remain a number of puzzling aspects to the theory that do not readily fall into place. The first of these is the question of the relevance of the exercise of our capacity of critical or reflective judgment (=taste) to our aesthetic experience or appreciation of beauty. In other words, what is the relation between criticism and appreciation in Kant's aesthetic theory? In order to place Kant's position on this question in proper perspective, we can compare it to two radically different contemporary views.

It might be maintained that the two activities of experiencing or appreciating an object aesthetically and of passing critical judgment on it are quite distinct. Indeed, it is not an uncommon view that the critical evaluation of a work of art (or a natural beauty) involves a detailed analysis of it which may lead to a loss in enjoyment and subsequent appreciation, that to dissect is to destroy. Jerome Stolnitz, for example, has gone so far as to argue that "appreciation and criticism . . . are psychologically opposed to one another," that "the aesthetic and critical attitudes are such radically different ways of approaching an object that when one is uppermost in one's mind, it drives the other out." Stolnitz supports his claim by arguing that the activities of experiencing or appreciating an object as a work of art and criticizing it or forming a critical judgment of it are different in two major ways: (1) Criticism is analytic; the critic "must consider the components of the work both in isolation and in their relation to each other,"[1] while in "aesthetic perception" the work is grasped as a whole. (2) Criticism and appreciation have different *purposes*: the critic seeks knowledge about the work while the appreciator has no interest in anything beyond appreciating the work.

On the other hand, there are those who have argued that critical evaluation and appreciation are not opposed but are themselves both part of the total aesthetic experience. Roman Ingarden, for example, has maintained that if criticism and evaluation are antithetical to aesthetic experience and appreciation, then the entire process of evaluation has been misunderstood.[2] When separated from a specific appreciation of the work, Ingarden maintains, a value judgment can only proceed by preconceived canons or rules of criticism, whereas the appropriate aesthetic evaluation arises immediately out of the experience of the work. In fact, Ingarden wishes to distinguish between the valuation (*Bewertung*), which is itself part of the aesthetic experience, and the value judgment (*Werturteil*), which is something imposed from without. The valuation is not something accomplished in an act of judgment distinct from the aesthetic experience, but actually is part of the aesthetic response-experience, the natural outcome of an act of appreciation. Otherwise, it is a wholly intellectual and usually worthless non-aesthetic activity of applying preconceived standards to works of art.

Kant's view of the relation between appreciation and criticism is certainly opposed to that of Stolnitz and is closer to Ingarden's. Both Kant and Ingarden emphasize the activity of the mental powers, especially the imagination, in the aesthetic experience; and both want to emphasize how the objectivity of our judgments in aesthetics necessarily depends upon such judgments being grounded in an activity of apprehending a common object of experience. With respect to the single point at issue, both argue that some assessment of the object of experience is part of the aesthetic experience of that object—indeed, a natural part of it. This view of the necessary, intimate connection between experience and evaluation in aesthetics has an important consequence: Any reason adduced in support of an aesthetic evaluation must have reference to features of the object as experienced; in other words, verbal criticism in this sense only articulates what we have already perceived or felt. This requirement for the activity of criticism is what prevents it

1. Jerome Stolnitz, *Aesthetics and the Philosophy of Art Criticism: A Critical Introduction* (Boston: Houghton Mifflin, 1960), pp. 377, 378.

2. Roman Ingarden, "Bermerkungen zum Problem des aesthetischen Werturteils," *Rivista di Estetica* 3 (1958):414–23; "Artistic and Aesthetic Values," *British Journal of Aesthetics* 4 (1964):198–213.

from interfering with the experience or appreciation of the work. Contemplating the object, considering the components of the work in their relations to one another and whether they relate meaningfully, is gaining knowledge of the object and at the same time attempting to grasp the work as a whole. Far from being opposed to and interfering with each other, the components are really part of the same activity. Even if a formal judgment of taste is not made, if the activity of contemplating the form of the painting, sculpture, or musical composition has occurred, then the material for the judgment of taste is available. All that is left is to re-mark it—to take note of what has happened and its causes; apart from that, no further dissection or critical activity remains to be done.

In the above remarks, the notions of aesthetic experience and aesthetic appreciation of an object have not been distinguished. Have they, in fact, coalesced? For Kant, to experience an object aesthetically is to grasp the significance of the relationships of its parts, and thus to appreciate it; to fail to appreciate a work is to fail to grasp such significance, even if one has independent reasons for supposing it to have significance, and hence either to arrive at a negative judgment about the object or to decide that one hasn't fully experienced the object in question. Thus, for Kant, aesthetic experience and appreciation mutually entail one another.

In conclusion, in Kant's aesthetic theory the activity of judging the beautiful is intimately connected with the appreciator's experience of the beautiful in art or nature. Verdictive judgments of taste are, for Kant, the natural culmination of the process of experiencing beauty, at least in the social context in which we wish to communicate our knowledge and feelings to others. Kant explains the existence of the institution for making judgments of taste in terms of our innate desire to obtain and share knowledge, our desire to reach and communicate that which lies beyond the realm of our sense experience, and our desire in society to impress others by our taste. Thus, although the verdictive judgment is a social act, it is the making public of a product of a natural human activity—exercising our reflective power of judgment in order to apprehend a unity (purposiveness) in a manifold of intuition.

8.2   Criticism and Creativity

Taste, as the faculty of judging the beautiful, is not something connected only with the experience of the beautiful on the part of the appreciator. It is, in Kant's view, also necessary for the *creation* of beautiful objects of art. An art deserves to be called a fine art[3] only if it displays taste. Taste is the "indispensable condition (*conditio sine qua non*), the most important thing one must look for in judging art as fine art" (§ 50.1, Ak. 319, my translation, cf. B. 163). This remark makes it clear that Kant is speaking of necessary but not sufficient conditions. He says earlier that "for *judging* beautiful objects as such, *taste* is requisite; but for fine art, i.e., for the *production* of such objects, *genius* is necessary" (§ 48.1, Ak. 311, B. 153). Kant is saying that "taste is merely a judging and not a productive faculty (§ 48.7, Ak. 313, B. 156), even though it is necessary for the successful production of beautiful objects.

The fine arts include poetry, music, painting, and the plastic arts. They are contrasted with the useful, functional, and mechanical arts on the one hand and with natural beauties on the other hand. The creator of fine arts must have imagination, understanding, spirit, and taste (§ 50.3, Ak. 320, B. 164). Kant remarks in a footnote that the first three of these faculties are united by means of the fourth, and that in some works proclaimed as fine art we find genius without taste, while in others we find taste without genius (§ 50.3n, Ak. 320n, B. 164n). The creative artistic genius may not be the most successful artist, since he may find it difficult to communicate his artistic insights (imaginings). He may not be able to subject them to the proper form for artistic communication. The successful artistic genius must subject his creative spirit to discipline. Criticism (the exercise of aesthetic judgment) and creativity must interact for good art to be produced.

Although originality is the first and most important characteristic of the creative artist, the artist's finished products, if successful, must display a rule-governedness (purposiveness without a purpose) which is not itself the result simply of following rules. Thereby it creates a rule by providing a model and serving as a standard or rule of judgment for others. But genius itself is diametrically opposed to construction in accordance with determinate rules; that is the path of imitation, not of imaginative genius (§ 46.4–§ 47, Ak. 307–10, B. 150–53). Because Kant characterizes the fine arts as the expression of aesthetic ideas and ties his analysis of artistic genius so closely to originality and the faculty of imagination, he must compromise his position and reintroduce taste and judgment. Since the significance of art is in the communication of aesthetic ideas through sensible forms and since this communication can occur only if the cognitive faculties are harmoniously engaged, judgment is necessary for the artist in the perfection of his product (as a successful expression of aesthetic ideas).

3. *Schöne Kunst,* which I translate "fine art," deviating from Bernard, in the quotations to follow.

Kant avoids an about-face by claiming that genius provides the *matter* for the products of fine art through the exercise of imagination, while the execution and *form* of works of art require that this innate talent be cultivated "in order to make such a use of this material as will stand examination by the judgment" (§ 47.3, Ak. 310, B. 153). Thereby the exercise of the faculty of judgment is also necessary for the successful creation of works of fine art. Given the goal of the communication of aesthetic ideas, in a conflict between the two faculties of imagination and judgment, the latter carries the most weight:

Taste, like the judgment in general, is the discipline (or training) of genius; it clips its wings, it makes it cultured and polished; but, at the same time, it gives guidance as to where and how far it may extend itself if it is to remain purposive. And while it brings clearness and order into the multitude of the thoughts [of genius], it makes the ideas susceptible of being permanently and, at the same time, universally assented to, and capable of being followed by others, and of an ever progressive culture. If, then, in the conflict of these two properties in a product something must be sacrificed, it should be rather on the side of genius; and the judgment, which in the things of fine art gives its decision from its own proper principles, will rather sacrifice the freedom and wealth of the imagination than permit anything prejudicial to the understanding. (§ 50.2, Ak. 319–20, B. 163–64)

The artist's continual examination of his product is thus necessary for the production of beautiful objects of fine art. The activity of creation of art is recognized by Kant as a process of considerable complexity, not a blind activity of imagination or the arbitrary employment of judgment:

By taste the artist estimates his work after he has exercised and corrected it by manifold examples from art or nature, and after many, often toilsome, attempts to content himself he finds that form which satisfies him. Hence this form is not, as it were, a thing of inspiration or the result of a free swing of the mental powers, but of a slow and even painful process of improvement, by which he seeks to render it adequate to his thought, without detriment to the freedom of the play of his powers. (§ 48.6, Ak. 312, B. 155–56)

Critical control by the artist is thus part of the successful creation of products of art; such control requires the exercise of the faculty of judgment generally as well as the making of specific judgments of taste in the course of creating an object of artistic beauty.

8.3   Reason-Giving in Kant's Aesthetic Theory

Kant denies the possibility of deductive arguments, rules, principles, and hence any set of conclusive reasons in aesthetics. But Kant recognizes that we do more than simply disagree about our judgments of taste; indeed, he insists on the point presupposed by our disputing them, arguing about them, defending them, questioning them—that they are in principle universally valid by being based on a rule or principle, even though that rule or principle is indeterminate and therefore does not provide us the means for strictly proving our judgments. Kant unhesitatingly denies the existence of reasons for judgments of taste in the same sense that he believes there are reasons available for cognitive judgments (knowledge claims about objects). In the sense in which there is empirical proof for judgments such as "Robin eggs are blue" and "Copper dissolves in sulphuric acid," Kant denies such proof is available for judgments of taste.

In contemporary aesthetics this denial of conclusive reasons has led to fresh inquiries into the nature, procedures, and characteristics of the activity of reason-giving in aesthetics. Far from making a fresh inquiry, which would not have required much in the relatively dark ages of eighteenth-century aesthetics, Kant seems to have made no inquiry at all. The first part of the *Critique of Judgment,* the "Critique of Aesthetic Judgment," has been interpreted in this book as consisting largely of an extended discussion of what the judgment of taste must be based upon if it is to have even so much as a claim to universal validity. But there is little said in the *Critique of Judgment* itself on how we determine whether this basis for the universal validity of the judgment of taste is being adhered to in a given case, and almost nothing on how reference to such a basis enters into critical discourse and the resolution of aesthetic disagreements. Thus one is led to ask what place reason-giving has in Kant's aesthetic theory—whether, in fact, reason-giving is possible at all.

If the latter question seems far-fetched, it should be remembered that the judgment of taste is, in Kant's analysis, *subjective* in that it is based upon a personal feeling of pleasure or displeasure in the contemplation of the object. The deduction has shown that, if judgments of taste are legitimately to claim the assent of others, this pleasure must be based on what is universally communicable—harmony of the cognitive faculties—and that this harmony is based on the purposiveness of the way the form of the object appears to us. But this is purposiveness without any objective purpose, and so is itself a subjective factor. The degree to which, or indeed whether, one is or can be conscious of these subjective elements is a question Kant does not discuss. On analogous points, the *Critique of Pure Reason* is similarly confusing. To what extent is or can one be conscious of the transcendental subjective principles underlying synthetic a priori judgments? The harmony of the cognitive powers in their free play on the formal purposiveness of the way an object appears to us seems a far cry from the harmony upon which verbalized reasons in support of an individual judgment of taste are or should be based. Kant's paucity of examples of the application of this theory may belie its inapplicability to the activity of criticism. At the very least, the status and nature of reasons in support of judgments of taste in Kant's aesthetic theory are problematic. Yet we must assume that Kant believes there is a point of some importance in making judgments of taste. He would hardly have devoted the attention he did to an activity if he viewed it to be of only marginal importance. In other words, Kant's linguistic turn in the formulation of the problem of a critique of taste seems to have no counterpart in the application of his solution to the problems of the nature of art criticism and reason-giving. On the assumption that judgments of taste are important, this section explores the nature and function of reason-giving in support of judgments of taste as entailed by or consistent with Kant's aesthetic theory.

The judgment that an object is beautiful depends, according to Kant, on a particular feeling of pleasure or displeasure on the part of the individual making the judgment. It follows that disagreements in matters of taste, if they can be resolved at all, must be dealt with at the level of differing responses to objects. The fact of disagreement in matters of taste is only too evident to Kant; as pointed out earlier, it is one of the two reasons he gives for merely empirical (psychological, physiological, anthropological) accounts of these judgments always being incomplete. No one can get me to change my judgment of taste simply by disagreeing with it; there are no authorities in aesthetics who, merely by their contrary judgment, force me to change mine. However, disagreement can cause me to doubt or to become suspicious of the validity of my judgment, in which case I am led to examine what, specifically, I was considering when I made the judgment, that is, the basis on which it was made—and whether it was made on the formal purposiveness of the object of my experience (§ 34.2, Ak. 286, B. 128).

What, in Kant's theory, could such an examination show? It could indicate, perhaps, that my judgment of taste was "impure," that it was based on sense pleasure, charm, emotion, or on a preconceived idea (a concept) of what the object should be, rather than on the pleasure or displeasure felt in the act of judging its formal purposiveness. This shows the nature of at least some disagreements of taste in Kant's theory —when one or the other or both disputants are making impure judgments of taste or what we now might call "extra-aesthetic judgments."

Kant here is setting up what is essentially a criterion of aesthetic relevance. Of course, showing that a judgment of taste is impure is not sufficient to show it is false; it simply shows it is ill-founded. One can always be right for the wrong reasons. But to be able to show, in a given case, that the judgment is impure (wrongly based) provides a possible way of resolving an aesthetic dispute. In judging the beauty of an object, one must abstract from any concept of what it ought to be and from its mere sensuous or emotional appeal.[4] Thus, insofar as one can become conscious of the grounds on which his judgment of taste is being made, one can know whether his judgment is pure:

It may be uncertain whether or not the man who believes that he is laying down a judgment of taste is, as a matter of fact, judging in conformity with that idea [a universal voice]. . . . He can be quite certain of this for himself by the mere consciousness of the separating off [of] everything belonging to the pleasant and the good from the satisfaction which is left. (§ 8.6, Ak. 216, B. 51)

In this way we see that the discovery of a given judgment of taste being impure results from becoming aware of (what one would give as) reasons for the judgment. Kant may have erred in the details of his criterion of relevance, namely, in his uncertainty as to the aesthetic relevance of colors and tones and in his rejection of the aesthetic relevance of the "lower senses," but this does not preclude the possibility of reason-giving within his theory or necessarily change its nature.[5] Kant must allow for reasons inasmuch as he holds that one can become conscious of and point to the ground of one's judgment. And Kant does consider "showing that one is speaking of free, the other of dependent beauty" to be a method by which "we can settle many disputes about beauty between judges of taste" (§ 16.8, Ak. 231, B. 68). To show that someone is speaking of dependent beauty (the beauty of perfection or "good-of-its-kind") or mere pleasure of sensation, either that person is aware of it and tells us, or we can somehow show him the grounds on which he made his judgment. This simply is to give reasons for or against the judgment in question.

Reasons of this sort, however, seem to be wholly negative in character. In somehow finding that the person was basing his judgment on, for example, the sensuous charm of the work and nothing more, we can show why his judgment is impure and hence ill-founded as a univer-

---

4. See note 11, chap. 4.
5. For the aesthetic relevance of colors and tones, see §§ 14.3–4, 51.10, 53.2; Ak. 224, 324–25, 329; B. 59–60, 168–69, 173. For the lower senses, see §§ 51.7, 51.9; Ak. 322, 323; B. 166, 167.

sally valid aesthetic judgment. We could be said thereby to have uncovered a prima facie reason for rejecting the judgment, but not a conclusive reason. Kant's account so far seems to assume that positive reasons are available and to give us one basis for distinguishing relevant from irrelevant considerations, but it does not yet show us which of the relevant considerations are in this case good reasons, reasons in support of the judgment that this object is beautiful.

Not all disagreements on particular aesthetic judgments can be reduced to one or the other or both of the judgments being impure. Some disagreements of taste, some differences in aesthetic response and evaluation seem to be the result not of the wrong kind of attention or attitude ("impure" as opposed to "pure," "interested" as opposed to "disinterested"), but rather of an incomplete attention to or awareness of the aesthetically relevant features of the work being considered. For example, one might have failed to notice and to incorporate into the grounds of his judgment on Beethoven's Ninth Symphony the important structure of the opening of the final movement—the juxtaposition of the string bass recitative with the main theme of each of the preceding movements in turn, giving way to a bass voice recitative and finally to a full statement of the main theme of the final movement. Not infrequently one retracts an earlier evaluation of a particular work of art in the light of a fuller knowledge and understanding of the work obtainable only through repeated experience and reflection, sometimes aided by the remarks, advice, and encouragement of others. Disagreements are often resolved through pointing out or discovering a different basis of evaluation, even though neither party was basing his initial judgment on extra-aesthetic ("impure") considerations. That is, it seems to be the nature of some of our disagreements on judgments of taste that one or the other or both persons were basing their judgments on inadequate material resulting from an incomplete or inadequate experience.

Kant allows for and can give an account of such disagreements within his theory as it stands, though he never does so explicitly. Kant, I think, would say: Such disagreements are only apparent; the two judges apparently in disagreement in fact are judging different objects—the "this" in each of their judgments of taste refers to a different object of awareness (not just in the trivial sense that in Kant's epistemology we always judge *our* awareness). It follows from Kant's analysis of judgments of taste as aesthetic that we can only judge the object as we have experienced it. Thus, some disagreements over judgments of taste can be accounted for by the experience of the objects judged being significantly different, and this may be the result not of attending to what would make the judgment impure but rather of an incomplete or inadequate experience.

The account Kant might have given within his theory of this second kind of aesthetic disagreement and of the nature of its possible resolution does depend on the ability to give positive reasons in support of a judgment of taste. Resolution of disagreements resulting from inadequate or incomplete attention depends on being able to become conscious of and point to the grounds of the pure judgment of taste, to delineate precisely what one has judged and to be able to establish a common basis of judgment. It is here, in the attempt to establish a common (intersubjective) object of experience and hence of evaluation, that Kant's aesthetic theory anticipates the problem of the phenomenological description of the aesthetic object.[6] Kant realized that the existence of a common object of awareness is a necessary condition for agreement about a particular judgment of taste; conversely, some disagreements of taste may be resolved through the discovery that the objects being judged were not common to the parties in disagreement. One rationale for the activity of art criticism within Kant's aesthetics has been unearthed and its nature partly determined—namely, to aid in the creation of a common object of experience, or common controls of individuals' experiences.

But someone might object: To call what need be adduced in accounting for and resolving this type of disagreement 'reasons' is unjustified, since they are merely identifying descriptions of the objects of their respective experiences and judgments. But these are not reasons; reasons cannot be mere descriptions. Reasons in aesthetics must serve as support for an evaluation by referring to some feature or aspect of the work as contributing to or detracting from its supposed beauty, aesthetic merit, or success.

Even if we drop the requirement, as Kant does, that reasons be conclusive, a reason must (claim to) show how something contributes to or forms the basis of our evaluative judgment in a reasonable way. But the above criticism neglects the fact that, in Kant's theory, aesthetic merit or beauty is itself a relation. More specifically, it is a *relation of relations: purposiveness of form*. Kant must and does allow for the awareness and articulation of the ground on which a given pure judgment of taste has been made. This ground is the form of the work of art under consideration. The judgment is made on the basis of whether the form is purposive, that is, whether the spatial and temporal relations of the elements themselves relate in a purposive manner without our bringing them under the concept of a determinate purpose. Pleasure in the beautiful is the result of experiencing this purposive form—the

6. See Roman Ingarden, *Das literarische Kunstwerk* (Halle: Max Niemeyer Verlag, 1931).

formal elements of the object are interrelated as if it had a purpose. Hence, for Kant, a description of the object of experience and a description of the features or characteristics contributing to the beauty of the object are not on different levels. Kant in this way attempts to avoid the fact-value or descriptive-normative dichotomy by insisting that there can be no criterion in terms of determinate natural qualities necessary and sufficient for something to be called beautiful. Analyzing aesthetic value in terms of pleasure allows it to remain at the level of being felt; by giving it a basis in purposiveness of form, Kant allows for the possibility of positive reasons.

Thus, in Kant's aesthetic theory we see a necessary, intimate connection between experience and evaluation: (1) Any reasons adduced to support a judgment of taste must have reference to the formal features of the object as experienced. When elaborated, this provides a criterion of relevance. (2) Criticism only articulates what we have already felt. In this way the activity of criticism is prevented from interfering with the experience or appreciation of the work. Considering the components of the work in their experienced relations is gaining knowledge of the work and at the same time attempting to grasp the work as a whole; they are part of the same process.

Point (2), together with the doctrine of a Common Sense as the subjective principle underlying the judgment of taste, has the implication that there can be no authorities in aesthetics, in the sense that anyone whom we should call an authority in aesthetics is a very different kind of authority from those whom we ordinarily call and treat as authorities. Ordinarily, although anyone of normal intelligence is able to understand what an authority says, not everyone is in a position to call the authority to question. The substantiation of an authority, the proof of his being an authority, rests in a small group of individuals, and the members of that group are generally not the authority's normal audience. An authority on matters of taste, on the other hand, must be capable of proving his position of authority to everyone. We listen to him, follow his directions and advice, and pay him respect, but usually only insofar as our own experience bears him out. And our own experience puts us—everyone—in a position to evaluate his competence as authority and critic. The position of an authority in matters of taste is not held merely by virtue of an ability to respond, but more importantly by virtue of an ability to articulate one's response. In Kant's aesthetic theory, the major task of the critic is to make objects of beauty accessible to us, thereby helping us in our critical development, and aiding in the delineation of a common object for our experience which enables us to share our responses with others.

But we must not give Kant more credit than he deserves. Kant nowhere elaborates a theory of the nature and function of art criticism. What I have tried to show is that his theory does not preclude one. His central concept for a theory of criticism is purposiveness of form, but this is inadequate for two reasons. (1) Kant's assumptions surrounding the form-matter or form-content distinction are confused (for example, in holding that we can only communicate the form of our experience and never the content, and in identifying formal properties with the traditional philosophical category of primary qualities). (2) Kant provides us little direction for determining how, in a given case, such purposiveness or the lack of it is to be discovered or discussed. The form is there, but the content of a Kantian theory of criticism remains to be given.

8.4 Kant's Analysis of the Arts

Kant's own work provides an almost perfect example of the gap between traditional philosophical aesthetics and art criticism. Although his aesthetic theory is compatible with a theory of and the usual procedures for art criticism, Kant barely provides a hint of the application of his theory. He engages in no discussions of particular works of art beyond the occasional illustration of single points, such as an aesthetic idea being expressed in a poem. However, Kant does provide an analysis of the various fine arts and attempts to rank them in terms of their "aesthetical worth." This section is concerned with these two points.

Kant's Classification of the Fine Arts

In §§ 51–52 (Ak. 320–26, B. 164–70), Kant presents a classification scheme for the arts based upon the analogy between elements in a given art medium and the modes of expression in speech communication. Although Kant declares that his classification is not a deliberate theory and invites other attempts at classifying the arts, even suggesting another himself, his classification and the analyses he bases upon it should be taken very seriously—indeed, as part of his aesthetic theory. The reason is that the principle underlying his extended classification by analogy is the important conclusion he reached earlier, namely, that fine art in general is the communcation of aesthetic ideas through their expression. The general principle is thus communication, and, since the model for communication is speech, Kant's schema is designed to display the ways in which the various arts communicate aesthetic ideas by analogy to the ways in which men express themselves and thereby communicate in speech (§ 51.9n, Ak. 323n, B. 167n). A further reason for taking Kant's classification scheme seriously relative to his aesthetic theory is that his ranking of the various arts according to their aesthetic worth is based upon the analyses in terms of which the various arts are classified.

Kant delineates three modes of communication in speech: (1) by the words themselves—their articulation; (2) by deportment and gesticulation; and (3) by tone—the modulation or inflection of sound in time. These modes combine in a given case of speech to yield communication between a speaker and his listeners. To these three divisions correspond three kinds of fine art. Kant implies that, since the remaining arts are either combined fine arts or are not fine arts, the classification is exhaustive for the fine arts. What follows is a summary of Kant's classification of the fine arts and his analyses of the various art forms.

(1) *The arts of speech.* The arts of speech express aesthetic ideas by means of representations of the imagination (that is, thoughts) aroused by words; namely, rhetoric and poetry.

Rhetoric is the art of carrying on a serious business of the understanding with words as if it were a free play of the imagination. The orator thus gives us less than he promises; he "promises a serious business, and in order to entertain his audience conducts it as if it were a mere *play with ideas*" (§ 51.5, Ak. 321, B. 165). Kant's low estimate of the orator thus emerges in his very characterization of the art, since, in Kant's view, the orator "fails to supply what he did promise, which is indeed his announced business, viz. the purposive occupation of the understanding" (§ 51.6, Ak. 321, B. 165).

Poetry is the art of conducting a free play of the imagination through words as if it were a serious business of the understanding. The poet thus gives more than he promises; he "promises merely an entertaining play with ideas" (§ 51.5, Ak. 321, B. 165), but "he provides in this play food for the understanding and, by the aid of the imagination, gives life to his concepts" (§ 51.6, Ak. 321, B. 165–66). Because of its nature, then, in order to be fine art the poem must appear to be undesigned and without constraint.

Kant does not discuss other types of literature, perhaps because poetry is very broadly characterized and distinguished from the only other verbal art form, rhetoric, merely by the manner in which it is put forth and in no way by a delineation of its elements.

(2) *The formative arts.* The formative arts express aesthetic ideas through sensible intuitions—figures in space—either by sensible truth or by sensible illusion, which are represented by the plastic arts and painting, respectively.

The arts of *sensible truth*, the *plastic* arts, make figures cognizable by two senses, sight and touch (though Kant indicates again that beauty is not concerned with touch). They embrace sculpture and architecture. *Sculpture* is the art of expressing aesthetic ideas by corporeally presenting concepts of things as they might have existed in nature. *Architecture* presents concepts of things that are possible only through art and the art form has for its determining ground not nature, but an arbitrary purpose, with a view of presenting them with aesthetic purposiveness (that is, purposiveness without a purpose). For an architectural work, the suitability of an object for a certain use is the essential thing and limits the aesthetic ideas able to be expressed in the building. Kant includes functional furniture in this category of fine art.

The arts of *sensible illusion* are represented by *painting*, which combines sensible illusion with ideas, either by the beautiful depiction of nature or by the beautiful arrangement of the products of nature. Kant uses the term "painting" in a special sense, as defined by the above disjunction. *Painting proper* is the art of the beautiful depiction of nature, which gives only the illusory appearance of corporeal extension. Painting proper is thus two dimensional, in contrast to sculpture, which presents things having extension and not merely a surface portrayal. *Painting in the broad sense* (landscape gardening, ornamentation, and the decorative arts) is the art of the beautiful arrangement of the products of nature, which gives the illusory appearance of corporeal extension in accordance with truth, but only the appearance of utility and availability for purposes other than the mere play of the imagination in the contemplation of its forms. The beautiful arrangement of natural objects in landscape gardening is like painting, Kant says, because all that counts is the visual arrangement, how it looks—just as in landscape painting. This is a curious view, as Kant himself recognizes (§ 51.9n, Ak. 323n, B. 167n). The arrangement, however, is in conformity with certain ideas, although it has no definite theme. Kant includes nonfunctional furnishings (like tapestry and bric-a-brac) and furniture in this category, when they are made just to be looked at (§ 51.9, Ak. 323, B. 167).

Kant remarks that the formative arts generally "may be compared (by analogy) with deportment in speech" since "the artist supplies by these figures a bodily expression to his thought and its mode, and makes the thing itself, as it were, speak in mimic language"; lifeless things take on a "spirit suitable to their form by which they speak to us" (§ 51.9, Ak. 323, B. 168).

(3) *The arts of sensory modulation.* The art of the beautiful play

of sensations, externally produced, is concerned with only the proportions and relations in time between the modifications of sense qualities of tone (either color or sound). *Music* is the art of the play of the sensations of hearing. The *art of color* is the art of the play of the sensations of color. By the art of color (*Farbenkunst*), Kant does not mean the use of color in painting, which he has previously ruled out as aesthetically irrelevant to the judgment of the beauty of the painting (§ 14.5–7, Ak. 224–25, B. 60–61). Rather, he has in mind the autonomous art of color modulations in time, as produced in his day by the color organ or color piano.[7]

(4) *The combined arts.* Under the combined arts, Kant lists the *theater*, in which rhetoric is combined with a pictorial presentation of its subjects and objects; *song*, poetry combined with music; *opera*, song combined with pictorial (theatrical) presentation; and *dance*, the play of sensations in music combined with the play of figures. Kant also briefly considers combining the sublime and the beautiful, as in tragedy in verse, didactic poetry, and oratorios; he notes that in such cases many different kinds of satisfaction cross one another (§ 52.1, Ak. 325, B. 170).

He concludes his discussion of the classification of the arts by reiterating his central view that "in all fine art the essential thing is the form, which is purposive as regards our observation and judgment" (ibid.). But this return to an emphasis on form does not last long.

Scaled Comparison of the Fine Arts

Kant introduces the topic of "the comparison of the respective aesthetical worth of the fine arts" (title to § 53) by initially returning to his conception of art serving as a vehicle of communication through the expression of aesthetic ideas. If the fine arts are to have any lasting significance and their satisfaction is to endure, they must be brought into "more or less close combination with moral ideas" (§ 52.2, Ak. 326, B. 170); otherwise, as mere enjoyment, they will gradually become distasteful, dulling the spirit, making the mind discontented with itself and peevish (§ 52.1, Ak. 326, B. 170), and serve only as a distraction, rendering our minds ever more useless and discontented (§ 52.2, Ak. 326, B. 170).

In § 53, Kant is concerned with the relative aesthetic value of the major types of fine art as he had classified them in § 51. His primary standard seems to be the communication of aesthetic ideas, but he actually uses several different criteria for his rankings, although he fails to state in any precise way what these criteria are.

7. See Herbert M. Schueller, "Immanuel Kant and the Aesthetics of Music," *Journal of Aesthetics and Art Criticism* 14 (1955–56):218n.

Given his overall analysis of the nature of the fine arts as the expression of aesthetic ideas, poetry comes out on top:

It [poetry] expands the mind by setting the imagination at liberty and offering, within the limits of a given concept, amid the unbounded variety of possible forms accordant therewith, that which unites the presentment of this concept with a wealth of thought to which no verbal expression is completely adequate, and so rising aesthetically to ideas. It strengthens the mind by making it feel its faculty—free, spontaneous, and independent of natural determination—of considering and judging nature as a phenomenon in accordance with aspects which it does not present in experience either for sense or understanding, and therefore of using it on behalf of, and as a sort of schema for, the supersensible. (§ 53.1, Ak. 326, B. 170–71)

Not so surprisingly, the other art of speech, rhetoric or the art of oratory, Kant considers treacherous. He has no respect for it whatsoever, since it is essentially persuasion, the aim of which is solely agreement, even at the price of using man's weaknesses. It is thus a deceitful art, unlike poetry, which Kant believes makes no serious pretensions even though it provides food for thought. Kant seems to be condemning rhetoric on moral grounds; he does not really consider the extent to which it satisfies the criterion he utilized for ranking poetry so high.

In the next paragraph (§ 53.2), Kant seems to shift his ranking criterion again, this time to the ability of the art form to provide "charm and mental movement." He ranks music next to poetry—apparently thinking that this criterion had provided some grounds for ranking poetry first. Insofar as music is more than the play of sensations (tones) in time, and is thought of as providing ideas for reflection, it does so by mere conventional associations. (§§ 54.2, 54.4; Ak. 331, 332; B. 176, 177). As has been noted, Kant is quite uncertain about the status of music. He cannot decide whether "colors or tones (sounds) are merely pleasant sensations or whether they form in themselves a beautiful play of sensations" (§ 51.10, Ak. 324–25, B. 168–69). As discussed in chapter 4, section 4, Kant seems to think that the decision rests on the factual question, as yet undecided, whether the individual elements themselves —colors or tones—are the result of formal relations of which we can be conscious. Because of his view on the nature of formal qualities (see chap. 5, secs. 2–4), he believes this has a bearing on the resulting composition of colors or tones, and hence on the status of these art forms as fine arts or mere pleasant arts.[8]

The formative arts rank second to poetry if their aesthetic worth is judged in terms of "the culture they supply to the mind," using "as a

8. Ibid., pp. 218–47.

standard the expansion of the faculties which must concur in the judgment for cognition" (that is, the imagination and the understanding).
In putting the imagination in free play, the formative arts "at the same
time carry on a serious business" (§ 53.4, Ak. 329–30, B. 174–75). Painting ranks first among the formative arts "partly because as the art of
delineation it lies at the root of all the other formative arts, and partly
because it can penetrate much further into the region of ideas and can
extend the field of intuition in conformity with them further than the
others can" (§ 53.5, Ak. 330, B. 175).

Kant's discussion of the issue of the aesthetic worth of the fine arts
is brief and does not advance his general theory very far, if at all. It
does reinforce certain important aspects of his theory, like the view that
art is the communication of aesthetic ideas. And his conflicting criteria
also indicate how he wants to pack more into the notion of formal purposiveness than a strict formalistic theory will allow. What else he
wishes to pack into formal purposiveness was indicated in chapter 6,
section 2, and in more detail in chapter 7: the extension of the faculties
to supersensible use, achieving an idea of the supersensible as the basis
for judgment generally and for morality in particular. Thus, his emphasis on the arts that most directly can communicate or express ideas follows from his conception of the function of art as the expression of
aesthetic ideas.

8.5 Conclusion

Kant's aesthetics is a theory concerning our exercise of the faculty of
judgment. The activity of aesthetic perception consists in disinterestedly judging the object with respect to the purposiveness of its form.
Discovering a purposiveness of form results in a feeling of pleasure
(satisfaction, delight) because the cognitive faculties (imagination and
understanding) are in harmony in the general way necessary for knowledge to be acquired. On a more profound level, the pleasure is the result
of having symbolized before us, in sensible intuition, the possibility of
nature being organized for our purposes. It is the idea that the forms
of nature are purposive for our faculties and hence that, at a supersensible level, nature is determinable by means of our intellect and,
further, that the freedom necessary for morality, again at a supersensible level, is real. Kant's transcendental deduction of judgments of taste
is complete only when this final transition to beauty as the symbol of
(the basis of) morality has been effected. Here, in conclusion, it is appropriate to place some of the preceding interpretations of Kant's aesthetic theory in a slightly different perspective.

A process-product ambiguity pervades both Kant's terminology and his way of dealing with the central problems of philosophical aesthetics. The term "judgment of taste" in one sense ($=$judgment$_1$) may refer to the activity or process of experiencing something and finding it beautiful; in another sense ($=$judgment$_2$) it may refer to the resulting product of this activity, to the judgment or proposition that something is (or is not) beautiful. Kant's aesthetic theory reflects this ambiguity in the following ways: on the one hand, Kant discusses at length what he takes to be the logical features of judgments$_2$ of taste—the sections of the "Critique of Aesthetic Judgment" in which his attention is concentrated on these features he titles the "Analytic of the Beautiful"; on the other hand, he presents us with the epistemological details of a theory of judgment$_1$ of taste, that is, of the faculty of judging the beautiful in nature and in art. Kant does not inquire into the relationship between these two philosophical activities, and he engages in no meta-aesthetic investigation on this point. But his procedure commits him to the view that the solutions to the problems of aesthetics lie in the successful presentation of a theory of judgment$_1$ that can explain all the logical features or peculiarities of judgments$_2$ of taste. In this way, Kant's aesthetic theory is saved from the obsolescence of faculty psychology by simultaneously being a philosophical inquiry into the logical grounds of judgments$_2$ of taste. In other words, however much he dips into a faculty psychology, Kant is simultaneously engaged in answering the philosophical question of what kind and degree of support our judgments$_2$ of taste are capable. His acumen and rigor in this activity rightly earn him his reputation as one of the major founders of philosophical aesthetics.

In categorizing Kant's aesthetics as analytic and critical, one should not lose sight of the fact that Kant's theory still is basically a theory of aesthetic experience. But, for Kant, this is analyzed in terms of aesthetic *judgment$_1$*, which in turn links the form of an aesthetic object with the felt pleasure of the experience. Only in this way does Kant think that two basic facts of the aesthetic context can be given proper weight: the claim that judgments of taste can have objective validity and the claim that the touchstone of such judgments is an actual "tasting"—personal experience. The key to the theory has already been discussed at length: the felt pleasure in tasting is based on the formal purposiveness of the object of experience, thus allowing it to be universally communicable and objective.

Kant's theory is clear enough at this point. Still, one can become puzzled by the question, What is the object of aesthetic appreciation according to Kant? The obvious answer is that the object of aesthetic appreciation is the beautiful object—the rainbow, seashell, peacock, sculpture, musical composition. Deeply committed to a property-ascriptive theory of judgment and meaning, Kant puts forward this model: the felt pleasure (a fact about the experiencing subject) based on the formal purposiveness of the object (a fact about the object as it appears to the subject) is marked by the judgment that the object is beautiful. Hence the judgment has the form of ascribing a property (beauty) to an object, though in fact it reports a characteristic (felt pleasure) of the subject in relation to an object on a basis allowing one to impute that this characteristic is objective (a universal pleasure, so to speak). But this analysis is inadequate at a deeper level; it is too neat a bridge between the subjective and the objective—because, for Kant, the basis of appreciation is not simply the formal properties of the object, but rather the harmonious correspondence between our mental powers in their most active cognitive roles and the forms of nature (or art made to look like nature). Kant sometimes speaks of this as the suitability of the object for cognition. Thus, the ultimate source of our pleasure in the beautiful is in the sensible awareness of the idea that nature was designed for us (see chap. 6, sec. 3, and chap. 8, sec. 3). Consequently, although the mediate object of appreciation is indeed the object we call beautiful, in a deeper sense of Kant's theory the object of appreciation is the idea which is given sensible expression in that object, although only symbolically. In this way the sustained argument of the first part of the *Critique of Judgment* naturally leads to the concern of the second part (the "Critique of Teleological Judgment")—judging the objective purposiveness of nature by means of understanding and reason. But that is another lengthy and complex subject, beyond the scope of this book.

Reference Matter

Bibliography

This is a bibliography of works, principally in English, concerned with Kant's aesthetic theory; it contains only a selected number of works in other languages.

Axinn, Sidney. "And Yet: A Kantian Analysis of Aesthetic Interest." *Philosophy and Phenomenological Research* 25 (1964):108–16.

Baeumler, Alfred. *Kants "Kritik der Urteilskraft": Ihre Geschichte und Systematik.* Halle, 1923.

Basch, Victor. *Essai critique sur l'esthetique de Kant.* Paris, 1927.

Beardsley, Monroe C. *Aesthetics from Classical Greece to the Present,* pp. 209–25. New York: Macmillan, 1966.

Biemel, Walter. *Die Bedeutung von Kants Begründung der Ästhetik für die Philosophie der Kunst.* Kantstudien Ergänzunghefte, vol. 77. Cologne: Kölner Universitäts Verlag, 1959.

Blocker, Harry. "Kant's Theory of the Relation of Imagination and Understanding in Aesthetic Judgments." *British Journal of Aesthetics* 5 (1965): 37–45.

Bretall, R. W. "Kant's Theory of the Sublime." In *The Heritage of Kant,* edited by G. T. Whitney and D. F. Bowers, pp. 379–402. Princeton: Princeton University Press, 1939.

Caird, Edward. *The Critical Philosophy of Immanuel Kant.* Glasgow, 1889.

Carritt, E. F. "The Sources and Effects in England of Kant's Philosophy of Beauty." *Monist* 35 (1925):315–28.

Cassirer, H. W. *Commentary on Kant's "Critique of Judgment."* 1938. Reprint. London: Methuen, 1970.

Cerf, Walter. Translator's Introduction and Translator's Comments to *Analytic of the Beautiful,* by Immanuel Kant. Indianapolis: Bobbs-Merrill, 1963.

Cohen, Hermann. *Kants Begründung der Aesthetik.* Berlin, 1889.

Copleston, Frederick. "Aesthetics and Teleology." In *A History of Philosophy,* vol. 6. New York: Doubleday, Image Books, 1964.

Crawford, Donald W. "Reason-Giving in Kant's Aesthetics," *Journal of Aesthetics and Art Criticism* 28 (1969–70):505–10.

Denckman, Gerhard. *Kants Philosophie der Ästhetischen; Versuch uber die*

*Philosophischen Grundegedanken in Kants Kritik der Ästhetischen Ur-
teilskraft.* Heidelberg, 1947.

Dunham, Barrows. "Kant's Theory of Aesthetic Form." In *The Heritage of
Kant,* edited by G. T. Whitney and D. F. Bowers, pp. 359–76. Princeton:
Princeton University Press, 1939.

————. *A Study in Kant's Aesthetics: The Universal Validity of Aesthetic
Judgments.* Lancaster, Pa.: Science Press, 1934.

Elliott, R. K. "The Unity of Kant's 'Critique of Aesthetic Judgment.'" *British
Journal of Aesthetics* 8 (1968):244–59.

Genova, A. C. "Kant's Complex Problem of Reflective Judgment." *Review of
Metaphysics* 23 (1970):452–80.

————. "Kant's Three Critiques: A Suggested Analytical Framework." *Kant-
Studien* 60 (1968–69):135–46.

————. "Kant's Transcendental Deduction of Aesthetic Judgments." *Journal
of Aesthetics and Art Criticism* 30 (1971–72):459–75.

Gilbert, Kathryn, and Helmut Kuhn. *A History of Esthetics,* chap. 11. New
York: Macmillan, 1939.

Glen, John D. "Kant's Theory of Symbolism." Tulane Studies in Philosophy,
no. 21 (New Orleans, 1972), pp. 13–21.

Gordon, Kate. "Criticism of Two of Kant's Criteria of the Aesthetic." In *Essays in Honor of John Dewey,* pp. 148–55. New York: Henry Holt, 1929.

Gotshalk, D. W. "Form and Expression in Kant's Aesthetics." *British Journal
of Aesthetics* 7 (1967):250–60.

Greene, Theodore M. "A Reassessment of Kant's Aesthetic Theory." In *The
Heritage of Kant,* edited by G. T. Whitney and D. F. Bowers, pp. 323–
56. Princeton: Princeton University Press, 1939.

Hancock, Roger. "A Note on Kant's Third Critique." *Philosophical Quarterly*
8 (1958):261–65.

Handy, Willimm J. *Kant and the Southern New Critics.* Austin: University
of Texas Press, 1963.

Humayun, Kabir. "Introductory Essays," *Immanuel Kant on Philosophy in
General* (principally a translation of the First Introduction). Calcutta,
1935.

Hume, Robert D. "Kant and Coleridge on Imagination." *Journal of Aesthetics
and Art Criticism* 28 (1969–70):485–96.

Jordan, Elijah. *The Constitutive and Regulative Principles in Kant.* Chicago:
University of Chicago Press, 1912.

Kaminsky, Jack. "Kant's Analysis of Aesthetics." *Kant-Studien* 50 (1958–59):
77–88.

Knox, Israel. *The Aesthetic Theories of Kant, Hegel, and Schopenhauer.*
1936. Reprint. New York: Humanities Press, 1958.

Körner, S. "Kant's Theory of Aesthetic Taste". *Kant,* chap. 8. Baltimore: Pen-
guin Books, 1955.

Lang, Berel. "Kant and the Subjective Objects of Taste." *Journal of Aesthetics
and Art Criticism* 25 (1966–67):247–53.

Lee, Harold N. "Kant's Theory of Aesthetics." *Philosophical Review* 40 (1931):537–48.

McFarland, John D. *Kant's Concept of Teleology.* Edinburgh: Edinburgh University Press, 1970.

Macmillan, R. A. C. *The Crowning Phase of the Critical Philosophy: A Study in Kant's "Critique of Judgment."* London: Macmillan, 1912.

Marc-Wogau, Konrad. *Vier Studien zu Kants "Kritik der Urteilskraft."* Uppsala, 1938.

Menzer, Paul. *Kants Ästhetik in iher Entwicklung.* Berlin: Akademie Verlag, 1952.

Meredith, James Creed, trans. Introductory Essays to *Kant's Critique of Aesthetic Judgment.* Oxford: Oxford University Press, 1911.

Nahm, Milton C. "Falstaff, Incongruity and the Comic: An Essay in Aesthetic Criticism." *Personalist* 49 (1968):289–321.

———. "Imagination as the Productive Faculty for 'Creating Another Nature. . . .'" *Proceedings of the Third International Kant Congress,* Rochester, 1970, pp. 449–57. Dordrecht: Reidel, 1971.

———. "Kant and Some Problems of Criticism and Taste." *Proceedings of the Fifth International Congress of Aesthetics,* pp. 625–28. Amsterdam, 1964.

———. "Kant's 'Productive Imagination' and the 'Creation of Another Nature.'" *Journal of Philosophy* 67 (1970):816–17 (abstract).

Nivelle, Armand. *Les Théories esthétiques en Allemagne de Baumgarten à Kant.* Paris: Société d'Edition "Les Belles Lettres," 1955.

Oppell, Baron von. "Beauty in Shakespeare and Kant." *Hibbert Journal* 40 (1942).

Osborne, Harold. "On Mr. Elliott's Kant." *British Journal of Aesthetics* 8 (1968):260–68.

Pareyson, Luigi. *L'Estetica di Kant.* Milan: U. Mursia, 1968.

Park, Roy. "Coleridge and Kant, Poetic Imagination and Practical Reason." *British Journal of Aesthetics* 8 (1968):335–46.

Putnam, Caroline Canfield. "The Mode of Existence of Beauty: A Thomistic or Kantian Interpretation?" *Studies in History and Philosophy of Science* 5 (1970):223–41.

Rostenstreich, Nathan. "The Problem of the *Critique of Judgment* and Solomon Maimon's Scepticism." In *H. A. Wolfson Jubilee Volume* on the occasion of his seventy-fifth birthday, pp. 677–702. Jerusalem: American Academy for Jewish Research, 1965.

Schaper, Eva. "The Kantian 'as-if' and Its Relevance for Aesthetics." *Proceedings of the Aristotelian Society* 65 (1964–65):219–34.

———. "Kant on Imagination." *Philosophy Forum* (Boston) 2 (1971): 430–45.

Schlapp, Otto. *Kants Lehre vom Genie und die Enstehung der "Kritik der Urteilskraft."* Göttingen, 1901.

Schrader, George. "The Status of Teleological Judgment in the Critical Philosophy." *Kant-Studien* 45 (1953–54):204–35.

Schueller, Herbert M. "Immanuel Kant and the Aesthetics of Music." *Journal of Aesthetics and Art Criticism* 14 (1955–56):218–47.

Souriau, Michel. *Le Jugement réfléchissant dans la Philosophie critique de Kant.* Paris: Librarie Felix Alcan, 1926.

Stadler, Ingrid. "Perception and Perfection in Kant's Aesthetics." In *Kant: A Collection of Critical Essays,* edited by R. P. Wolff, pp. 339–84. New York: Doubleday, Anchor Books, 1967.

Tonelli, Giorgio. "La Formazione del testo della *Kritik der Urteilskraft.*" *Revue internationale de Philosophie* 8 (1954):423–48.

———. "Kant, dall'estetica metafisica all'estetica psicoempirica." *Memorie dell'Accademia delle Scienze di Torino,* ser. 3, vol. 3, pt. 2 (1955).

———. "Kant's Early Theory of Genius." *Journal of the History of Philosophy* 4 (1966):109–31, 209–24.

———. "Von den verschiedenen Bedeutungen des Wortes 'Zweckmassigkeit' in der *Kritik der Urteilskraft.*" *Kant-Studien* 49 (1957–58):154–66.

Uehling, Theodore E., Jr. *The Notion of Form in Kant's Critique of Aesthetic Judgment.* The Hague: Mouton, 1971.

Weiler, Gershon. "Kant's 'Indeterminate Concept' and the Concept of Man." *Revue internationale de Philosophie* 16 (1962):432–46.

Weingartner, Rudolf H. "A Note on Kant's Artistic Interests." *Journal of Aesthetics and Art Criticism* 16 (1957–58):261–62.

Wellek, René. "Aesthetics and Criticism." In *The Philosophy of Kant and Our Modern World,* edited by C. W. Hendel, pp. 65–89. New York: Liberal Arts Press, 1957.

Wilber, James B. "Kant's Criteria of Art and the Good Will." *Kant-Studien* 61 (1969–70):372–80.

Williams, Forrest. "Philosophical Anthropology and the Critique of Aesthetic Judgment." *Kant-Studien* 46 (1954–55):172–88.

Zimmerman, Robert L. "Kant: The Aesthetic Judgment." *Journal of Aesthetics and Art Criticism* 21 (1962–63):333–44.

Index

Abstraction: from non-aesthetic elements in the pure judgment of taste, 90–91, 95, 106, 132

Addison, Joseph: "Essays" compared to Kant's *Observations*, 8

Adherent beauty. *See* Free and dependent beauty

"Aesthetic": Baumgarten's use of the term, 12, 29–30; Kant's use of the term, 29–35

Aesthetic appreciation: and pleasure, 47–50; and cognition, 78, 90–91; and critical judgment, 160–62, 170–72; the object of, 177–78

Aesthetic attribute: means of expressing aesthetic ideas, 121–22

Aesthetic ideas: the beautiful as the expression of, 120–22, 134–35, 155; as a basis for ranking the arts, 121–22, 174–76; and the supersensible, 134–35

Aesthetic judgment: and the judgment of taste, 24, 29–36; defined, 31, 46; paradoxical in Kant's philosophy, 31–35

Aesthetic sensitivity: and moral virtue, 146–49

Aesthetic surface, 111–13

Aesthetic value of the fine arts, compared, 174–76

"Analytic of the Beautiful": how structured, 15–17

Antinomy of taste, 11–12, 35–36, 61, 63–65, 138, 155

Appearance [*Erscheinung*]: the object of intuition, 80–81

Appreciation: and critical judgment, 160–62, 170–72

A priori concepts: require transcendental deduction, 58

A priori intuitions. *See* Space; Time

A priori judgment: sense in which a judgment of taste is, 25–26, 58–60

A priori knowledge: as transcendental, 78–79, 101–2

A priori principle: underlies the judgment of taste, 4–5, 8–13, 23–26; determinate vs. indeterminate, 11–12; as a regulative idea, 12; governs the faculty of judgment, 14, 15

Architecture, 173

Art criticism: and aesthetic appreciation, 160–62, 170–72; Kant's aesthetic theory and, 164–71

Arts: Kant's analysis of, 7, 154, 171–74; Kant's scaled comparison of, 174–76

Baumgarten, A. C.: his use of "aesthetic", 12, 29–30; his view that beauty is perfection rejected by Kant, 56

Beautiful, the: compared to the pleasant and the good, 43, 54–55; experienced as pleasure, 47–50; expresses aesthetic ideas, 134–35; and the sublime have a common basis, 137, 140–41; the symbol of morality, 148–49, 152–59, 176. *See also* Judgment of taste

Burke, Edmund: Kant's characterization of his aesthetic theory, 4, 60; *Inquiry* compared to Kant's *Observations*, 8–11

Categories: as forms of synthesis, 86–87

Causality, inner: of the pleasure in the beautiful, 48–50

Charm: not a basis for the pure judgment of taste, 55–56

Cognition [*Erkenntnis*]: Kant's theory

of, 13–15, 20–22, 76; judgment of taste linked to, 67–68, 76–78; form and content of, 97; and aesthetic perception, 90–91

Color: aesthetic relevance of, 56, 100, 107–9, 167; as subjective, 105, 107

Color, the art of, 174–75

Common sense [*sensus communis*]: presupposed in all judgment, 28, 126–30; as the subjective principle of judgment, 68, 127–28, 137–38; as a feeling, 128–30; identified with taste, 129–30; as a postulate, 130–31; and morality, 131–33, 137–38; and the supersensible, 137–38

Composition. *See* Form

Concepts: indeterminate, 11–12, 65, 138–41; and synthesis, 21; role of in making judgments, 21; role of in cognition, 81–84, 138–39; Kant's analysis of, 138–39

Content. *See* Form-content

Content of intuitions, 80–81

Creation of art: involves critical judgment, 162–64

Creativity. *See* Critical judgment; Genius

Critical judgment, and creativity, 161–64

Critical philosophy: place of *Critique of Judgment* in, 17–20

Critique of Judgment: importance in aesthetic theory, 3–5; difficulties in studying, 3–7; and *Critique of Pure Reason,* 3, 13–16; and *Critique of Practical Reason,* 3, 14–15; inaccurate translation of title, 3*n*; structure of, 5–6, 15–17; possibility of, 7–13, 30; place in Kant's philosophical system, 13–15, 17–20; why necessary, 23–29

Critique of Practical Reason: relation to *Critique of Judgment,* 3, 14–15

Critique of Pure Reason: relation to *Critique of Judgment,* 3, 13–16; Kant's view on principles of taste in, 10–12; theory of cognition and perception in, 20–22, 78–91; use of "aesthetic" in, 30–32; form-content distinction in, 97–98

Critique of taste: the possibility of, 7–13, 30

Dance, 174

Deduction, empirical: distinguished from transcendental, 58–61; of the judgment of taste, 61–62

Deduction, transcendental: defined, 58; distinguished from empirical, 58–61

—of judgments of taste: summarized, 27–28, 66–69, 125–26, 145; why required, 36, 58–61, 65; and the antinomy of taste, 63–65; and morality, 68–69, 154–55

—of judgments on the sublime, 150–52

Dependent beauty. *See* Free and dependent beauty

Desire: and pleasure, 47–50

Disinterestedness: the concept of, 37–39; of the pure judgment of taste, 37–39, 55, 142–45; and the deduction of judgments of taste, 42–46, 61–62

Emotion: irrelevant basis of judgment of taste, 55–56

Evaluation, aesthetic: of the arts, 7, 154, 171–74; and appreciation, 160–62, 170–72; and reason-giving, 164–71

Faculties of the mind: Kant's assumptions about, 6–7

Feeling [*Gefühl*]: a kind of sense perception, 30–31, 80

Figure. *See* Form

Fine arts: analysis and classification of, 154, 171–74; scaled comparison and evaluation of, 174–76

Form: of intuitions, 80–81; as figure and composition, 98–100; and color, 107–8; and expression, 123–24. *See also* Purposiveness of form

Formalism: the limitations of Kant's, 118–19, 123–24

Formal purposiveness. *See* Purposiveness of form

Form-content: as distinguished by Kant, 96–98; difficulties with Kant's distinction, 110

Free and dependent beauty, 56–57, 107, 113–17, 167

Freedom, idea of: as a presupposition of morality, 157

Free play: of cognitive powers in the experience of the beautiful, 28, 50, 67–68, 75–77, 89–91, 95–96

Genius: Kant's theory of, 119–20, 121–22; and artistic creation, 163–64

Good: the beautiful neither an instrumental nor an intrinsic good, 43; compared with the beautiful and the pleasant, 54–55. *See also* Moral feeling; Morality; Moral virtue

Harmony: of the cognitive faculties in the experience of the beautiful, 28, 67–68, 75–78, 89–91, 95–96

Hume, David: "A Standard of Taste" compared to Kant's *Observations*, 9–11; his theory of the imagination compared with Kant's, 84–87

Hutcheson, Francis: his *Enquiry* compared with Kant's *Observations*, 8

Ideas: principle of taste as a regulative idea, 12; as representations of the imagination, 120; rational vs. aesthetic, 120–21; moral ideas and the beautiful, 156–57. *See also* Aesthetic ideas

Imagination, faculty of [*Einbildungskraft*]: role of in making judgments, 21–22; and understanding harmonize in free play in the experience of the beautiful, 28, 67–68, 75–77, 89–91, 95–96; function of in cognition, 81–84; Kant's theory compared with Hume's, 84–87; productive and reproductive use of, 87–90; in conflict with reason in the experience of the sublime, 99–100; and artistic genius, 117–21

Indeterminate concept: the resolution of the antinomy of taste, 65; underlying the judgment of taste, 65, 69, 138; and the supersensible, 65, 138–41

Ingarden, Roman: on appreciation and critical judgment, compared with Kant, 161–62

Interest: and pleasure, 38–41; in the beautiful in society, 44–45, 50–51, 142–45, 153–54; and aesthetic objects, 50–54; in natural beauty a mark of a good person, 146–49. *See also* Disinterestedness

Intuitions [*Anschauungen*]: in Kant's theory of cognition, 80–81; form and content of, 97–98; space and time as the pure forms of, 101–2

Judgment, faculty of [*Urteilskraft*]: the principle of, 18–20; identified with the understanding, 20; role of in cognition, 20–23; characterized, 20–23, 177–78; determinate vs. reflective use of, 22–23, 73–74, 89–90

Judgment of sense: aesthetic, 24, 26, 34; contrasted with judgment of taste, 24, 26–28, 34; wholly subjective, 27–28, 34; characterized, 55

Judgment of taste: a singular judgment, 16–17, 23, 32, 37; a necessary judgment, 17; purposive, 17; universal, 17; a reflective judgment, 22–23; characterized, 23, 24–25; compared to judgment of sense, 24, 26–28, 34; aesthetic, 24, 26, 29–36; pure vs. impure, 24–26, 37, 45, 166–68; requires a transcendental deduction, 26–27, 58–61; claims universality, 34, 38, 65; subjective, 34–35; cannot be proved, 35–36, 63–64, 65; disinterested, 37–54; not based on charm or emotion, 55–56; not based on the perfection of the object, 56; sense in which it is a priori, 58–61, 65; distinguished from the judging of the object, 69–74; abstraction from non-aesthetic elements in, 90–91, 95, 106, 132. *See also* Deduction, transcendental

Judgments: judgments of experience vs. judgments of perception, 33–34; form and content of, 97; products of the faculty of judgment, 177–78. *See also* Judgment, faculty of; Judgment of sense; Judgment of taste

Knowledge [*Erkenntnis*]. *See* Cognition

Landscape gardening, 117, 173

Locke, John: on primary and secondary qualities, 102–4

Matter. *See* Form-content

Moral feeling: and the experience of the sublime, 149–52

Morality: and Kant's aesthetic theory, 19–20, 142–59; and the deduction of judgments of taste, 68–69; and common sense, 131–33; and the sublime, 137, 157; and the immediate interest in natural beauty, 146–49, 154; sym-

bolized by beauty, 148–49, 152–59, 176; and the supersensible, 155
Moral virtue: and aesthetic sensitivity, 146–49
Music: aesthetic worth of, 156, 175; Kant's analysis of, 174

Natural beauty: characterized, 115; and aesthetic ideas, 134-35; immediate interest in, a mark of moral virtue, 146–49; as the symbol of morality, 156, 158; like art, 158
Non-representational painting, 111–13, 117–18

Observations on the Feeling of the Beautiful and Sublime, 7–9
Opera, 174
Originality, the most important mark of the creative artist, 163–64

Pain [*Unlust*]: and the experience of the sublime, 136–37
Painting: Kant's analysis of, 173; aesthetic worth of, 175–76
Perception, Kant's theory of, 78–91
Plastic arts, 173
Pleasant, the: compared with the beautiful and the good, 54–55. *See also* Judgment of sense
Pleasure, feeling of [*Lust*]: cannot be connected a priori with an object, 26–27, 59; an aesthetic sensation, 32; a subjective sensation, 32; and interest, 38–41, 42–43; how distinguished, 42, 75
Pleasure in the beautiful: compared with the pleasant to sense, 43, 49, 54–55; disinterested, 46; characterized, 47–50; compared with pleasure in the good, 49, 54–55; an immediate satisfaction, 64; a consequent of judging the object, 69–74
Poetry: characterized, 121–22; aesthetic worth of, 121–22, 156, 175
Postulate: common sense as, 130–31
Postulates of practical reason, 130, 130n
Primary qualities: Kant on the primary-secondary quality distinction, 102–5
Principles of taste. *See* Standards of taste

Proof: absence of proof for judgments of taste, 35–36
Pure and impure judgments of taste, 24–26, 37, 45, 166–68
Purpose [*Zweck*]: defined, 93; and purposiveness, 93–96; necessary for an object of fine art, 116–17
Purposiveness of form [*Zweckmässigkeit*]: in the two parts of the *Critique of Judgment*, 5–6, 93; and the pure judgment of taste, 18–19, 38–39, 42, 56, 68, 91; as the a priori subjective principle of judgment, 18–19, 95–96, 151–52; and pleasure, 19; characterized, 93–96; and the sublime, 135–37, 151–52; and the supersensible, 137–41, 155, 176; of nature only an ideal, 155; and reason-giving, 165–66, 169–71

Reasons: in support of judgments of taste, 164–71
Representation [*Vorstellung*]: Kant's use of the term, 21, 30–31, 39–41; in art and Kant's aesthetic theory, 111–18
Rhetoric, 172, 175

Sculpture, 173
Secondary qualities: Kant on the primary-secondary quality distinction, 102–5; cannot yield knowledge, 105–6; and the experience of the beautiful, 106–10
Sensation [*Empfindung*]: one kind of sense perception, 30; Kant's characterization of, 30, 32, 79–81; and cognition, 81–84, 101–2; form and content of, 97–98
Sensibility, faculty of [*Sinnlichkeit*]: defined, 32, 79–81; role in cognitive perception, 81–84, 101–2; space and time as the subjective conditions of, 101–2
Smell, subjectivity of, 105–7
Society: interest in art arises only in, 44–45
Song, 174
Space: as an a priori (pure) form of intuition, 80–81, 101–2, 105–6
Spatial relations. *See* Form
Spirit [*Geist*]: the faculty of genius, 120
Standards of taste: Kant on the possi-

bility of, 7–13, 30; Hume on, 9, 11n; discussed in *Critique of Pure Reason*, 10–12; Burke on, 11n

Sublime: disinterestedness of judgments on, 39; formless, 99–100; the mathematically sublime, 135–36; Kant's theory of, 135–37; and the supersensible, 135–37, 140–41; the dynamically sublime, 136–37; and moral feeling, 137, 149–52; and the beautiful have a common basis, 137, 140–41; as the symbol of morality, 137, 157; deduction of judgments on, 150–52

Supersensible, the: and purposiveness of form, 19–20, 139–40, 176; and the antinomy of taste, 65, 138; and Kant's aesthetic theory, 133–41; and aesthetic ideas, 134–35; and the sublime, 135–37, 140–41; and a common sense, 137–38; an indeterminate concept, 138–41; and morality, 140–41, 155; idea at the basis of the judgment of taste, 155; three ways of describing, 155; and freedom, 157

Synthesis, in Kant's theory of cognition, 81–84, 86–90

Taste: faculty of judging the beautiful, 156, 162–64. *See also* Judgment of taste

Tastes (gustatory), subjectivity of, 105–7

Temporal relations. *See* Form

Theater, 174

Time: as an a priori (pure) form of intuition, 80–81, 101–2, 105–6

Tones: aesthetic relevance of, 100, 107–9, 167

Transcendental: how the critique of taste is, 27; Kant's method, 78–79; status of Kant's theory of cognition, 85–87, 88–89. *See also* Deduction, transcendental

Understanding [*Verstand*]: faculty identified with judgment, 20–22; and imagination in the experience of the beautiful, 28, 67–68, 75–77, 89–91, 95–96; function in cognition, 81–84

Universal voice. *See* Common sense

TEXT DESIGNED BY GARY GORE
MANUFACTURED BY IMPRESSIONS, INC., MADISON, WISCONSIN
TEXT AND DISPLAY LINES ARE SET IN CALEDONIA

Library of Congress Cataloging in Publication Data
Crawford, Donald W   1938–
    Kant's aesthetic theory.
    Bibliography: p. 181–184
    1. Kant, Immanuel, 1724–1804 — Aesthetics.
               I. Title.
    B2799.A4C7   111.8'5   73-15259
             ISBN 0–299–06510–3